I0487701

Posing For The Camera

By Harriett Shepard & Lenore Meyer

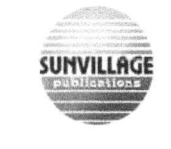

SUNVILLAGE
publications

www.sunvillagepublications.com

Posing For The Camera
By By Harriett Shepard & Lenore Meyer

Copyright © 2010

No part of this publication may be reproduced, stored in a retrieval system or transmitted in any form or by any means, electronic, mechanical, photocopying, recording or otherwise, without prior written permission from the publisher.

Disclaimer: Neither the author nor the publisher accepts any responsibility for any injury, damage, or unwanted or adverse circumstances or conditions arising from use or misuse of the material contained within this publication. While every effort has been made to ensure reliability and accuracy of the information within, the liability, negligence or otherwise, or from any use, misuse or abuse arising the operation of any methods, strategies, instructions or ideas contained in the material herein is the sole responsibility of the reader.

Cover image credits: © Frank Janssen/Dreamstime.com

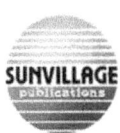

SUNVILLAGE
publications

Cover design by www.WebCopyAlchemy.com

POSING
FOR THE
CAMERA

contents

TABLE OF CONTENTS

SECTION I

(BASIC POSING)

SECTION II
(ADVANCED TECHNIQUE)

WHAT IS A POSE?

It is not possible to be entirely precise, for definitions vary, the meanings change with the times and a good deal of healthy controversy exists.

The dictionary says it is, first, a *position of the body ...an attitude.* Its secondary meanings, however, have negative connotations of artificial appearance - *placing or putting, mere affectation, pretense, rigid stance,* etc.

The modernist winces and avoids its use, for photography has advanced with the speed of its lenses and films and left the word *pose* - as it maintains inflexibly its old meaning - draining life and vitality out of action.

Although, we too, must use the word -we ask you to accept it in its new and broadest sense. *Pose* (or *Posing)* today includes something more basic, a state of composure, balance ... poise before the camera.

A pose may be deliberately assumed with gestures and attitudes designedly adapted to mood or position... yet that does not preclude candidness.

The manner is which the body achieves a position before the camera (the action can be as candid or deliberate as you please) is *posing* in the modern sense, and the state in which it is recorded (in either poised consciousness or oblivion to the camera) is the *pose.*

FOREWORD

This book is not a compilation of 'Do's and Dont's.' It seeks to organize thought on the part of photographers, directors and models as to where posing begins and how it is accomplished. Step by step, we will take the major and minor components of the posing figure and show how they function in relation to the camera - their possibilities and their limitations.

Once you know how the figure functions, and the results thereby obtained, it is up to you to decide whether the pose is desirable or undesirable for the job at hand. For instance, a certain hand position may be generally recognized as awkward or conspicuous. This position would be undesirable if you wanted your picture to express grace and loveliness. On the other hand, it could very well serve to characterize a gangling teenager or call attention to an object or important copy in an advertisement.

This book is not meant to impose our personal opinions upon you. Its intent is to increase your awareness of how symmetry of figure in pictures follows a consistent pattern. That pattern, when analyzed, establishes basic truths that beat like a motif throughout prize-winning and time-tested pictures. These truths are the fundamentals of which we speak.

All art (and we do consider posing an art) as well as a science, has its basic fundamentals. Teachers readily admit that rules have a tendency, at first, to be confining. However, after they are learned well, creativity springs from the sound foundation they form.

As your skill and knowledge develop, you yourself will burst the confines of these basics to improvise in good taste. No longer will you be laden with technicalities; you will be free to create.

There are no rules for the director or model who know what they are about and specifically set out to accomplish the *taboo* with a confident flourish. We realize that 'murder' for the meek is 'meat' for the master and encourage you, when you have the talent, to utilize it on these special effects.

However, neither personal flourishes, style changes nor photographic trends will ever radically affect the value of good fundamentals. They can always be intelligently adapted to fit the times and situation.

Throughout this book, references are made to the model, the director and the photographer. Let us define these terms so that we have a clear understanding:

The model is any person, regardless of experience, age or sex, who appears before the camera. Although we refer to the model as *she* because the majority of models are female this term also includes any male subject who appears before the camera. **The director** is the person who has the completed picture in mind and whose job it is to call forth the needed position and response from the model. Regardless of whether he is called *floor* director, *talent* director or *production* director, his specific responsibility is control of the personnel and not the camera.

The photographer whether amateur or professional, is the person responsible for the camera's behavior and, in most instances, is also the director of model action. It is to this *director* phase of his photographic endeavors that this book is addressed.

A quick glance through the illustrations in this book may provoke the questions:

'Why all the clocks and geometric symbols?' 'What have they to do with posing?'

These objects, familiar to all of us, have purposely been selected as a means of simplifying, through association, the form and movement of various parts of the human body. They evoke clear, indelible pictures in your mind, pictures that become invaluable aids in directing yourself or someone else ... camera-wise.

You will also note, this book is divided into two parts, the basic and the advanced techniques of posing. The purpose of this has been to separate the fundamental repertoire of the beginner from the varied and creative potential of the advanced photographer and model.

If you are a beginner, start at the beginning. Concentrate on a few basic positions of each part of the body. Learn them well and then go on to others. Worthwhile creation in any art cannot begin until you have gone through and graduated from your basic rules and fundamentals.

A good illustration of this happened several years ago when a disheartened young model poured out her troubles to us. She had become a popular model with no effort at all. Directors and photographers had been eager to photograph her. She was wholesomely attractive, vibrant and spontaneous in her poses. Her pictures had been an immediate success. Modeling was the perfect profession for her. Everyone had told her so.

Then, all of a sudden nothing was right. Assignments were increasingly difficult and tedious. Results were amateurish and disappointing. Photographers were no longer satisfied. Something had gone wrong and she could not put her finger on the cause.

We could picture what had happened,

for it happens over and over again. She had skipped through one assignment to another in happy oblivion until one day she was asked to do something different, something more exacting - and she didn't know what to do first. From that moment on everything went wrong. As she lost confidence, her posing became stiff and frozen. Fear crept into her pictures and all signs of her *natural* ease and talent disappeared.

We explained to the young model that there is a big difference between being natural and acting natural. One is a happy accident and the other is a studied and consistent talent. Once you know how, this *pseudo-naturalness* can be called forth over and over again at command.

Nothing is so fatal to talent as too early success based only upon *beginner's luck;* nothing is so damaging in the long run, as the brash assumption that a bright smile, or flash inspiration can ever be a satisfactory substitute for experience.

A good craftsman must learn his art in all its dimensions. This girl had the courage to go back and start at the beginning. She had to study the fundamentals of what comprises a natural body position and what thought will photograph as a spontaneous expression. Once these tools and knowledge were hers, combined with her individual charm, she had a permanent combination that was hard to beat. And today, she enjoys a career as a top-flight model.

This example also holds true of the beginning director or cameraman whose first or second series of pictures show promise, natural flair and are successful. But no matter who you are, or what your profession, if you are a talented beginner, and do the right thing without knowing why,

you must eventually retrace your steps and learn basic principles if you wish to step into the ranks of reliable craftsmen and have your work maintain a consistent professional level.

If you are experienced in the posing field - you can start anywhere in the book. The beginning chapters will, however, acquaint you with some of the terminology used in the advanced section as well as give you insight into working with a beginner, while the second section of the book is intended to serve as source for creative variations of all basic positions.

You will find these variations in movement and thinking organized into a mental filing system which makes hundreds of positions and their changes available to your searching mind at the moment when you need them most.

Each of the two sections of the book, basic and advanced, has been similarly divided into four major parts - the body, the legs, the arms and the head. This is no arbitrary arrangement. It is the logical order of posing.

Body - because it is the largest and most prominent mass, is your starting point.

Legs - support the body and must therefore be considered next.

Arms - coordinate the design of the picture and act as liaison between the body and the facial message.

Head - is posed last because expressions must be caught at their peak of spontaneity. Facial expression climaxes the mood and message of the complete arrangement.

This progression of posing, whether basic or advanced, makes no rules but states facts and proven results. Use what you will and discard what seems unimportant.

BASIC
BODY
TECHNIQUE

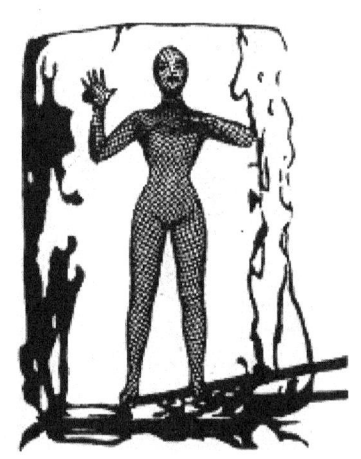

LET'S BREAK THE ICE!

Let's free ideas that sometimes freeze when posing starts!

Has it ever happened to you? That moment when your mind stopped and you asked yourself 'Now what? Where should I begin?'

Posing begins with the body...

so let's forget all else and focus our attention on the body in a new light... a shadow!

A

shadow devoid of detail...

no buttons... no
bows... no
pockets.

Simply begin to think of the body in terms of its *silhouette*.

THIS SILHOUETTE

is an actual black-and-white photograph. All
graduated tones have been eliminated, leaving
only the true outline of the model.

*The figure has been sliced to two dimensions
height and width.*

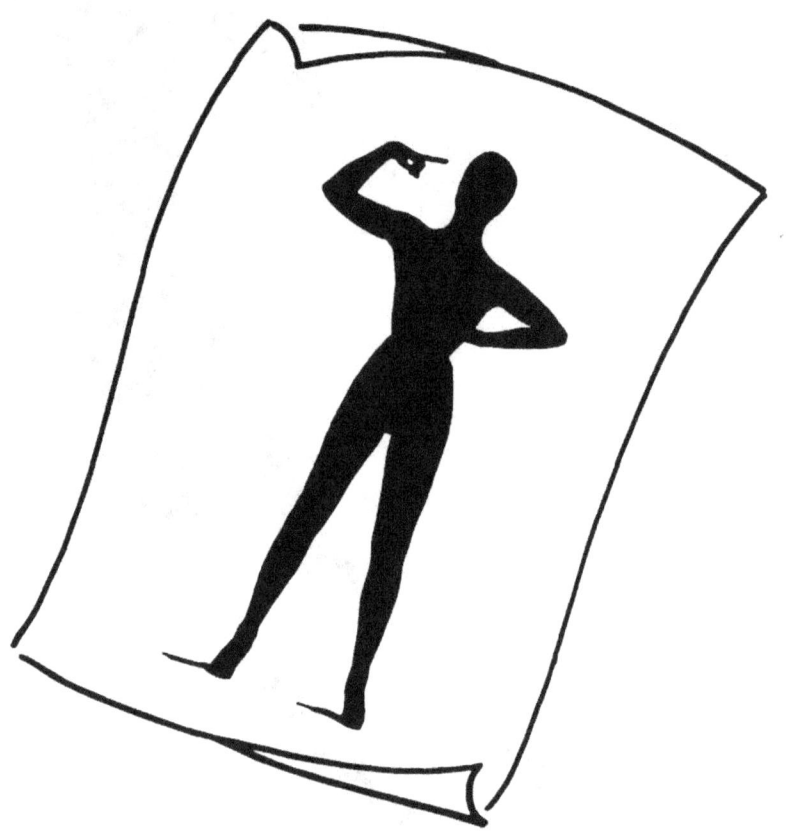

IT'S TRUE

that in silhouette you can't see the model's features, what she is holding in her hand, or the expression on her face...

But...

notice how the stark simplicity of the silhouette carries your mind's eye directly to the position of her

... body

 ... legs

... arms

... and head!

When you...

strip the body of distracting trivia and you discover the foundation of all posing -the form in silhouette.

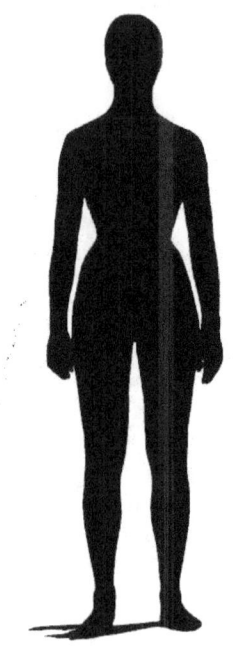

As you focus your attention on a silhouette, you begin to notice things you never saw before. For even in outline the body has character and feeling.

Notice the position of this model. Her stance makes her appear broad, heavy and masculine.

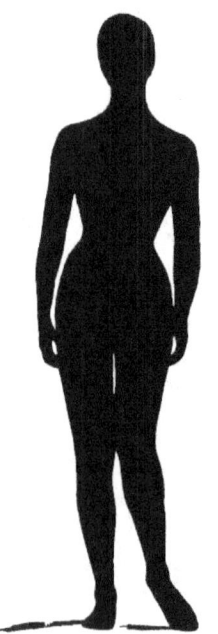

Yet here - when she shifts her weight to one foot - her pose immediately becomes more relaxed, lighter and more feminine.

Slight change ... big difference! Do you suppose that other apparently minor changes make comparable differences in the impression communicated by a photograph?

OF COURSE THEY DO!

The slightest twist or turn of the subject, easily detected in outline, alters both the silhouette and its meaning.

When you can translate the rounded human figure into a flat silhouette, and associate its lines with a familiar symbol, you have the key to duplicating or creating any pose.

17

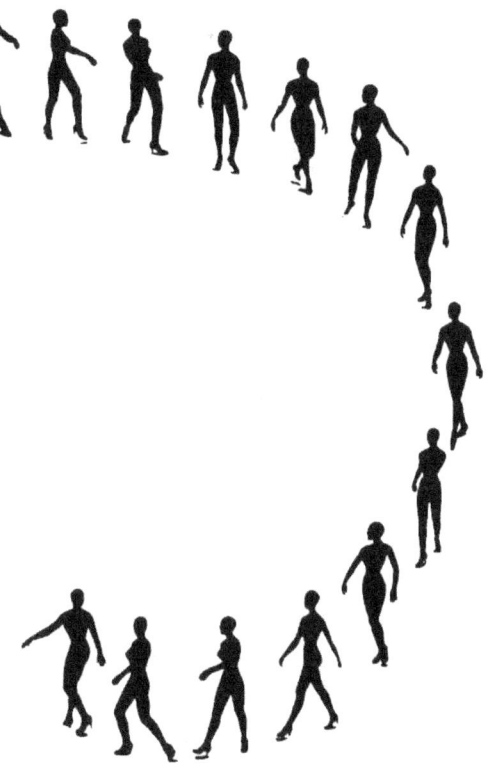

All silhouettes can be translated into simple lines. Some have long lines; others tend to zigzag.

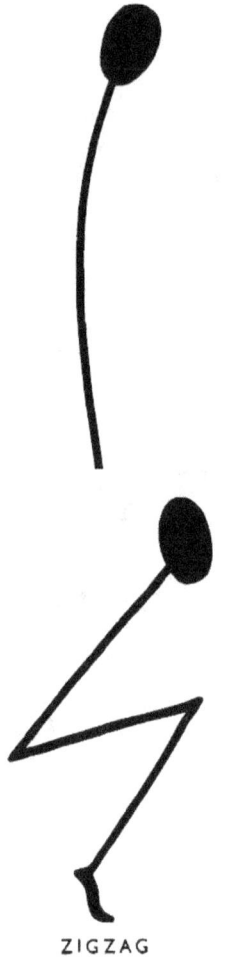

ZIGZAG

Long-line silhouettes . . .
are usually those in a standing or reclining position, or any other stance where the body is, or almost is, at its fullest length.

Zigzag silhouettes . . .
are usually created by sitting or kneeling poses that shorten the body into positions of angularity.

These, you will agree, are two very general classifications. However, each can be diagrammed for careful analysis and specific identification.

18

A LONG-LINE SILHOUETTE

is simple to diagram. Find a full-length picture of a person. Think of it in terms of its silhouette. With a heavy black pencil or crayon, get ready to draw the lines that will permit you to classify it.

Draw a dotted line...
from one shoulder joint to the other. (This **we will call the *shoulder-track.)***

Draw another dotted line...
from one hip joint to the other. (This we will call the *hip-track.)*

Now draw a heavy **solid line**...
from the center top of the head to the middle of the shoulder-track. Continue this line down to the middle of the hip-track and on to the tip of the foot that is not supporting the weight of the body. (If the weight is equally distributed, the line is drawn to a point half-way between the feet.)

The solid line you have just drawn is the *long-line* of the silhouette.

If you will diagram at least five more standing figures, you will discover an interesting fact:

HEAD-LINE + BODY-LINE + LEG-LINE = LONG-LINE

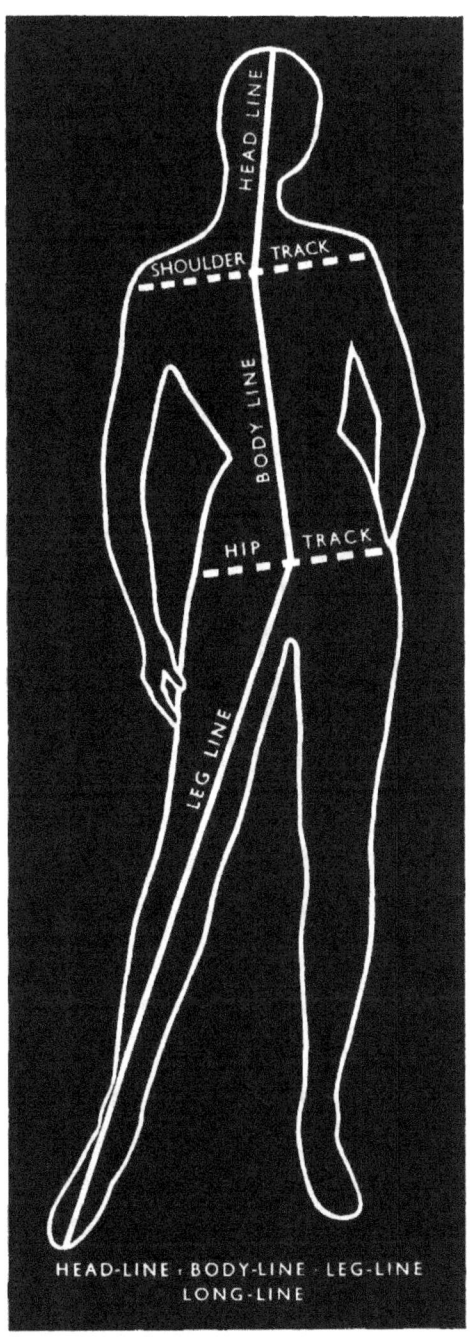

HEAD-LINE · BODY-LINE · LEG-LINE
LONG-LINE

ALL LONG-LINE SILHOUETTES FORM LETTERS

that are easy to remember. Separate the pictures you have diagrammed and you will find that each solid line simulates one of three letters of the alphabet - an T, a 'C or an 'S'!

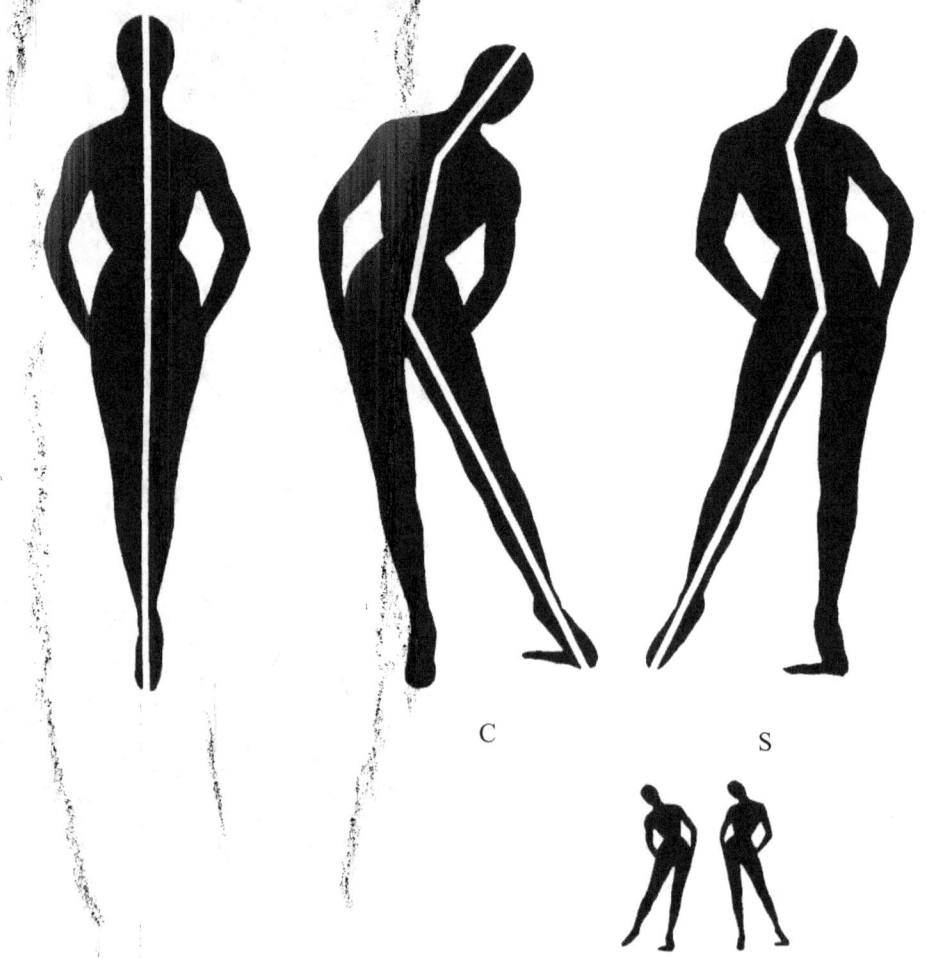

C   S

SOMETIMES C[1] AND *'S'* ARE BACKWARDS

A long-line silhouette does not always appear in a vertical position. Sometimes you'll find an 'I', 'C' or 'S' slanted on the diagonal.

Sometimes the silhouette will be presented in a horizontal arrangement.

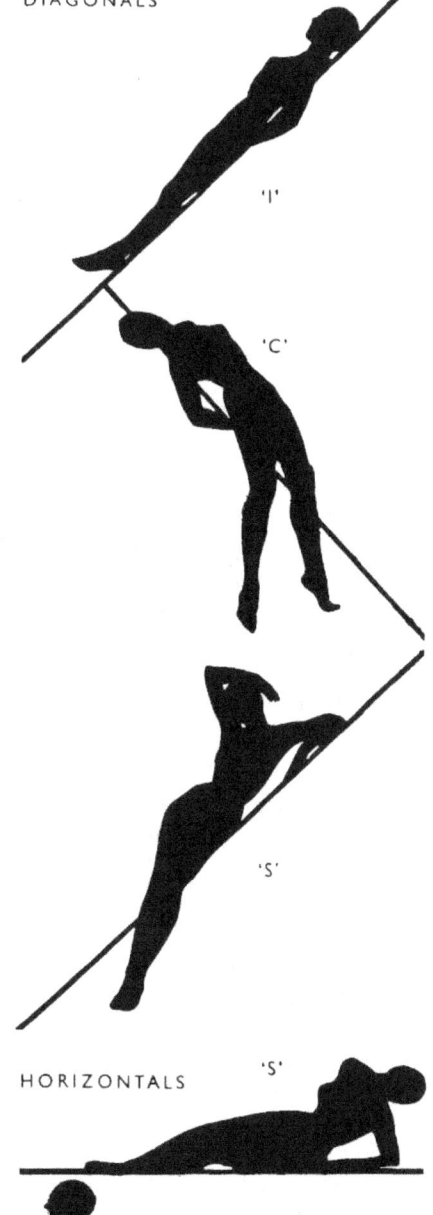

DIAGONALS

'I'

'C'

'S'

HORIZONTALS   'S'

'C'

21

VERTICAL SILHOUETTES

are formed by the model who stands on her feet, using the ground as her primary means of support. In this vertical position her body is capable of forming an 'I', 'C or 'S' line, regardless of which view is presented to the camera.

Vertical 'C silhouettes are simple to execute with effective results. They form the basic poses that the beginner can use without encountering complications and are the basis of creative posing for the more advanced. 'C silhouettes tend to lighten the body and manifest a feeling of femininity, grace and ease.

VERTICAL 'I'

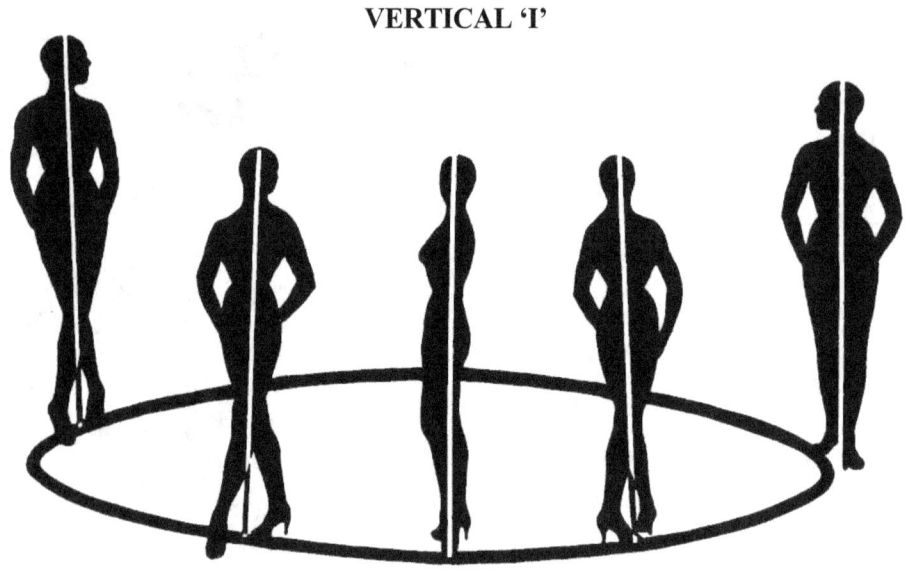

| FRONT | 3/4 FRONT | SIDE | 3/4 BACK | BACK |
| VIEW | VIEW | VIEW | VIEW | VIEW |

Vertical 'I' silhouettes have an exacting quality overlooked by the casual eye. They are the most inflexible of all poses and require experience and skill. Contrary to common belief, an interesting straight vertical silhouette is difficult to execute without giving the body a stolid appearance. However, when expertly used to express strength, masculinity, elegance, regality, it is a very effective long-line silhouette.

Vertical 'S' silhouettes are interesting to work with and, although they require more practice, they are worth the extra effort. The slight shift of the head-line or the leg-line to the opposite side that changes a 'C silhouette to an 'S' makes a rewarding difference. The graceful line created by the 'S' silhouette appeals to the artistic eye. It flows with femininity, flexibility and symmetry.

22

VERTICAL 'C'

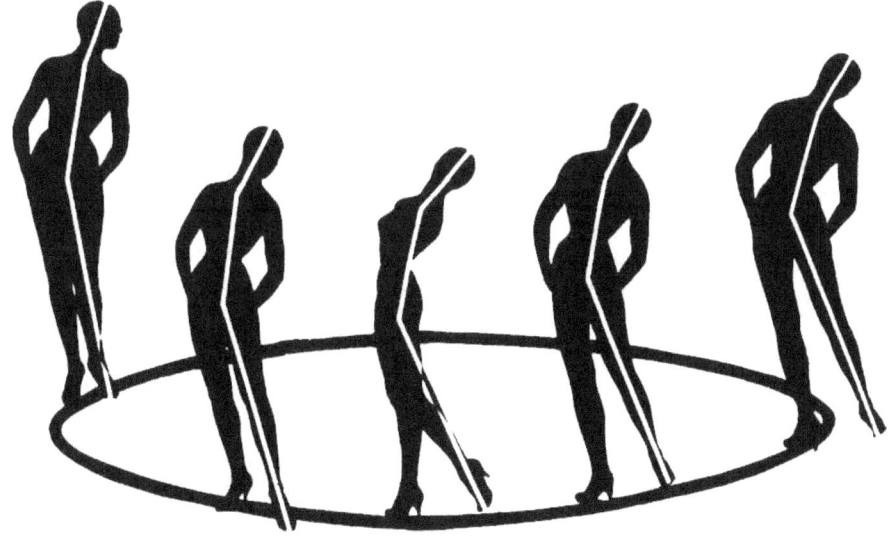

VERTICAL 'S'

| FRONT VIEWS | 3/4 FRONT VIEWS | SIDE VIEWS | 3/4 BACK VIEWS | BACK VIEWS |

HORIZONTAL SILHOUETTES

are created by the body in a reclining position. In this horizontal arrangement, the body's silhouette can still be classified by its 'I', 'C or 'S' lines. As the body rotates to present a different view to the camera, the individual characteristics of each letter formed can be noted.

In horizontal posing, the weight of the body is supported by various parts of the body other than the feet. Because of this, opportunity presents itself for certain poses which the standing figure could achieve only with considerable strain.

Horizontal silhouettes can be arranged leisurely. Many poses are deliberately taken in this position - inverted or tilted later. For instance, a picture may be set up, with the model in a horizontal position, for the express purpose of inverting the picture later to simulate a standing pose. When this is the intent, extra attention should be given certain details. Hair and clothing should be arranged in the position in which they would fall naturally. All props and accessories must appear to conform to the law of gravity if the finished picture is to be believable and realistic.

The reclining figure is best supported by hard parts of the body such as the foot, wrist, hand, elbow or fingers. These are not distorted by weight or pressure. Soft parts of the body such as the hips, arms, thighs, calves, etc., bulge when they are pressed against a hard surface to support weight.

When soft flesh must contact a hard surface with pressure, shift the major weight to the opposite side so that the flesh facing the camera touches the surface lightly, maintaining its most effective line.

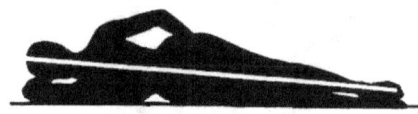

FRONT VIEW

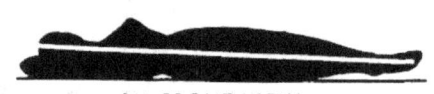

3 4 FRONT VIEW

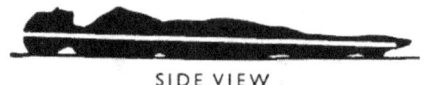

SIDE VIEW

3/4 BACK VIEW

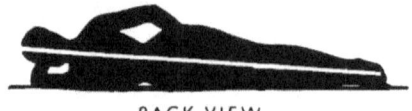

BACK VIEW

HORIZONTAL 'C'   ## HORIZONTAL'S'

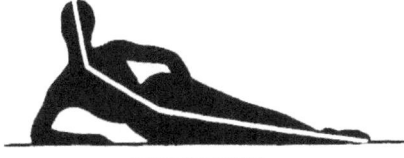

FRONT VI EW

FRONT V I E W

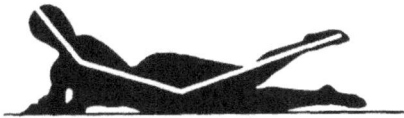

3/ 4   FRONT V I E W

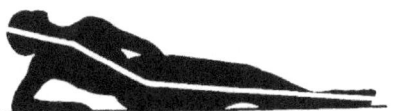

3/ 4   FRONT V I E W

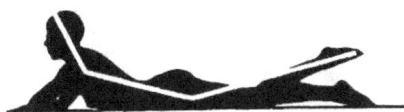

SIDE VI EW

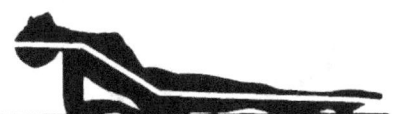

SIDE VIEW

3/ 4   BACK V I E W

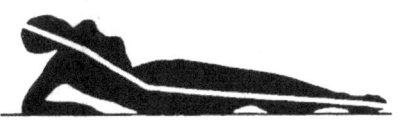

3/ 4   BACK VI E W

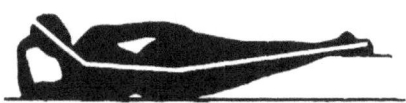

BACK V I E W

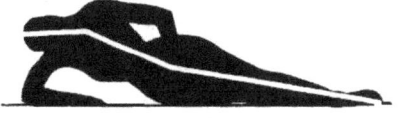

BACK VI E W

DIACONAL SILHOUETTES

may slant at any angle between vertical and horizontal. Still figures, classified as diagonals, usually require specific support other than the feet, while diagonals taken in action do not need additional support. The diagonal silhouette, supported by an object at any height, can present any view to the camera and still form 'I', 'C' or 'S" lines that permit classification.

Diagonal C is the most commonly used diagonal body silhouette. The average girl supported by an object, curves her body naturally in a C. Although this silhouette is the easiest of the diagonal lines to achieve, it expresses grace nevertheless, and gives the effect of being softly feminine and generally pleasing. Many outstanding photographers favor this 'C curved silhouette and beginners would do well to remember it.

DIAGONAL 'I'

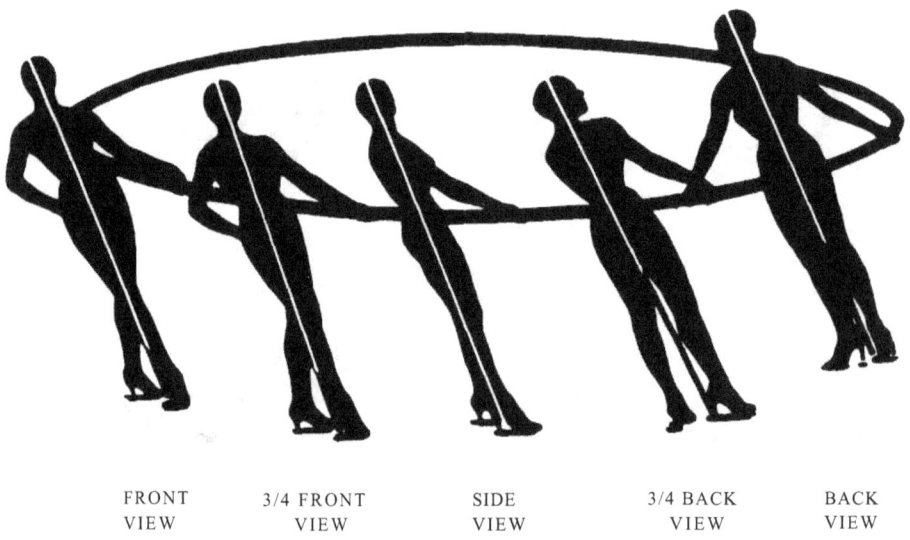

| FRONT VIEW | 3/4 FRONT VIEW | SIDE VIEW | 3/4 BACK VIEW | BACK VIEW |

Diagonal 'I' is the most difficult of all 'I' silhouettes to sustain in a true line. It is stark and exact - demanding rigid control on the part of the experienced model. It maintains the feeling of directness and strength which is characteristic of all straight-line silhouettes and can be prosaic unless done with deliberate intent.

Diagonal 'S' silhouettes have that extra something that adds flair to a picture. This flowing reverse of curves is reminiscent of Hogarth's classic *line of beauty*. With a bit more expert handling than is needed for the 'C silhouette, the 'S' long-line is both highly artistic and adaptable to distinctive work.

26

DIAGONAL'S'

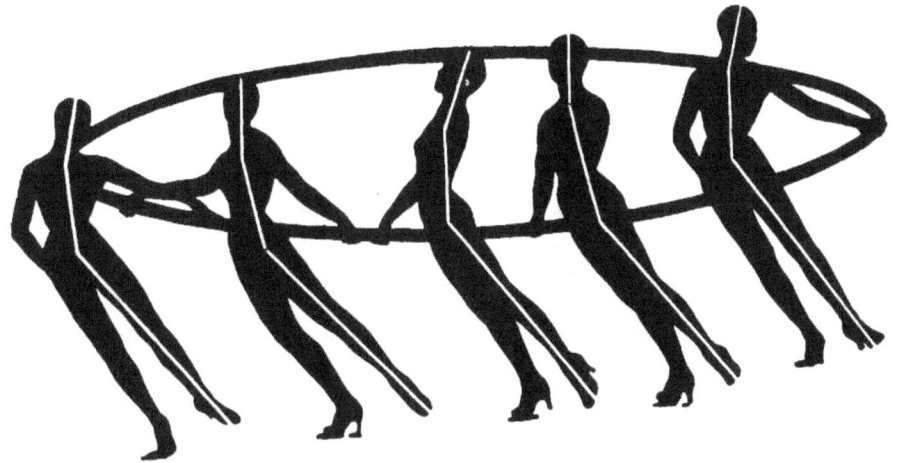

DIAGONAL 'S'

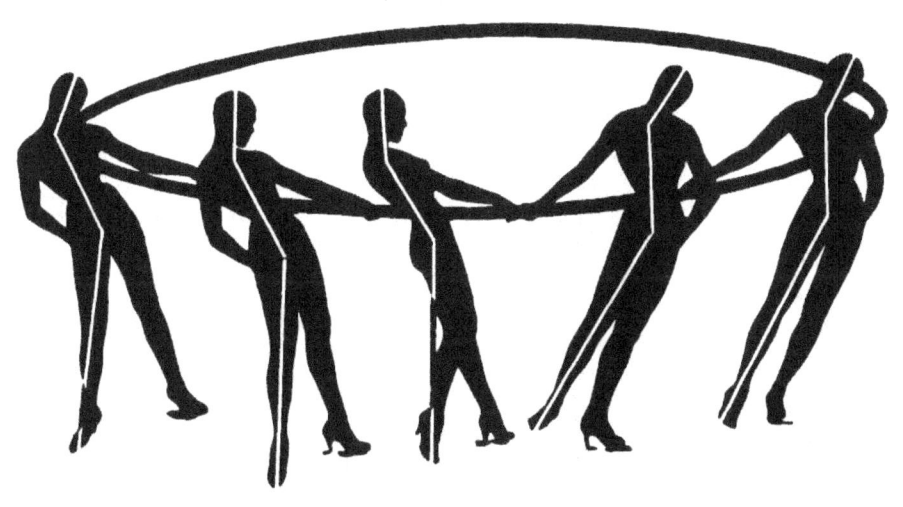

| FRONT
VIEWS | 3/4 FRONT
VIEWS | SIDE
VIEWS | 3/4 BACK
VIEWS | BACK
VIEWS |

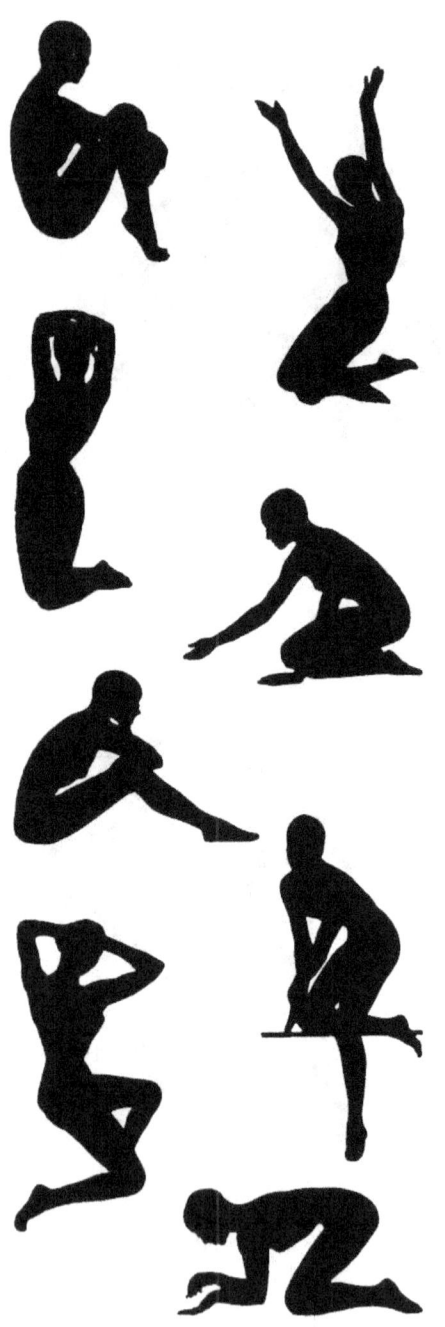

THE ZIGZAG SILHOUETTE

should be examined only after you have familiarized yourself thoroughly with the long-line silhouette.

As you know, the zigzag silhouette is formed primarily by sitting and kneeling figures. A simple line diagram of the body in these positions will do just what the name implies. It will zig and then zag. Most of the time it will zig, zag, and then zig again to form a figure 'Z'.

These are tricky silhouettes and can, if not carefully handled, look like one big lump! Good zigzag poses are best directed by the photographer from the camera position. When hips and shoulders face the camera, in a zigzag position, the immediate impact of the pose is often lost. Therefore, those unsure of which sitting or kneeling position to use, will find that side or | views present a silhouette that defines the body's outline.

For the clean body-line popular today, use the arms in a lace-work around the torso. An open silhouette gives the feeling of freedom, space and lightness. Arms that appear glued to the sides, thicken the silhouette and can give the impression of an undesirable bulge or a heavy waistline.

Sitting and kneeling figures cannot be diagrammed like the long-line silhouettes. They are so angular that even their classification is different.

Ah! There's our key ... *angular!* Let's study them by the angles they form.

HOW TO DIAGRAM
ZIGZAG SILHOUETTES

Collect at least five sitting or kneeling pictures. With a heavy black pencil or crayon draw the following three lines so that you can examine the angles they form:

1. **Body-Line.** Ignore the head mass and draw a line from the center of the shoulder nearest the camera to the center of the hip nearest the camera. (If shoulders or hips are the same distance from the camera, the line is drawn from the center of the shoulder-track or the center of the hip-track.)
2. **Thigh-Line.** Continue the line from the hip nearest the camera to the center of the knee nearest the camera. (If knees are equidistant, continue with a line to each.)
3. **Shin-Line.** Extend this line from the knee to the ankle of the same leg.

The two angles formed by this zigzag line can be used to identify any zigzag pose.

So let's look to see what kind of an angle any two of these lines form. Are they perpendicular to each other? If so, they form a *right* angle. If the angle is less, we call it *acute;* if it is more - *obtuse.*

Note: Except for the rare occasions when the camera is centered on the subject in a side view, the actual angles assumed by the model are not necessarily the same angles that are formed on the ground glass of the camera, or subsequently appear in the finished picture. Therefore all final corrections of the zigzag pose must come from the man behind the camera.

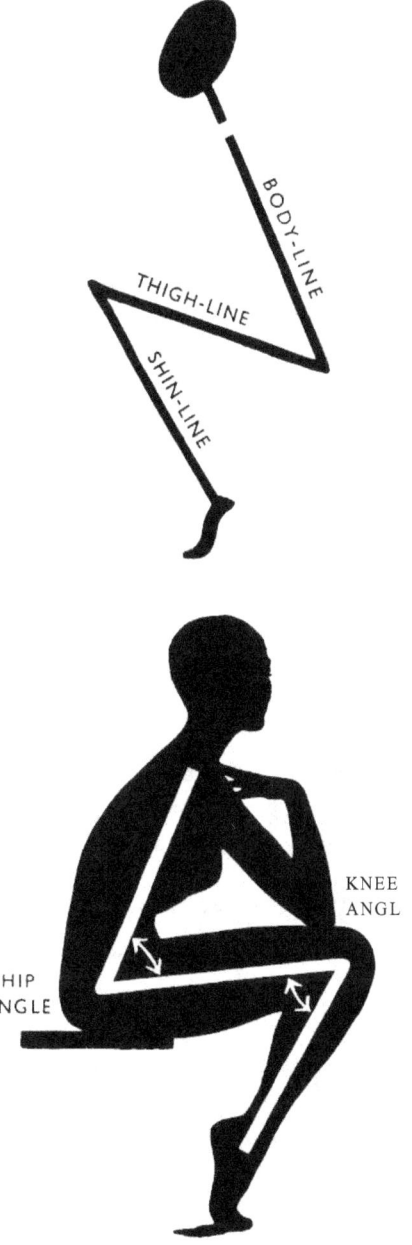

BODY LINE + LEG LINES   ZIGZAG LINE

ZIGZAG SILHOUETTES

form either a pair or a combination of angles whether their support is higher-than-chair-level, or on the floor. There are four basic zigzag silhouettes:

1. The geometric silhouette...
consists of two right angles, whether the figure is sitting or kneeling. Pairs of right angles are usually used when the purpose of the pictures is to create an effect of masculinity, strength, stylization, or, to depict a pose characteristic of certain dance postures. Right angles, unless deliberately used for their geometric form, prove stilted and sometimes even ludicrous.

varied by muscle tension to express anything from an athletic crouch to a relaxed curl of the body.

Acute angles often close the space between limbs and body causing parts to lose their individual outlines as they press against one another. Thus, great care must be exercised to see that the body maintains a clean-cut outline defining character and situation even in its compactness.

3. The obtuse silhouette...
contains two obtuse angles whether the figure is sitting or kneeling. It has a flowing

TYPICAL GEOMETRIC SILHOUETTES-SITTING

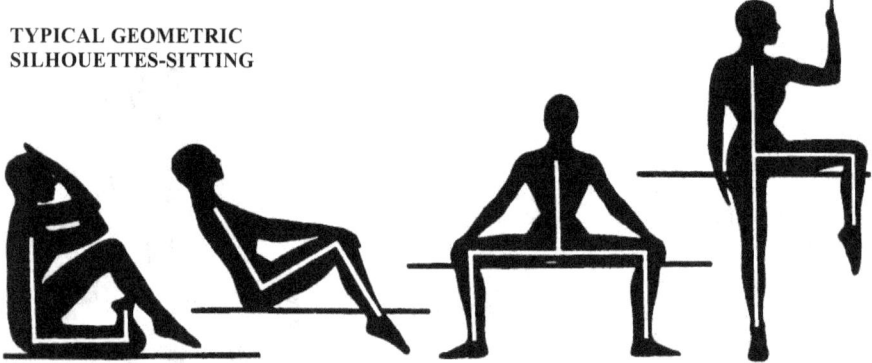

Note: In bathing suit and nude posing, where the form is not covered by clothing, the weight of the body may distort the buttocks. Correction can be made by placing a spacer, such as a book, under the side away from the camera upon which the weight of the body can be supported. The camera side of the body is then lifted slightly to relieve pressure and exhibit a firm line.

2. The acute silhouette...
formed by a pair of acute angles, may also be a zigzag figure in any position. It can be

line and expresses a relaxed, luxuriant and casual feeling.

4. The mixed-angle silhouette...
is the most widely practiced form of the four silhouettes used in sitting and kneeling figures. It is usually arranged by combining an acute angle with an obtuse angle. A right angle is rarely compatible with an angle of another kind and is seldom used in mixed-angle silhouettes.

TYPICAL ACUTE SILHOUETTES-SITTING

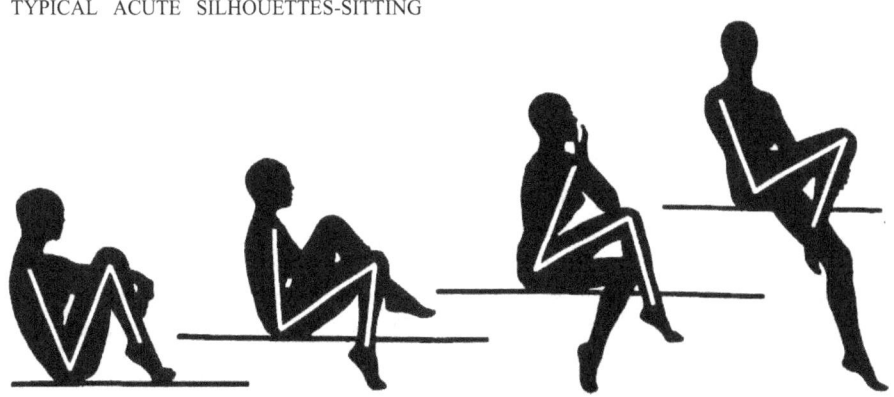

TYPICAL OBTUSE SILHOUETTES-SITTING

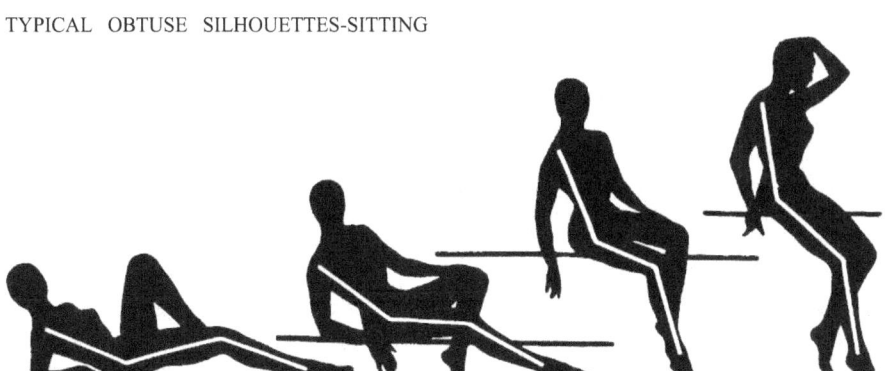

TYPICAL M I X E D - A N G L E SILHOUETTES-KNEELING

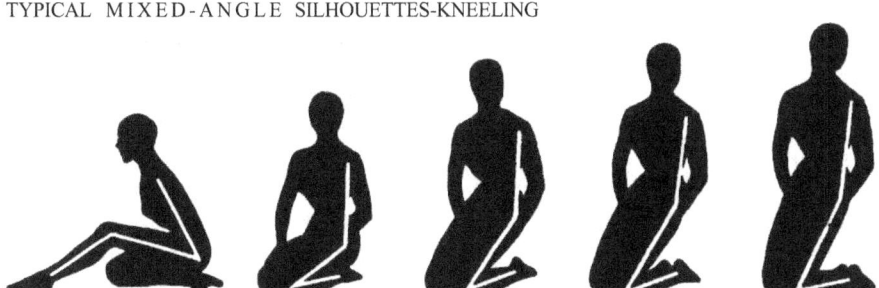

BUILDING THE POSE
- DIRECTOR

These notes (and others that end subsequent chapters) are not meant for the casual reader, the detached spectator or the procrastinator. They are offered to those willing to analyze their work in a new light.

You're the man with a definite plan. You are ready to start building poses before you take another picture!

Analysis helps you build, for it gives you a target for future shooting. Go into your files and diagram some of your full-length pictures - the not-so-good as well as your best prints. (Those that you do not care to deface may be diagrammed on an overlay sheet of onion skin paper.) Diagram at least 50 long-line pictures and separate them into three main groups:

'I' silhouettes
'C silhouettes
'S' silhouettes

Divide each group into its five possible views.

You'll probably find that you have favored the front view of either the T or the 'C long-line silhouette. In fact, you may discover that you have repeated the exact pose on different occasions. Too much repetition denotes lack of creative repertoire and it is so easy to direct those small changes that make the big difference!

Let's get busy and see how working with the figure in silhouette helps clear your mind for action.

An hour or so of practice with a *live silhouette* can eliminate countless hours of 'If

only -' mistakes, reams of paper and fruitless hours. In no time at all you'll be able to direct the body like a master puppeteer!

A friend, your wife or a model who also wishes to benefit by the training, can be your *silhouette.* Your first step is to thumbtack a white sheet over an open doorway. Place an ordinary, unshaded 100 watt lightbulb 9 feet behind the sheet and about 30 inches from the floor.

Your *silhouette,* dressed in a form-fitting bathing suit or leotard should stand close to the sheet on the same side as the light, while you direct her from the opposite side of the sheet in a darkened room.

Brief your model on what you mean by an T, 'C and 'S' silhouette. If she is inexperienced, all the better ... more opportunity for you to practice directing!

As your model poses in silhouette, see if you can direct her in:

3 different vertical silhouettes 3

different diagonal silhouettes

Check each pose for:
(a) Clearly defined T, 'C or 'S' line.
(b) Clean-cut body outline... especially at the waistline.
(c) Positions that specifically appeal to you.
(d) Slight alterations - twists or turns that im prove figure proportions or the pose.

When you have gained insight into the positions you repeat through preference, study the work of others and analyze their favorites. Magazines and catalogues are filled with poses for illuminating comparison.

Fashion magazines offer an unlimited source of full-length pictures by topflight photographers. As you diagram and analyze their pictures, you will notice that they too, favor one type of silhouette over another ... but careful observation will reveal their flair for the slight changes that make the big difference.

Practice of the following exercises will help you plan body positions:

1. Bend an ordinary pipe cleaner to fit the vertical 'C' body-line on page 20.
2. Straighten this extreme 'C' slightly to form a modified 'C'
3. Change this modified 'C' into a very subtle or slight 'C'.
4. Reverse the 'C' position by flipping the pipe cleaner between your fingers.
5. Change the 'C' to an 'S' by placing the head-line on the opposite side of the body line.
6. With the same or other pipe cleaners, duplicate some of the long-line poses in your collection.
7. Now visualize a model against the background before you. Hold one of your pipe cleaner figures at arm's length in front of you pretending it is she. Answer these questions:
a) How far away would she be?
b) What would support her weight?
c) Which direction would she face?
8. Try directing a person into the position you have visualized.

This pipe-cleaner figurine is almost a magic wand in planning body-lines. In actual directing, the pipe cleaner can also be a great aid. Arrange it in a 'C' long-line. Hold it between you and your model. As you manipulate and change its position, see if she can follow its lines with a minimum of further explanation. Try reversing some of the positions. You will find that although she views the line from a different side, her response will be exactly what you want - greatly simplifying the mental gymnastics of reversing commands.

To familiarize yourself with the directing of zigzag poses go back to your basic classifications of zigzags. Direct your *silhouette* in each of the poses shown. Create

and direct her in some positions not shown:

acute kneeling obtuse
kneeling geometric
kneeling mixed-angle
sitting

Now that you are actually ready to start taking pictures you will be able to *break the ice* as well as cope with unchangeable factors that dictate the direction the model must face - existing light; natural background; clothing details; pre-determined picture layout ... or, even the figure liabilities of the model.

After you have weighed the importance of these factors establish her general body direction, plan approximately what she will need to support her figure and what she will be doing.

Now is the time to communicate your plan to the model in clear and definite terms:

1) The idea we want to get across is -.' (Purpose, picture format, how much of model will be revealed, what she will be doing, etc.)
2) 'You will be sitting on the stairway.' (Relate a long-line or a zigzag silhouette to the existing staging.)
3) 'Face the camera,' (body view)

With all these decisive steps in the right direction, you are ready to start building the pose, accepting, rejecting or adding to positions the model might assume.

As you know, the time element in posing is important. Some models fatigue easily and sag with loss of interest. Others tense and become immobile. If the basic position you have chosen permits easy balance, your model can rearrange arms, legs or head deftly before she wilts or rigor mortis sets in.

BUILDING THE POSE -MODEL

Have you ever seen yourself in silhouette? You will be amazed to discover that your silhouette can tell you more about modeling than your mirror! Your silhouette, more than anything else, can give you a clear idea of many points:

1. The variety of positions your body is capable of forming.
2. A workable understanding of weight distribution and poise.
3. The changes, resulting from *slight* movement.
4. Basic conveying of mood and character.
5. The vital changes that result when the camera transforms your rounded figure into a two dimensional picture.
6. How your silhouette proportions change in different body positions.

Once you mentally control yourself in silhouette, you can create poses or take instructions from your director with ease. A model who does not know how her body moves and balances itself, seems to fall apart when asked to shift a hip or move a hand. Working with your silhouette at home will give you an understanding of what the camera sees and practice will help you call forth what's needed to adjust or hold any pose.

Long-line practice...
is started by first analyzing the work of some of the successful models whose pictures appear in current women's magazines and fashion catalogues. Cut out and diagram:
25 'S' silhouettes
25 'C' silhouettes
25 'T' silhouettes

Separate each category into vertical, horizontal and diagonal poses.

To practice duplicating these poses in silhouette, set an unshaded table lamp on the floor. The bulb should be about hip high and about 10 feet from a smooth, light colored wall. Darken the room by turning off all other lights.

In a form-fitting bathing suit or leotard, stand about two feet from the wall, facing it. The shadow you cast on the wall is a pretty good replica of the silhouette a camera sees. Notice how each move alters your form. Remember — every alteration represents a change the camera will record in the outline of a real position. Spread your collection of diagrammed magazine poses before you on the floor. Duplicate each in turn. Note the following in each pose:

1. The direction the body is facing.
2. Which leg supports the bulk of the body weight.
3. The identity of the letter formed by its long-line.
4. The position and proportion of the hips and shoulders.
5. Clean-cut waistline.
6. Lowered shoulders and definite neckline.
7. Expression of character.

Close your eyes and think of a silhouette in an 'S' or 'C' long-line. Make your body conform to the mental picture and when you think you have achieved it, open your eyes. Notice how close or how far you were from what you thought you were doing. Make the necessary changes that would give you what you pictured and any minor adjustments that will create an interesting or flattering silhouette. Remember those changes ... how little or how much movement was necessary.

If you find after considerable practice that you tend to repeat posing faults in silhouette, you will now know where weakness lies.

Practice all the silhouettes in this first section. Memorize the front view and one of the 3/4 views of the 'C' and 'S' long-lines and practice balancing in each while moving your arms around. Practice these four body positions in silhouette until they become part of you. Don't put this off another day ... remember that body positions are the basis of all your posing. Practice frees you of mechanics and soon you will be able to go full speed ahead.

Another practice exercise: take your four basic long-line poses and see if you can reverse each one. Same symbol line - different direction. If this is hard at first, trace an outline of the pose on a sheet of thin paper and turn it over. Hold it up to the light and you will have the position reversed. It is important for you to know how to do this in case the photographer wants the exact pose in a reverse view. A view, impractical from one position because of unalterable background, props or lighting conditions may be exactly the position wanted - transposed left to right or vice versa.

Practice duplicating the silhouettes in your collection and gradually add to your posing repertoire.

Zigzag practice is important too. Find and diagram at least:

5 acute sitting figures,
5 obtuse sitting figures,
5 geometric sitting figures,
10 mixed-angle sitting figures.

Also find at least:

5 acute kneeling figures (these may be on one knee or two),
5 obtuse kneeling figures,
5 geometric kneeling figures,
10 mixed-angle kneeling figures.

If you are unable to find the required number of each of these figures, roughly sketch the zigzag line you are looking for and you will find that you can work from it just as well as from a picture.

In silhouette, practice arranging yourself in a sitting or kneeling position with your eyes closed and after you think you have the pose ... open your eyes and examine what you have done. Would your silhouette be improved if you ... . . pulled in your tummy? . . raised your chest? . . dropped your shoulders for a better neck and chin line? . . shifted your weight slightly? . . separated your arms from your waistline?

Would anyone looking at your silhouette know what you are doing? In other words ... is your silhouette more than a blob?

A good exercise to get you thinking from the camera's point of view:

1. Select any spot in the room and pretend that it is a camera.
2. Face it.
3. Present a side-view to it.
4. Present a 3/4 front view to it.
5. Select another spot and try to present a 3/4 back view to it before you can count
ten.
6. Mentally compose a sitting position. Select another camera spot and see if you can arrange your body easily from that viewpoint.

Train your body to flow easily into positions that feel right - and look right. That's the job half done ... and the rest is fun!

BASIC LEG TECHNIQUE

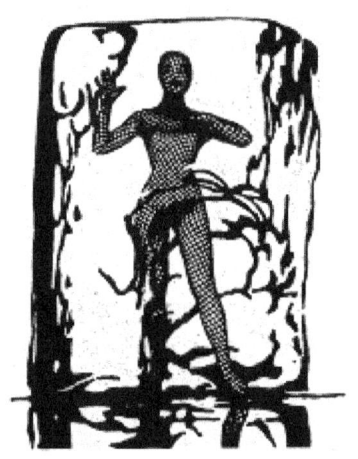

LEGS

in standing figures, contribute to the support of the body, while in sitting and reclining figures, they serve a more ornamental purpose. Whatever their prime function, when properly posed, legs add to the natural balance of the body and the design of the picture as a whole.

The *leg,* as defined by the dictionary, is 'That part of the lower limb from the knee to the toe'. Universal use of the term however, has extended that meaning to include ... 'that part of the limb extending from the hip to the toe'. For posing purposes, we will take the longer view.

Parts of the leg are also referred to in various terms in different regions of the world and so to avoid confusion and establish a common basis for understanding, let us define the parts of the leg as they will be referred to from time to time throughout this book.

UPPER LEG

LOWER LEG

FOOT

TOE

Thigh - the upper section of the leg from the hip to the knee.

Lower Leg - the lower section of the leg, from the knee to the ankle, which has the *shin* in the front and the *calf or* fleshy portion in the back.

Foot - the third section of the leg. It tapers from the ankle to the base of the toes, parts of it include the *heel, instep* and *ball-of-the-foot.*

Toe - the five terminal parts of the foot which work in unison and for photographic purposes will be referred to as one unit.

37

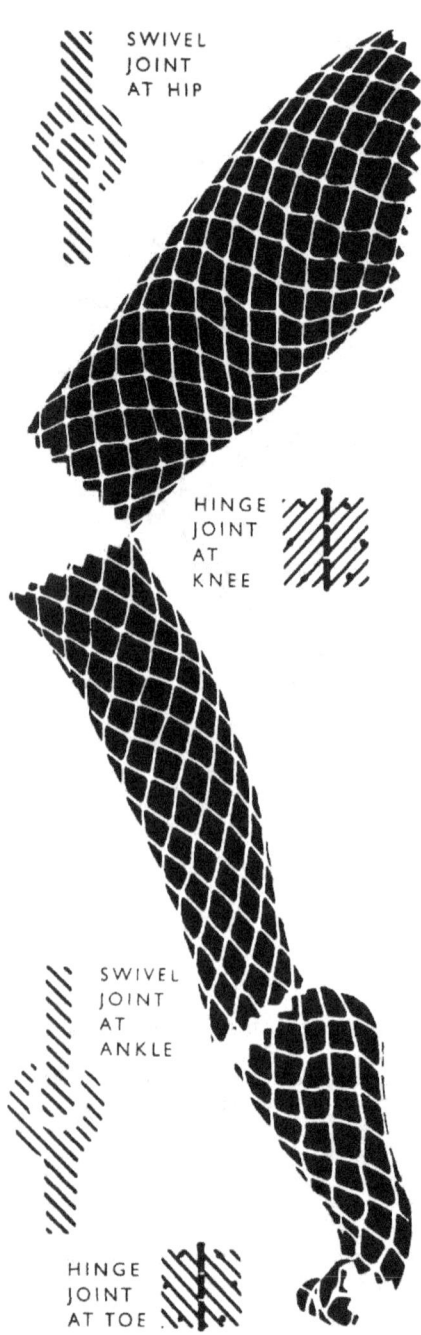

SWIVEL
JOINT
AT HIP

HINGE
JOINT
AT
KNEE

SWIVEL
JOINT
AT
ANKLE

HINGE
JOINT
AT TOE

LEG MOVEMENT

is governed by the flexibility of the joints that connect the four sections of the leg. Each leg has two kinds of joints; a hinge-type joint (which permits the connected parts to swing back and forth) and a swivel-type joint (which permits motion in almost every direction.)

Swivel joints

The *hip-joint* is a swivel-type joint connecting the thigh with the body. It frees the thigh to move in almost any direction.

The *ankle-joint* is another swivel-type joint connecting the lower leg with the foot. It permits the foot to rotate in almost unlimited freedom.

Hinge joints

The *knee-joint* is a hinge-type joint connecting the thigh and the lower leg. It permits the latter to swing back (150^0 arc) then forward to its original straight position in line with the thigh.

The *toe-joint* is a second hinge-type joint that connects the toes with the foot and permits them to bend either upward or downward.

These simple mechanical joints bring the sections of the leg into all photographic positions. Posing legs is simplified when you understand and use the many variations that their flexibility allows.

LEGS IN STANDING POSITIONS

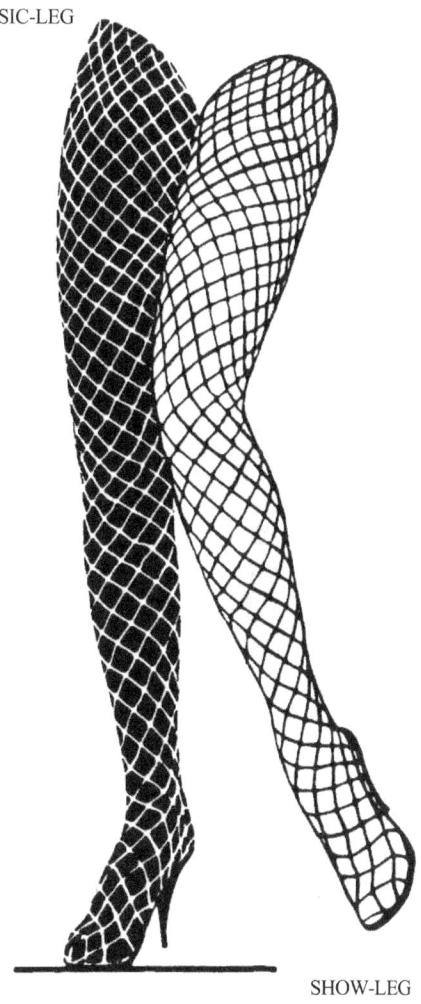

SHOW-LEG

support the body and are responsible for the natural balance of the picture as a whole. They may share equally or unequally in supporting the weight of the body.

When both legs carry an equal share of the burden, they give the body a strong, solid base. This feeling of solidity seems to disappear as the body weight is shifted to one foot. The body becomes pliant. An impression of elasticity or delightful informality flows into the body form.

When the legs share unequally in the support of the body, one leg carries the bulk of the weight while the other lightly touches the floor. These are the leg positions most frequently adopted and varied for photographic use. Let us study this uneven distribution of body weight, how each leg moves and its individual responsibility ... camerawise.

The basic-leg carrying the bulk of the body weight, can pivot on its heel while its toe can point in any direction. If you should compare it to the hand of a clock, it would remind you of the hour hand which indicates each hour.

The show-leg does not support the body to any great degree. It performs another function; it balances the body and adds to the artistic value of the picture.

This *show-leg,* in its freedom, can swing around the *basic-leg* in a wide circle. In fact, the sweeping movement of the *show-leg* is like the minute hand of the clock.

This becomes a significant simile, for, as you relate legs to the hands of a clock, you immediately find dozens of natural leg positions at your disposal.

The basic-leg shown here is dark while the show-leg is light. This difference in tone will be standardized throughout the illustrations to help you evaluate the position and activity of each leg separately, a very important factor in posing legs. Remember: basic-leg - dark, show-leg - light.

39

BASIC-LEG

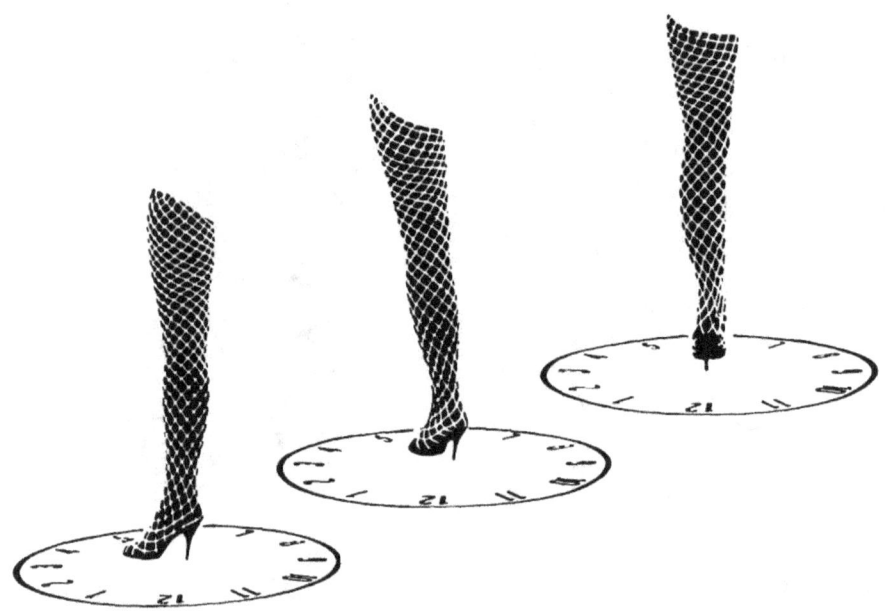

POSITIONS

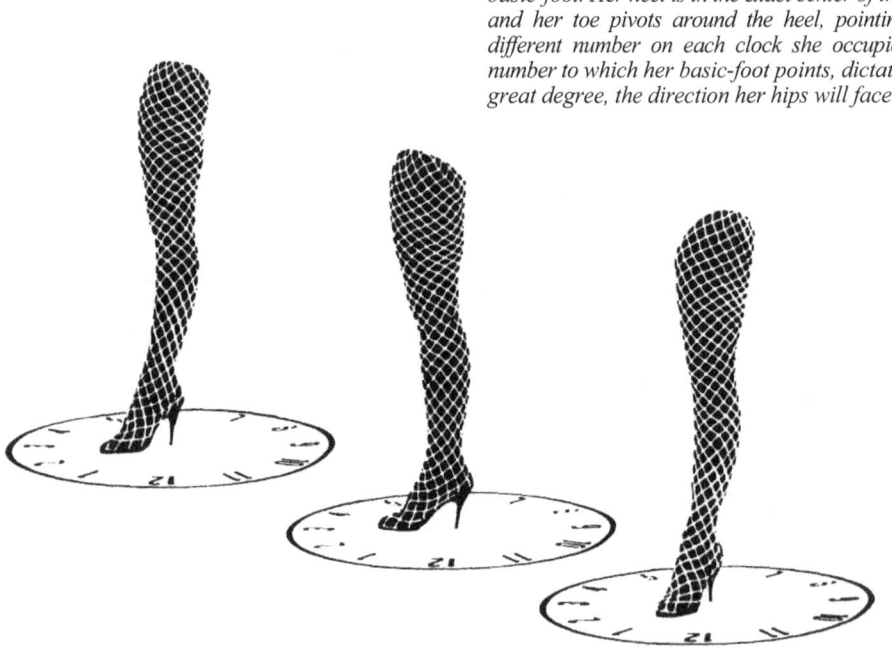

A FLOOR-CLOCK encircles this model's basic-foot. Her heel is in the exact center of the clock and her toe pivots around the heel, pointing to a different number on each clock she occupies. The number to which her basic-foot points, dictates, to a great degree, the direction her hips will face.

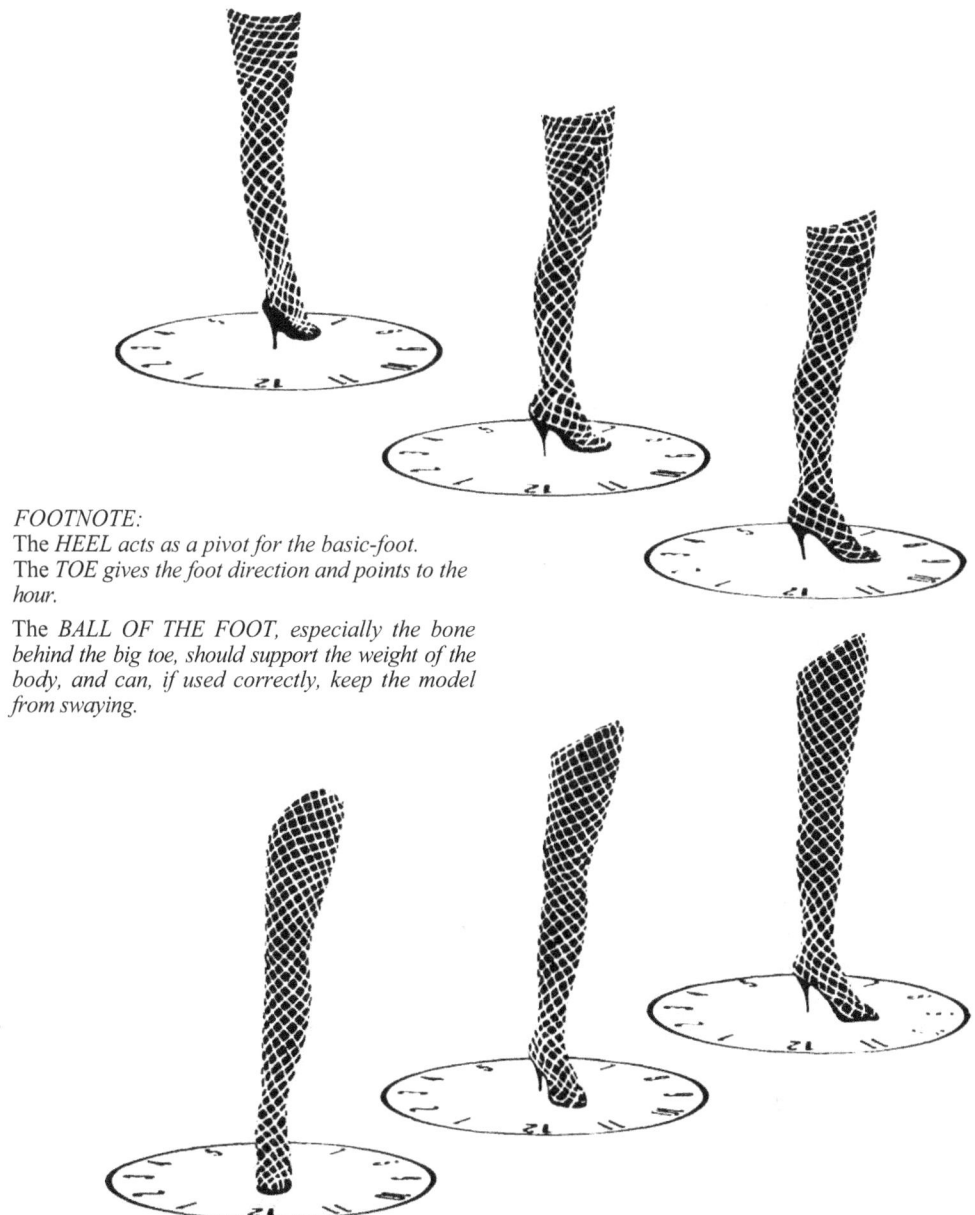

FOOTNOTE:
The *HEEL* acts as a pivot for the basic-foot.
The *TOE* gives the foot direction and points to the
hour.

The *BALL OF THE FOOT*, especially the bone
behind the big toe, should support the weight of the
body, and can, if used correctly, keep the model
from swaying.

41

SHOW-LEG
POSITIONS

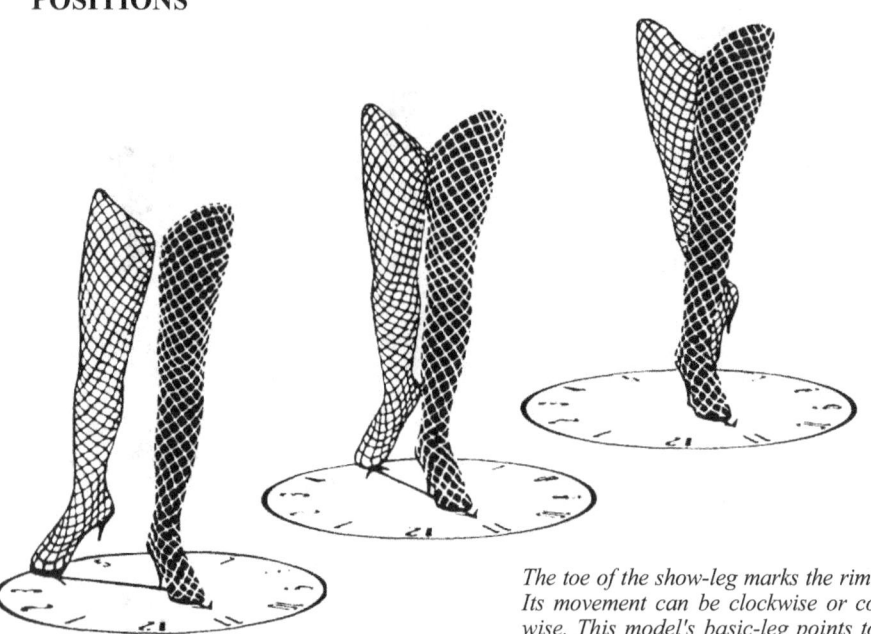

The toe of the show-leg marks the rim of the clock.
Its movement can be clockwise or counter-clock-
wise. This model's basic-leg points to eleven and
her show-leg stops at each of the twelve numbers
on the clock. Her exact leg position in each picture
can thus be identified.

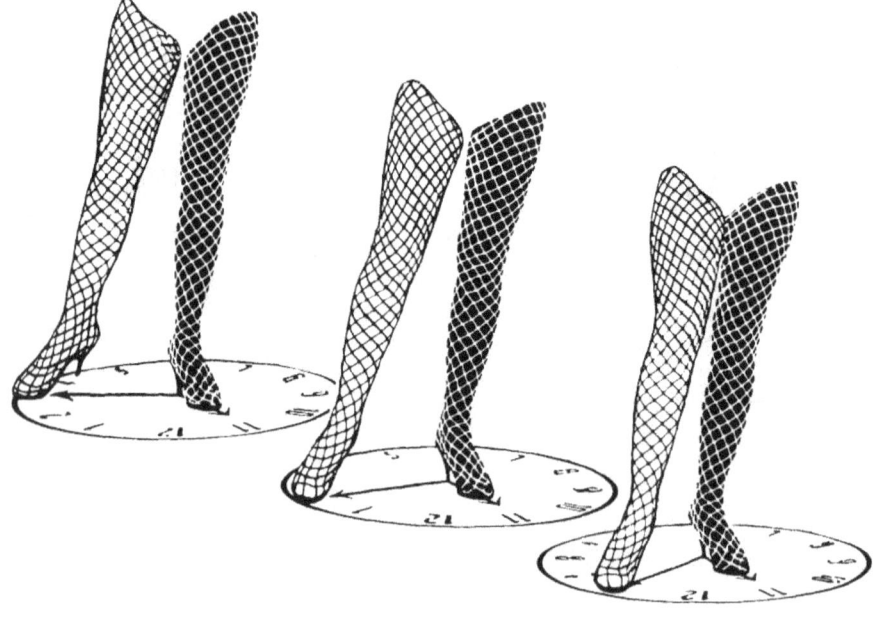

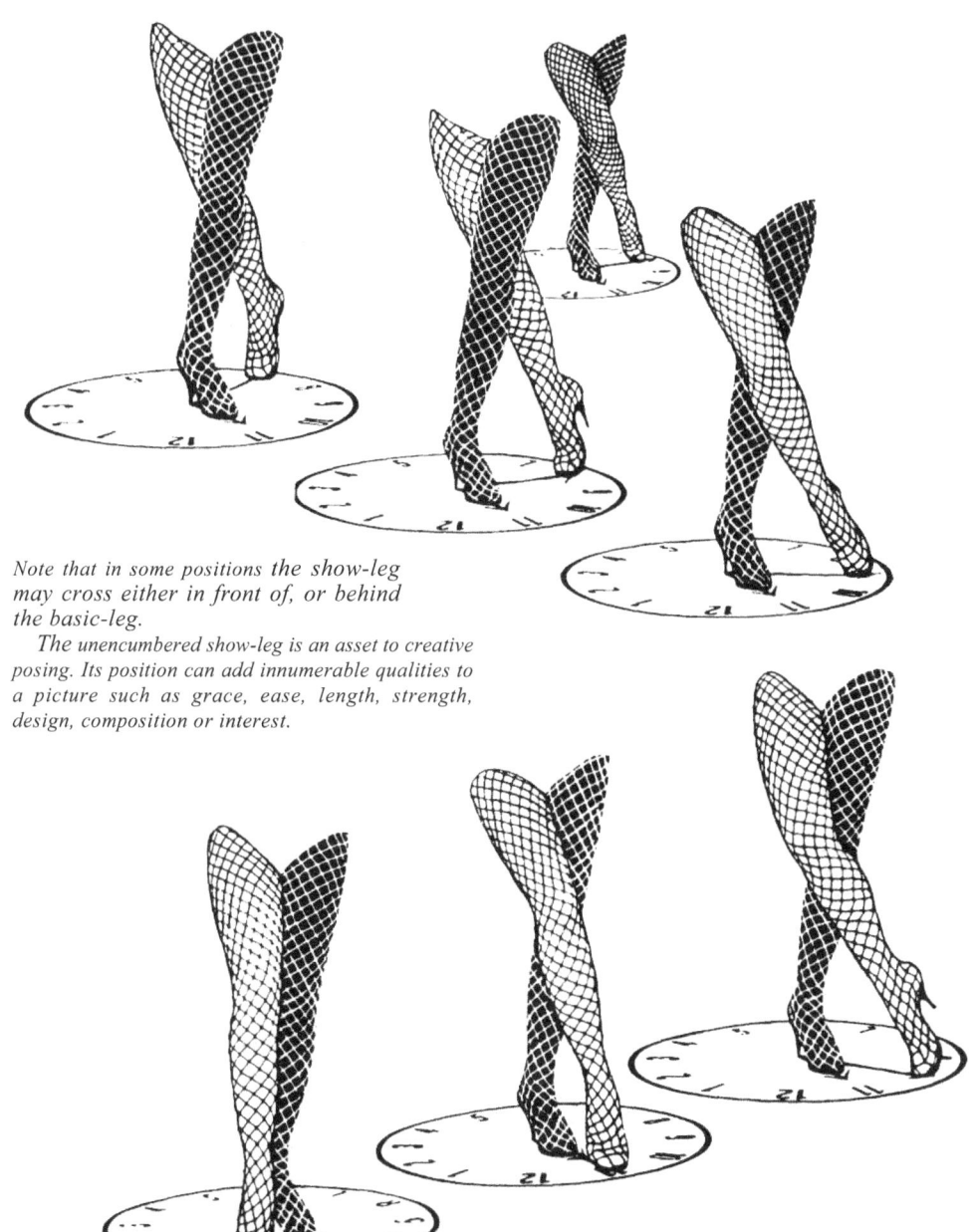

Note that in some positions the show-leg may cross either in front of, or behind the basic-leg.

The unencumbered show-leg is an asset to creative posing. Its position can add innumerable qualities to a picture such as grace, ease, length, strength, design, composition or interest.

43

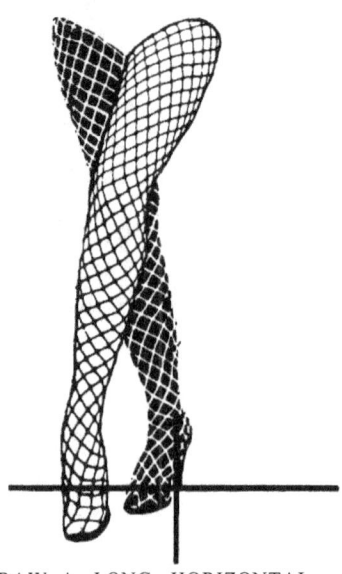

1) SELECT A STANDING LEG-POSITION

2) DRAW A LONG HORIZONTAL
   LINE THROUGH THE HEEL OF
   THE BASIC-FOOT
3) DRAW A SHORT VERTICAL LINE
   THROUGH THE SAME HEEL

HOW TO DIAGRAM A STANDING LEG-POSITION

for analysis and duplication.

The basic-leg and the show-leg in combination, with slight or great change, are capable of hundreds of positions. Certain combinations, however, are more usable than others and it is important to be able to recognize and remember a good foot-position when you see it.

Many times it becomes necessary, or desirable to know how certain illustrated leg-positions were executed.

A simple way to analyze a standing leg-position is to draw a rough *floor-clock* about the feet of the illustration so that you can quickly estimate leg placement. (Where it is undesirable to deface a fine photograph or a borrowed magazine, use transparent paper and draw your diagram over it.)

1) Select a sketch or a photograph contain ing a leg-position you would like to ana lyze.

2) With a heavy black pencil (or a red one) draw a long horizontal line through the heel of the basic-foot parallel to the bot tom of the page. This line should be of equal length on each side of the heel.

3) Draw a short vertical line through the heel of the same foot perpendicular to the bottom of the page. (When the foot is on the toes, as in high heels, the line should be drawn through the point at which the heel of the shoe touches the floor or would touch the floor if it were set down.)

4) Describe an elliptical circle to represent the edge or rim of the floor-clock. Start

the line at the tip of the show-toe and swing the circle to each end of the crossed lines.

5) Turn the picture upside down and ar range twelve numbers clock-wise around the circumference of the ellipse. Put 12:00 o'clock at the center-top of the page.

6) The basic-foot is the hour hand and the show-foot is the minute hand; read the time indicated by the leg position you have just diagrammed.

Our floor clock says seven minutes after 1 :00 o'clock. What does yours say?

In order to save time and space, most experienced photographers, directors and models use a direct method of indicating positions of the feet instead of saying the actual time. For example, twenty minutes until one o'clock on the floor-clock means that the basic-foot points to 1 and that the show-foot rests on 8. Such a position of the feet is said to be *one over eight.*

If the position is written, it is separated by a diagonal line thus:

    basic-foot number / show-foot number or, ı

If the basic foot is to be designated it might be written R -J or L 1, which would indicate, of course, that the (R)ight or the (L)eft foot is to be the basic one. Other positions might appear R •{, L \ or R J, and would be verbalized as *right 3 over 6, left 2 over 1, right 1 over /,* etc.

Could you duplicate a standing position from one of these simple diagrams?

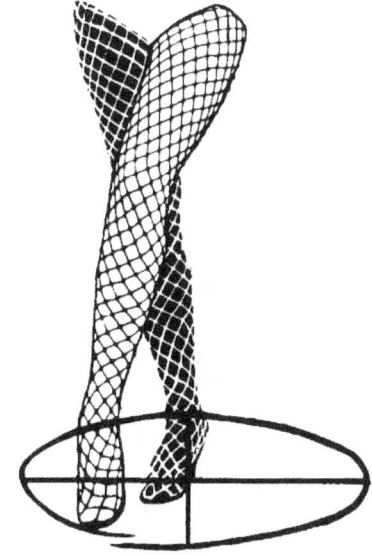

4) ENCIRCLE THE END OF THE CROSSED LINE

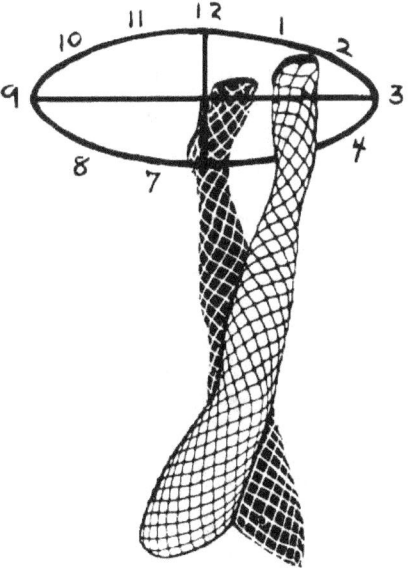

5) INVERT THE PICTURE AND NUMBER THE CIRCLE CLOCKWISE

45

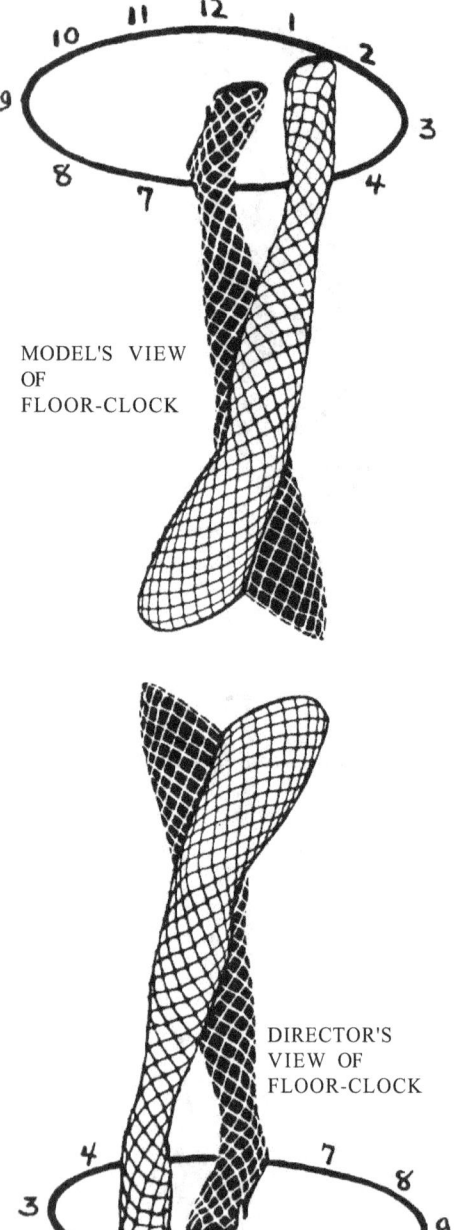

MODEL'S VIEW
OF
FLOOR-CLOCK

DIRECTOR'S
VIEW OF
FLOOR-CLOCK

DUPLICATING A
LEG-POSITION

is easy after you have diagrammed it.

Model
When you have turned your diagram up-side down, you will seem to be looking down your own legs to the floor-clock that surrounds your feet.

With your basic-toe pointing to the hour, and your show-toe indicating the minutes, you can tell time ... time and time again!

Director
It is best to interpret the position of each leg independently so that you can super-vise its movement without confusing your model.

With your diagram in hand, establish the position of the legs illustrated in your own mind before translating it, by com-mand, to your model. Tell her:

... which foot is to support her weight.
... to which number its toe points. ...
upon which number her show-toe
should rest.

It's as simple as that!

THE CONTOUR OF A LEG

in any standing position, depends upon the degree of tension at the knee. This affects the physical outline of the leg and influences the viewer's impression or interpretation of the position.

Too often and too late ... legs do not appear in a finished picture as you thought they would. The trick is to exercise control of the knee and see that it *adds to* the significance of the leg.

After a leg position is established, note the tautness and position of the knee. Is it tensed until it appears bowed? Does it look straight? Does it curve, or is it angular? Actually, none of these positions is wrong ... if it serves the right purpose.

The taut knee position with its bowed effect is associated with the young and awkward. It is often used to characterize a cocky individual or give a comic impression. Sometimes this position occurs unintentionally when a model shifts too much weight to one leg and forgets to ease the knee before the camera clicks.

When both knees are forced back with pressure or undue tension, they appear bowed like barrel staves.

The relaxed knee is actually a flexed knee. It is purposely relaxed or slightly bent to keep it from looking stiff. This position appears perfectly normal in a picture and lends ease and flexibility to a straight stance.

The bent knee can present the leg as a long curve or a sharp angle. A slight curve accentuates the flowing line of the leg and its natural contour. If it is bent at a sharp angle, the angle usually assumes more importance than the leg's contour.

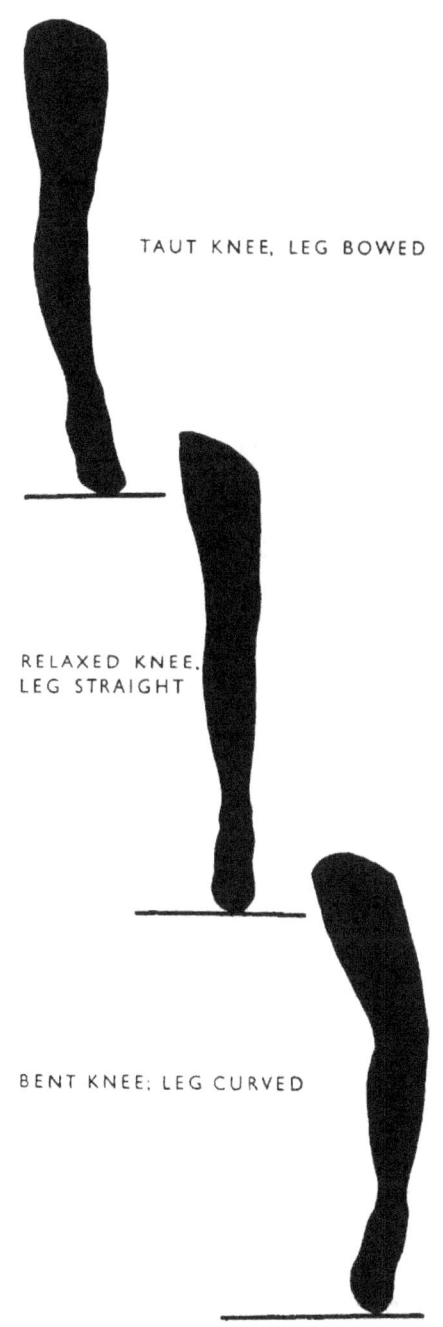

TAUT KNEE, LEG BOWED

RELAXED KNEE,
LEG STRAIGHT

BENT KNEE: LEG CURVED

47

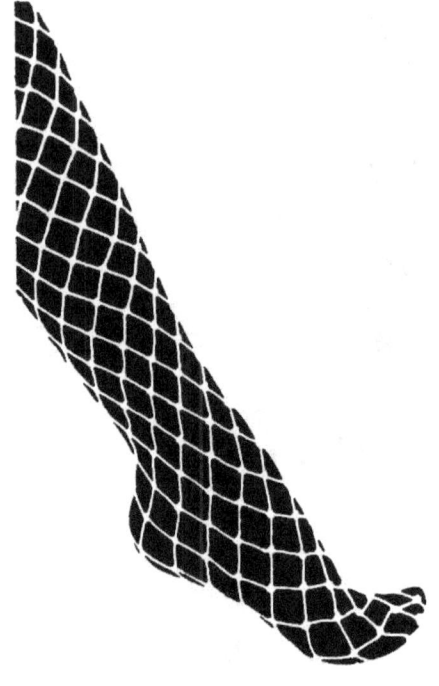

FEET

play an important part in the arrangement of leg positions and are interesting in themselves.

Did you know...

... the position of the feet can make the legs look cither long or short?
... that feet can make the legs appear graceful or awkward?
... that feet can indicate whether the legs are relaxed or tense and can express many other qualities important to you pictorially?

It is hard to realize that even though the ankle joint is a swivel-type joint, capable of moving in almost any direction, the important views, so far as the camera is concerned, all stem from simple movements.

There are just two of these movements; one is the hingelike action that elevates the heel or the toe (its action can be detected best from the side view or the foot).

The other movement is best seen from the front view of the foot: the ankle rolls in and out - from side to side.

These movements of the ankle, whether used singly or in combination, affect the appearance of the foot regardless of the camera's viewpoint.

Let's examine these simple movements of the ankle in detail:

FIRST MOVEMENT
OF THE ANKLE

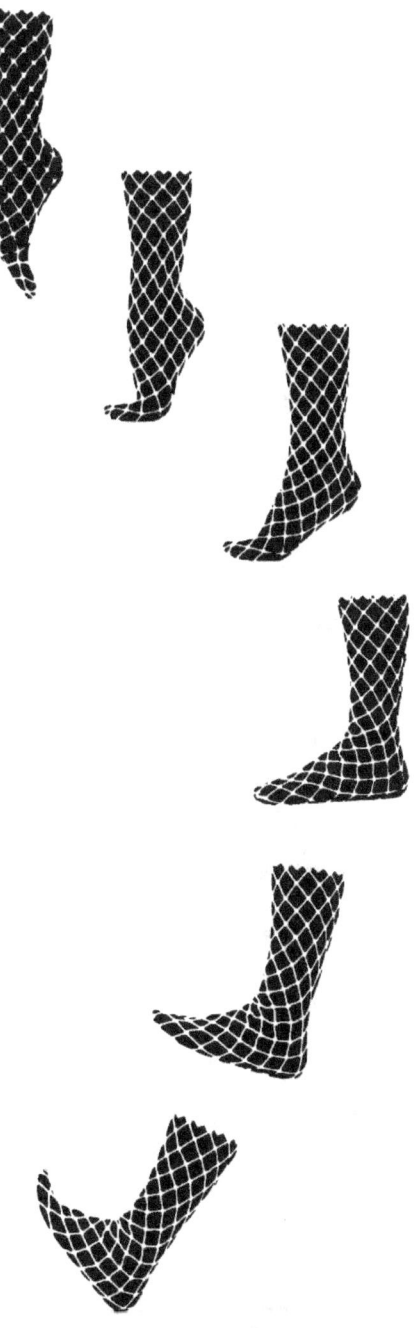

is an up-and-down action and is best illustrated in a side view of the foot. The relation
of the heel to the toe identifies its position.
The heel moves from a position higher
than the toe to a position lower than the toe.

With the heel in its highest position, the
toes curl back and form a continuous curve
with the instep. This position denotes train-
ed control and is used primarily by dancers, divers, acrobats and other skilled per-
formers because it adds maximum length
to the leg.

It is often misused by models in
would-be spontaneous or candid-type
pictures; tension in this position is easily
detected.

For naturalness and ease, without sac-
rificing the length of the leg to any notable
degree, the toes remain relaxed while the
instep alone arches down. This streamline
position is popular whether the foot is bare
or encased in high-heeled shoes, whether it
touches a support or is suspended in space.

As the heel drops closer to the ground, the
length of the leg diminishes. When the heel
touches ground, the leg looks quite stubby.

When the toe rises above the heel, a
more abrupt angle is formed and the leg
appears even shorter. The effort exercised
by the model to hold her toe up, gains
prominence, and qualities such as adoles-
cence, pertness, impudence, awkwardness or
comedy are inferred. Regardless of the
camera's viewpoint, these impressions remain the same. For instance, an arched
instep (from any camera view) makes the
leg look longer and more graceful than any
of the other positions.

SECOND MOVEMENT
OF THE ANKLE

**ANKLE ROLLED IN
(FEMININE)**

**ANKLE STRAIGHT
(MASCULINE)**

**ANKLE ROLLED OUT
(ADOLESCENT)**

is revealed primarily in the front view of the foot. It is identified by the position of the ankle in relation to the toes. The ankle moves from a vertical position over the toes either to the inside or the outside of the body.

Artists use the term *adduction* and *abduction* to indicate the movement of the ankle either toward the axis of the body or away from it, but because the terms are too similar, they are not useful in photographic work, either for determining or directing the position of a model. We talk about the model *rolling her ankle in* (toward the other foot) or, *rolling her ankle out* (away from the other foot.)

Like other movements of the foot, the three positions resulting from this action have definite meaning for the viewer. The ankle rolled - in toward the big toe side of the foot - makes a graceful curve that is used for very feminine positions.

When the line of the foot and leg becomes one and the ankle is straight, the position assumes a straightforward masculine significance. Though this position is often used by a female model to depict hoydenishness, formality or stylization; the top (feminine) position is never used by a male. An ankle rolled-out conveys immaturity.

In ballet, the position with the ankle rolled out is called *sickling* because it reminds one of the shape of the sickle used on a farm to cut grass. Most directors find the position *sickening* as it destroys poise, balance, grace and the form of the leg. If you use this position, be sure you are after adolescent, primitive or comic effects.

FAN-LIKE MOVEMENT
OF THE FOOT

must not be confused with *second movement of the ankle* although a quick glance at these two pages seems to indicate similarity in their action.

The *fan of the foot* affects only the show-foot. Its action does not involve any movement of the ankle at all; it stems from a twist of the whole leg.

Because its limited action involves only a twist of the leg, hips do not follow its rotation (remember, rotation of the basic-foot sometimes requires a change of hip position).

In *neutral position* the show-foot parallels the basic-foot. When *it fans-in*, the toe of the show-foot points toward the basic-foot; when it *fans-out*, it points away.

The degree of fanning is measured from the neutral position and although the show-foot can fan 90^0 to the right, or 90^0 to the left, it seldom does so. In fact, it is used almost exclusively in neutral position or slightly fanned-out.

Fanned-in positions are seldom used, for when the show-toe passes the line parallel to the basic-foot it *appears pigeon toed.*

We often associate the fan-of-the-foot with other characteristics and feelings:

Fanned-in it denotes awkwardness and inexperience, shyness.

The foot fanned-out about 90^0 presents the inside of the leg (when the body is in front-view) and is typical of ballet's precise control.

Fanned-out excessively and used *loosely* it is associated with the flatfooted, unsophisticated person of limited intelligence and is employed by comedians and clowns.

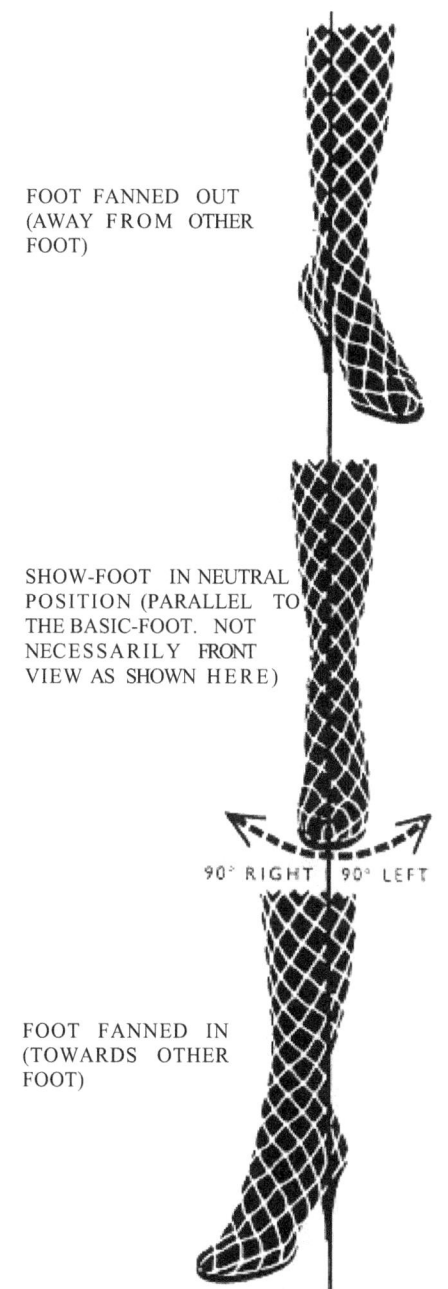

FOOT FANNED OUT (AWAY FROM OTHER FOOT)

SHOW-FOOT IN NEUTRAL POSITION (PARALLEL TO THE BASIC-FOOT. NOT NECESSARILY FRONT VIEW AS SHOWN HERE)

90° RIGHT | 90° LEFT

FOOT FANNED IN (TOWARDS OTHER FOOT)

BUILDING THE POSE
-DIRECTOR

Footwork is best initiated by your model because she usually knows her own balance and can, in most instances, suggest a stance that is not impossible to maintain while other parts are being adjusted. Before you begin to tell her exactly what to do, see if she herself can approximate a position. If you are striving for a more creative or unique leg position than she can offer or suggest, it becomes advisable and necessary to help her construct her leg position through your direction.

In order to translate your ideas into her action, you must have a keen understanding of body balance and leg mechanics. You must also be able to visualize and analyze both basic and creative leg positions.

Collect, for observation and evaluation, at least 50 illustrations of leg positions. Separate them into two piles according to weight distribution:
1) *Equal* (weight evenly distributed)
2) *Unequal* (a basic-foot and a show foot)

Invert pile 2 and diagram each picture with a floor-clock. Separate the pictures into piles that indicate the same hour. Note and compare the difference that the placement of the show-foot has made on each.

Select the leg positions you prefer. Remember them in terms of time. Try to execute them yourself. Of course you are no model, but if you will experiment with each position in private, you will learn several things:
1) Methods of directing a model you never thought of before.

2) How to think clearly and quickly from your viewpoint and that of your model.
3) Exactly how the legs balance the body as weight shifts from point to point.

Several years ago this floor-clock method of placing feet was used as a class experiment. A gawky teenage boy was selected as the subject for demonstration. Modeling was the furthest thing from his mind. He was given three simple rules of the game. He became interested. In less than five minutes he was complying with every foot position at command and feeling pretty proud of himself!

The three-point briefing he received was this:
1) 'There is an imaginary clock encircling your feet on the floor. 12:00 o'clock is directly in front of you'.
2) 'Pretend that the foot in the center is an hour hand (basic-foot) and your other foot is the minute hand on the clock.'
3) 'Put one heel in the center of this clock and shift all your weight to that leg. Notice how the toe of this same foot can point to any hour on the clock without taking your heel from the center.'

The instructor began to call time and the class watched him respond. Try it with your next inexperienced model. It is easy. And interesting.

Direct someone who has never heard of a floor-clock. Direct her into the positions you like. This will help you remember the leg positions that you prefer (or variations you have seen and liked) for the next time you want to use them.

If, instead of having your model's weight unevenly distributed, you want it equally distributed on each foot - give her these four simple directions:

1) 'Keep your weight on both feet.'
2) 'Let your body face - ' (direction)
3) 'Space your feet - inches apart.'
4) 'Bend (or straighten, or cross) your knees.'

Such leg positions, you'll notice, are generally used with the straight, long-line body and carry out the characteristics of the severe T silhouettes.

When the weight is shifted to one leg, you will probably use 'C and 'S' curves with the silhouettes carrying out their flow of line and character.

Here are answers to some of the problems we all meet in working with live models.

Hips are not facing the camera at a flattering angle.
If the change is to be great, assign a new number for her basic-foot. If it is slight she will be able to twist her hips without disturbing the position of her basic-foot.

Feet look 'pigeon toed Simply ask her to *fan-out* the toe of her show-foot until it is either parallel to, or pointed away from the toe of her basic-foot.

Foot appears too long. (Usually when the foot is at a right angle to the lens axis) Ask her to point it directly toward or slightly away from the camera. This will present the foot at an angle rather than at its greatest length. *Ankle looks thick.*
Ask your model to roll her ankle in carefully as she turns its narrowest line to face the camera. *Legs look heavy and masculine.* Select finer and more feminine positions for her. Get her to lift her weight off her heels, relax her basic-knee slightly. Ask

her to *break* or *flex* her show-knee and curve her instep (roll her ankle in).

Unsteady on her feet and swaying while trying to hold even a simple pose. Direct her to lift her heel physically and to suspend her weight mentally on the large bone at the base of the big toe of her basic foot. *Legs look bowed.*
Turn her basic-foot away from the camera so that its tell-tale inner or outer curve cannot be compared with the other leg. Then ask her to bend her show leg slightly at the knee. You can also arrange the leg nearest the camera in a flattering position so as to hide the leg supporting her weight. *Body position disturbing, even though her legs are not showing.*
Approximate the foot position she is using, determine its faults and start all over with her body correctly balanced on her legs.

As you become more conscious of the positions of legs in pictures, books, movies, magazines, TV, newspapers, etc. do you find any which would have been improved if:
The toe had been fanned out?
The heel had been raised a little?
The ankle had been rolled in?
One knee had been bent slightly?
The pose had been properly balanced?

In other words, how would you have directed the model to make the change to improve the picture?

Can you detect the difference in pictures, between the models who feel their balance instinctively and those who do not?

Can you detect the difference between models who were properly and improperly directed?

BUILDING THE POSE
- MODEL

You value your legs ... but, do you value them enough - picture-wise? Do you realize how very important it is know exactly what they are doing and how they look to the camera?

Inexperienced models exasperate directors and photographers by using the same, unimaginative cliche leg-position over and over for each pose. Capable models are expected to be - and are - more creative and flexible.

Imagine! You can perform dozens of different leg-positions, starting right this minute - without practice - if you only think of your feet as the hands of a clock. Practice will teach you how to hold your balance and to choose the ones best for you; but, just by thinking of the clock at your feet, you're off to a creative start. You won't even have to spoil every pose by looking down to see what your feet are doing. The correct arrangement of legs starts in your mind! So let's start your mind thinking about legs.

1) With your left foot as your basic-foot, execute 1:00 o'clock. Remember that your show-foot should barely touch the floor. It must be free to make changes (ankle move ment and foot positions) without leaving the spot. Remember, also, at all times, that 12: 00 on your floor-clock is always in di rect line with the camera regardless of the direction your body is facing.

2) With your right basic-toe at two, stop your show-toe at each number on the clock ... repeating the time out loud as you do so. Try each of the positions you just did and use the short-form for telling the time, as: *right 2 over* 1, 2 , 3, 4, etc.

3) Ask a friend to call out some time-posi tions and see if you can comply readily with them.

4) For practice in holding leg positions, see if you can balance without teetering while you count slowly to 100.

5) To help you plan ahead what you will do with your legs, watch the second hand on a clock and see how many times you can change leg positions every 10 seconds without losing the count or repeating the same position.

6) Clip at least 50 leg-positions out of sev eral different kinds of magazines. Sort out all the pictures in which the weight is even ly distributed on both feet and note how some of the legs are close together, some slightly separated and others are wide apart. Also note that the body can face any direc tion while the legs are in any one of those positions.

7) Here are some of the interesting things you can do with the remaining illustrations (where weight is on one foot):

(a) Separate them into two groups: those that use the left foot as basic and those that use the right.

(b) Invert and diagram all those in which the right foot is basic. With half of these still upside down, write the time indicated along with a big 'R' (Right foot basic) at the bottom of the page. Turn the rest of this group right side up and print 'R' again at the bottom of the page with the time beside it. Set this group of pic tures aside while you...

(c) Take all the positions in which the left foot is basic (separated in step a) and put a big 'L' (Left foot basic) at the bottom of the page. See if you can estimate the correct time for each picture without inverting it or diagramming it.

(d) Shuffle all your marked pictures together and stand before a full length mirror which represents the camera at 12:00 o'clock. Cover the illustrations one after the other except for the time you have written. Let your own legs be the hour and minute hands as you execute each time. After you have taken each position, hold the illustration in front of you (right side up and facing the mirror) and check to see if your position is the same as that of the picture.

(e) Now separate your illustrations according to the ones you prefer. Ask yourself why you like some more than others.
Is the body balanced right? Do the legs add to the over-all effect and character of the pose? Can you think of a slight movement that would have improved the positions you do not like?

(f) Memorize, according to time-position, at least five of these leg positions that you can use.

(g) Select any one of these five positions and try varying it with every possible foot movement; fan-like sweep of the toe, the two ankle movements and combinations of these three.

8) Experiment with leg positions in which your show-foot can cross either in front of, or behind your show-leg.

Conditioning Exercises

Strong and flexible ankles, displaying well curved instep are essential to any professional model. Strong ankles will help you hold any position your mind can conceive or your director can dictate.

To begin with, get in the habit, even when wearing high heels, of working as much as possible on the balls of your feet. Toes should be relaxed and not pointed stiffly downward unless you are directed to this.

The importance of actual ankle and instep exercises cannot be overemphasized. Take time to practise and strengthen the necessary muscles with these exercises and you will surprise yourself - with feet and legs that *know* what they are doing!

1) Stand barefoot, feet two inches apart and parallel. Rise high on the balls of the feet, ankles well forward and still evenly apart. Now bring ankle bones together while still on the toes. Keep your heels apart! Separate the ankles and return your heels to their original position on the floor.

Now, starting with the feet in the same position, roll each foot on its outside edge, back onto its heels with the toes off the floor, down on to the inside edges, up on the toes and down. Repeat about twenty times each day.

2) Place one foot in front of the other, toes slightly out, weight on the balls of the feet, heels high and ankles well forward. Let heels down, almost touching the front heel to the back toe. Rise to the fullest height on the toes again and walk around the room keeping your stride and rhythm even. This movement should lift your body upward rather than forward.

3) For *fluid* ankles, pretend that you are stirring a cake with your big toe. Stand erect and with your leg stationary and your toe pointed, move your ankle in circles. This will increase the flexibility of your ankle and condition your knee muscles. (Imperfectly formed legs need flexible knees to correct their natural formation as tense knees accentuate any discrepancy in shape.)

4) Put your toes and the balls of each foot on the edge of a fairly thick book. Leave your heels on the floor. Pull your heels up slowly until you are in the tallest possible position. Do not let your ankles *roll out* at any stage of this action.

5) Form a habit of holding your instep inward and downward at all times. Learn to do this naturally while you are sitting, walking about or lying down in various positions.

BASIC
ARM
TECHNIQUE

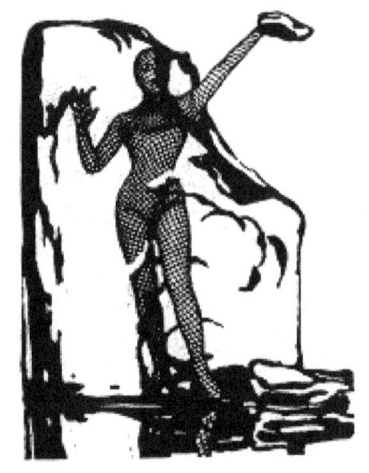

ARMS

can do one of two things: they can add to or detract from a picture! Legs may carry the weight of the model, but the arms carry the responsibility for balance, artistry and supporting expression.

Arms require more attention in posing because arms attract more attention in the finished picture.

Posing arms requires care for they can wander in many directions, while the camera limits them to relatively few usable positions.

Sound difficult? Tricky, yes, but not as

COTTER PIN JOINT (AT THE SHOULDER)

UPPER-ARM

COTTER PIN JOINT (AT ELBOW)

FOREARM

HAND

SWIVEL JOINT (AT THE WRIST)

involved as it may seem if you can begin to think of arms in three segments: upper arm, forearm and hand.

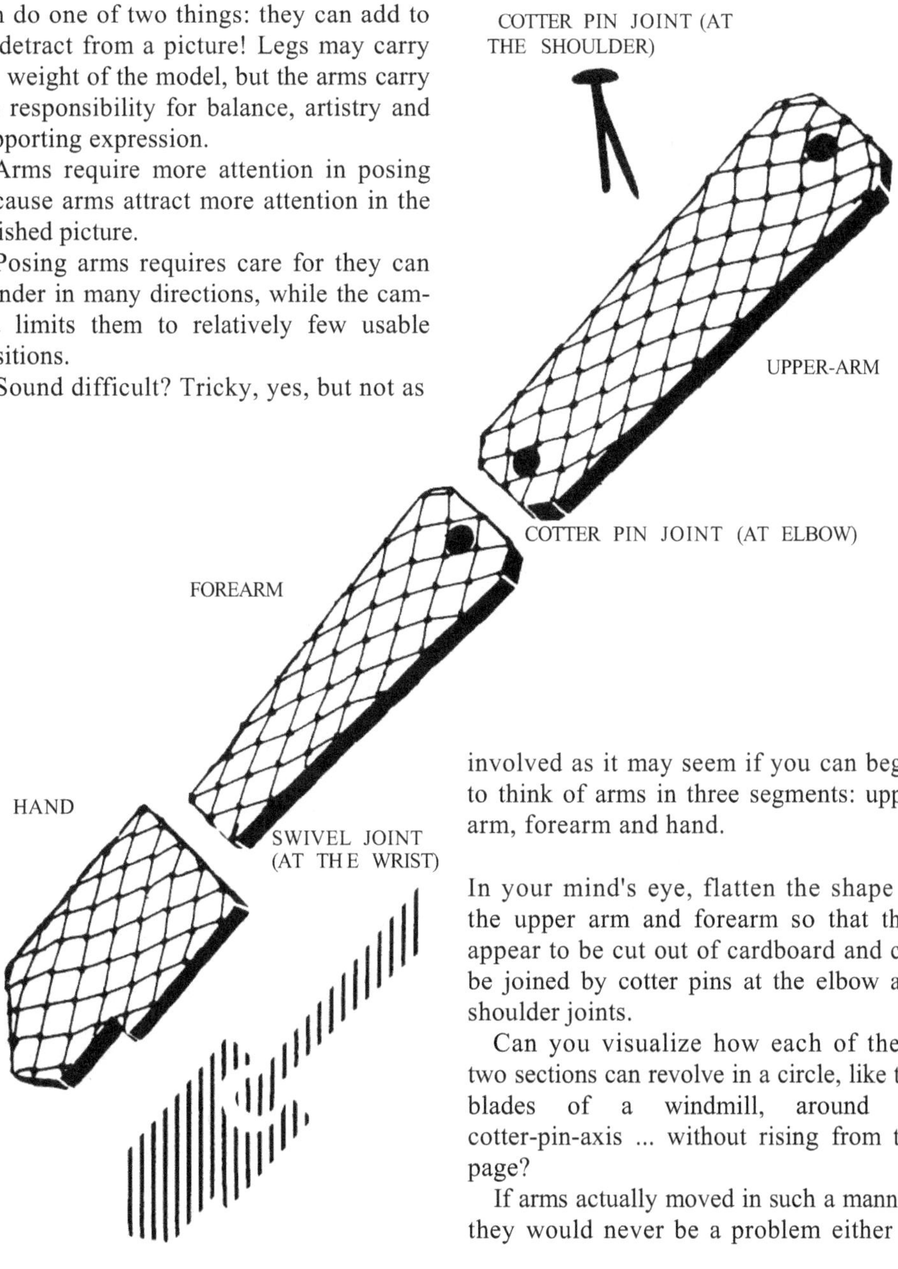

In your mind's eye, flatten the shape of the upper arm and forearm so that they appear to be cut out of cardboard and can be joined by cotter pins at the elbow and shoulder joints.

Can you visualize how each of these two sections can revolve in a circle, like the blades of a windmill, around its cotter-pin-axis ... without rising from the page?

If arms actually moved in such a manner, they would never be a problem either to

57

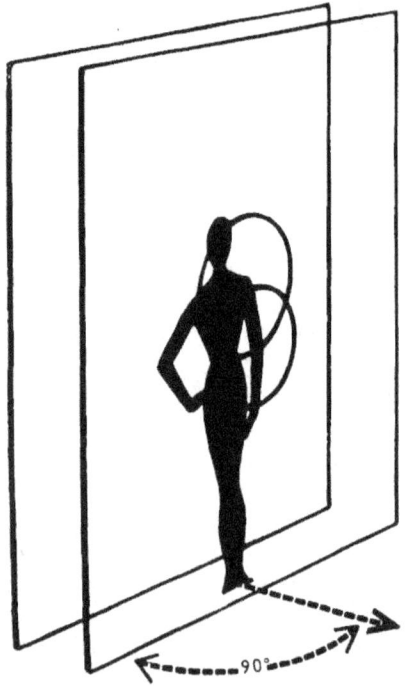

TO CAMERA

IMAGINE; MODEL AND GLASS
SANDWICH

SANDWICH FACES CAMERA
AT ALL TIMES (MODEL
MAY ROTATE WITHIN SANDWICH)

ARM MOVEMENT
CAMERA-WISE

cannot precisely duplicate the flat, flat conception of our schematic cardboard and cotter-pin figure, but the essential movement is correctly represented by its windmill-like motion sidewise, rather than toward or away from the camera.

The camera's viewpoint must be considered whenever the arms are moved. If an arm moves toward the camera, a part may be foreshortened or enlarged. If directed too far away, a part may lose its identity or be grotesqduely dwarfed. The closer the camera approaches the subject the more bizarre the distortion becomes.

The one-eyed cyclops establishes laws, restricts movement ...all must conform!

Although modern pictures are allowed more creative leeway with distortion and perspective than formerly, smart directors and models start compressing the pose into boundaries before it reaches the lens.

Posing boundaries take the form of two large panes of glass, parallel to each other and perpendicular to an imaginary line extending from the direct center of the lens (lens axis).

These two pieces of glass sandwich the model and restrict the movement of her arms. Even so, her arms can swing freely to either side, meet overhead, or cross her body in the narrow zone between it and the glass.

Thus we begin to see that these restrictions are not absolute. Each arm actually has great freedom within its limitations. Even though the movement of the forearm or upper arm is limited so far as depth is concerned, we discover many interesting positions still available to each arm.

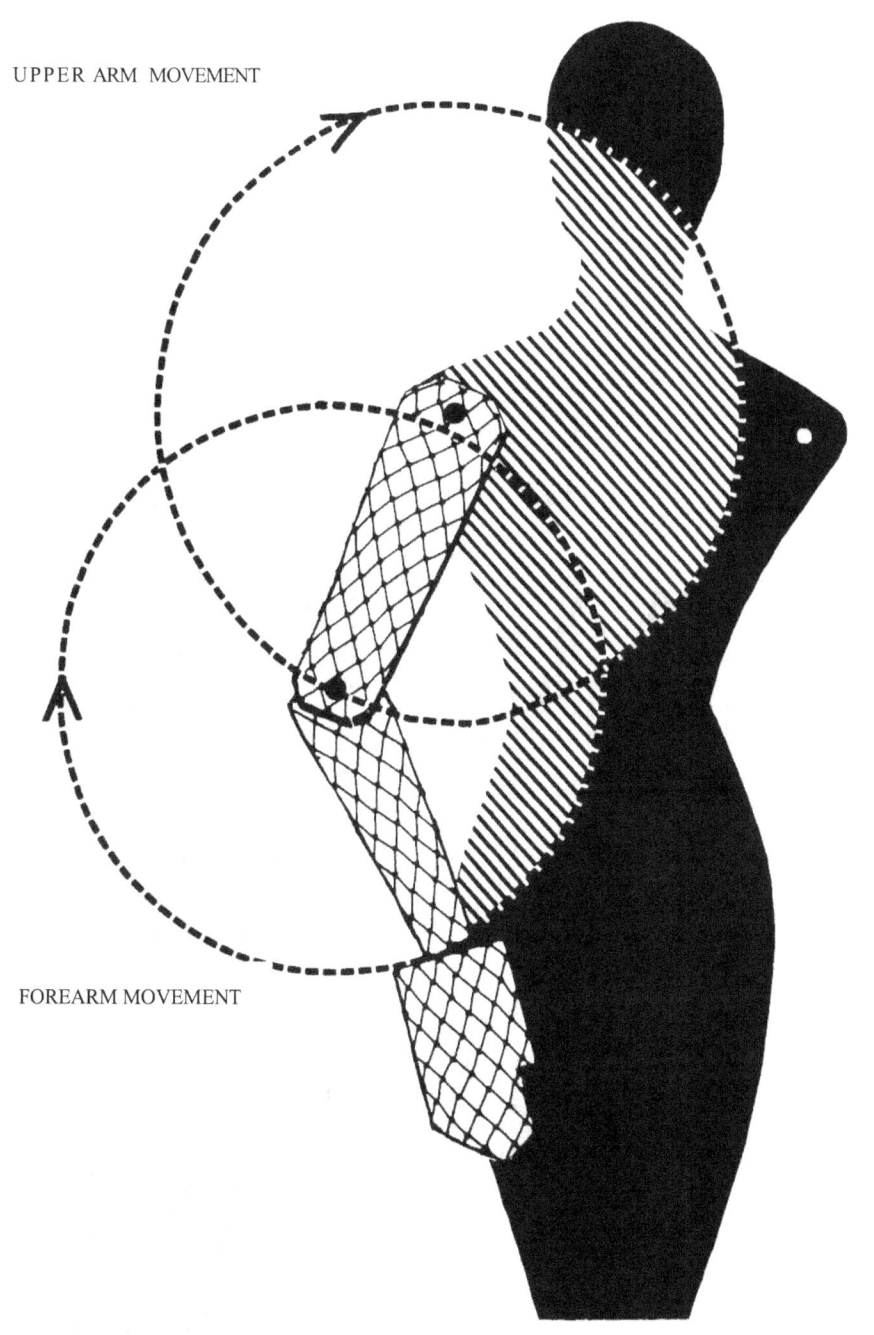

UPPER ARM MOVEMENT

FOREARM MOVEMENT

UPPER ARM

positions can be noted or directed by locating the elbow. When the body faces front, the elbow may move, within its restricted area, *out* (away from the body), *up, in* (toward the center of the body), and *down* again.

This circuit establishes four basic *stops*

or positions for the elbow with many intermediate positions.

In its normal position the upper arm hangs down from the shoulder and therefore the most used sector for the upper arm is *out and down.*

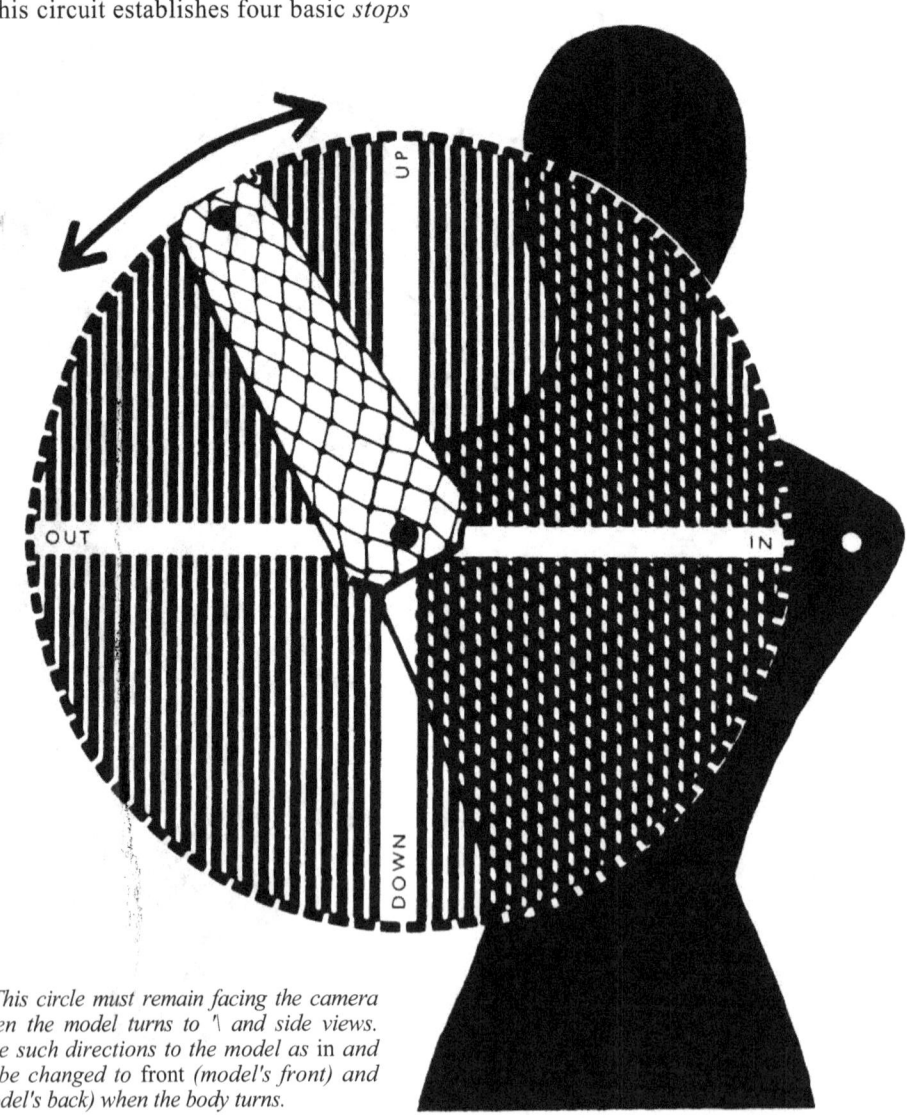

NOTE: This circle must remain facing the camera even when the model turns to \ and side views. Therefore such directions to the model as in *and* out *can be changed to* front *(model's front) and* back *(model's back) when the body turns.*

60

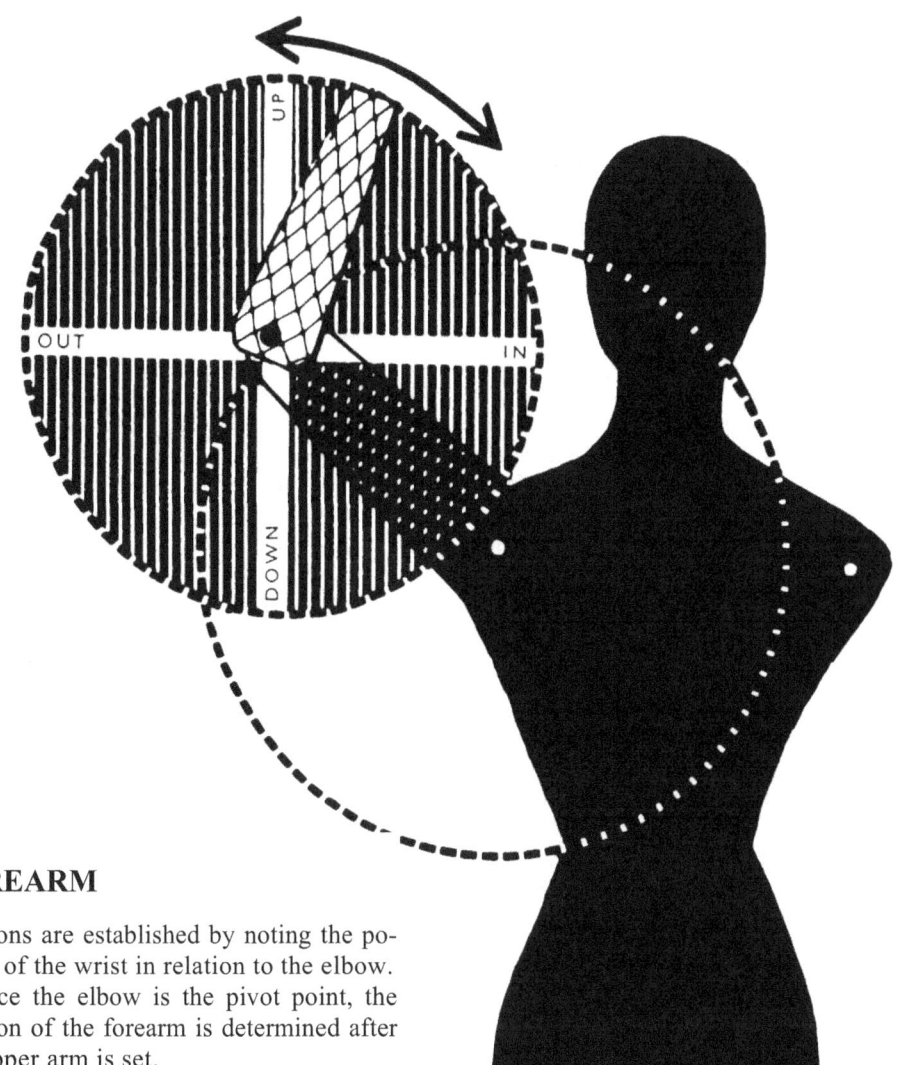

FOREARM

positions are established by noting the position of the wrist in relation to the elbow.

Since the elbow is the pivot point, the position of the forearm is determined after the upper arm is set.

In its normal position the forearm also hangs down and its four basic positions are designated by the same terms as the upper arm; *out, up, in* or *down* or by indicating intermediate positions as *in and down, up and out, in and up* and *out and down.*

This circle must also face the camera regardless of the direction the body turns while posing.

NOTE: In this schematic diagram the forearm describes a complete circle with one side remaining up. In practice the inner forearm sweeps half of this circle, then twists to let the outer forearm complete the circle.

61

COORDINATING UPPER AND FOREARM MOVEMENT

centers in the placement of their common meeting point - the elbow. Its location not only fixes the axial point from which the forearm takes action but it starts the line of the arm flowing from the shoulder in a specific direction. The placement of the wrist can continue this line or it can oppose it. When both elbow and wrist are in the same quarter of the circle, obtuse angles are formed and the arm is at its longest. When they are in opposite quarters, acute angles are formed and the arm is at its shortest. If the two segments of the arm are in adjoining quarters many different effects can be achieved.

The location of the elbow in relation to the shoulder joint is the key to determining the location of the upper arm. It is located *down, up, in* or *out* 'in toward the body or out away from the body' when the body faces either in full-front or full-back views.

If the body is in a 4 position (either front back) or in a side view, the positions to the right and to the left of the camera are designated in terms of the model's *front* or *back,* depending upon which way her body faces.

It is important to remember that both the upper and forearm circles always remain flat to the camera, regardless of which way the body faces or turns.

When the elbow is placed near the waistline several factors must be considered. If the elbow comes to rest in the edge of the waistline silhouette the arm often looks like part of the body, especially if the tone of the garment is the same at both elbow and waistline.

If the elbow is moved further away from the body on the same line, a lacework or *air space* develops between the two parts by separating them so that the background can show through. Such an area, surrounded by parts of the body is usually called a *trap* and can be very useful in designing a pose.

If the wrist and elbow are both placed on the waistline the forearm comes straight across the body and cuts it practically in half. Few pictures of women require such severe geometric treatment.

On the opposite page you will find a chart representing the range of possible views the camera can use of the arms while the body is facing the camera.

You might direct or try each of the combinations shown. Pay particular attention to the positions which are natural and easy to use. The impractical ones are marked with a *

For instance, if the upper arm is in an *out and down* position, the camera can see the:

Inner wrist with the forearm in either of the *out* positions or *up and in.*

Outer wrist with the forearm in any position on the circle; however, *up and out* is not practical.

Thumb edge of the forearm in any position on circle *(up and out is impractical).*

Little finger edge of the forearm in any position on the circle.

You might want to try these four combinations of the upper and forearm while the upper arm is in the *out and down* position. You might also like to experiment with the upper arm in each of the other seven positions shown.

62

COMBINING UPPER AND FOREARM MOVEMENT
PART OF ARM VIEWED BY CAMERA

UPPER ARM	FOREARM				ELBOW JOINT
	inner	*outer*	*thumb edge*	*pinky edge*	
'DOWN'					*inside*
'OUT & DOWN'					*inside*
out					*inside*
'OUT & UP'					*inside* *back**
UP'					*back*
UP & IN'					*back*
IN'					*back*
& DOWN'					*back* / *inside**

*The forearm has the freedom of each quarter indicated by the light area. *An arm can assume this position only under strain, tension or pressure.*

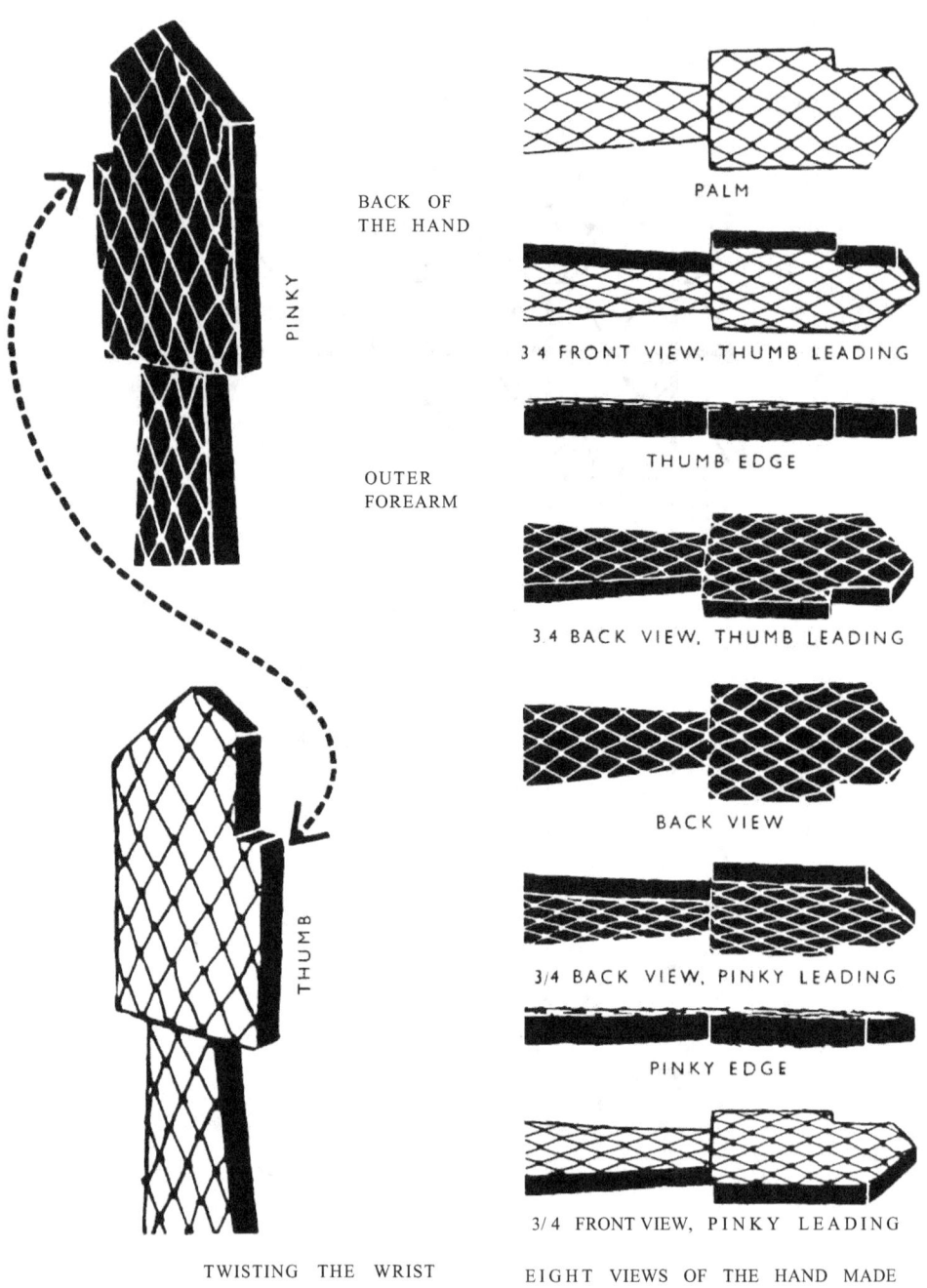

BACK OF
THE HAND

PINKY

OUTER
FOREARM

THUMB

TWISTING THE WRIST

PALM

3 4 FRONT VIEW, THUMB LEADING

THUMB EDGE

3 4 BACK VIEW, THUMB LEADING

BACK VIEW

3/4 BACK VIEW, PINKY LEADING

PINKY EDGE

3/4 FRONT VIEW, PINKY LEADING

EIGHT VIEWS OF THE HAND MADE
POSSIBLE BY TWISTING THE WRIST

64

THE HAND

is controlled by the wrist camerawise. Since, at this point, becoming involved with a handful of fingers might prove confusing, let's consider the hand as one mass. Imagine it gloved in a flat, pointed box conforming roughly to the hand's general outline.

This box, like the hand, has broad surfaces on the front and back. The narrow edges are easily identified as the *thumb* or *pinky* (little finger) edge. Many views become possible with two movements of the wrist called the *twist* and the *break.*

Twisting the wrist does not actually twist the wrist at all! To understand fully this movement, you must think of the forearm and hand as a single, flat, continuous bar; the palm and inner forearm on one side and the back of the hand and outer forearm on the other. As the wrist twists it flips the bar from one side to the other or stops part way to display the edges.

Breaking the wrist means breaking the continuous line formed by the hand and the forearm at the wrist junction.

The wrist can break in two directions 1) sidewise, or 2) front and back. When the wrist *breaks sidewise* it can *break in* (toward the thumb) or *break out* (away from the thumb.)

When it breaks front and back, it *breaks forward* (the palm toward the inner forearm) or it *breaks back* (the palm of the hand away from the inner forearm).

As these movements are used singly or in combination, many views of the hand become possible ... some more acceptable than others.

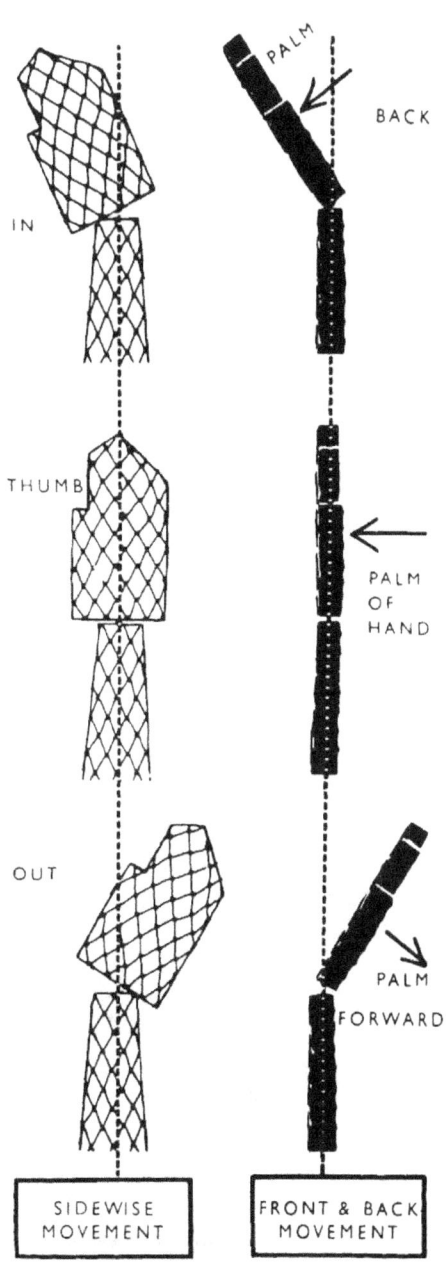

BREAKING THE WRIST

HAND POSITIONS
BOLD AND TAPERED

result from movements of the wrist, the forearm or combinations of the two.

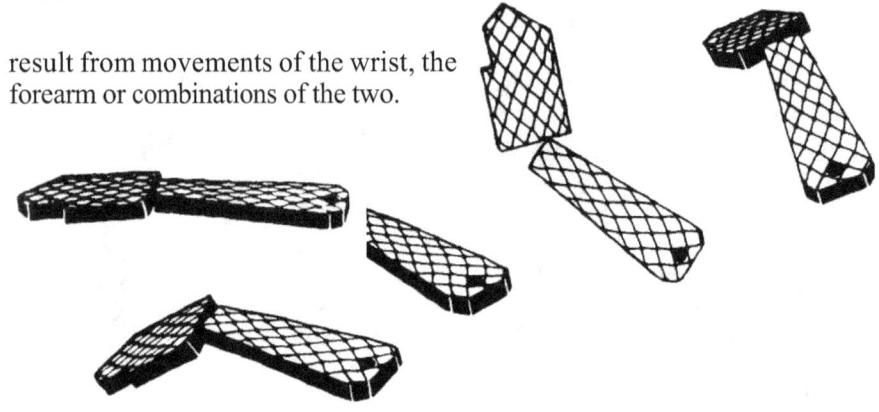

Side views of the hand, that form a long point at the finger tips and all other narrow positions which add length to the forearm are said to taper, while any position that stops the flow of line, foreshortens the hand or shows the hand as square or boxy is called bold *and shortens the overall effect.*

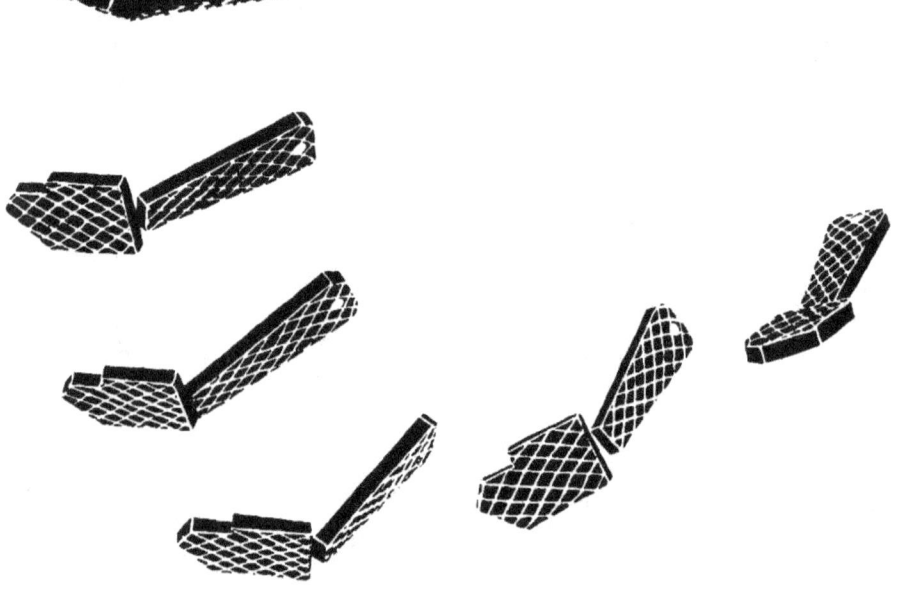

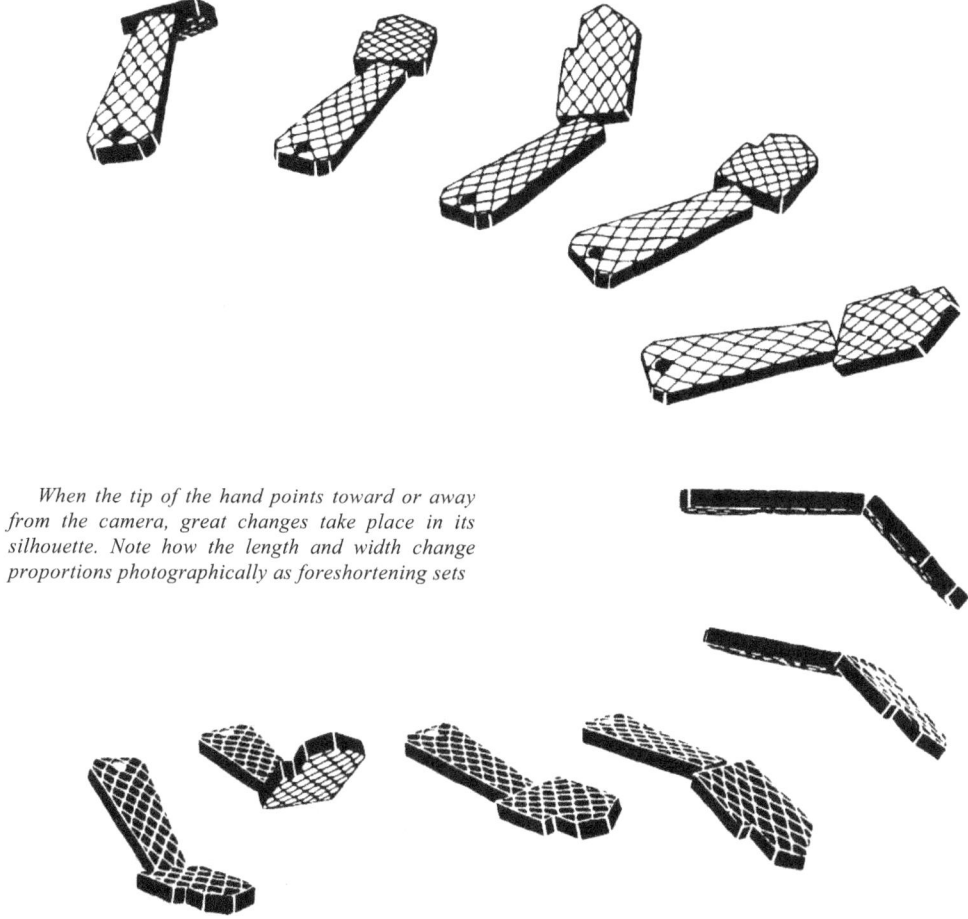

When the tip of the hand points toward or away from the camera, great changes take place in its silhouette. Note how the length and width change proportions photographically as foreshortening sets

Tapered hands . . .

primarily display the long inside or outside contours of the hands.

They add length to the arm and grace to the picture as a whole.

Since they are used to express finer emotion and character, their message is relayed in subtle differences of position and careful attention to detail is of utmost importance in their use.

Bold hands . . .

display the broad flat palm, back of the hand or geometric shapes, such as a clenched fist. They are deliberate attention getters ... masculine and massive. Their abrupt bulk stops the eye. Bulk transmits positive feelings of physical vibrancy, strength, dynamic emotion or authority. Sometimes bold hands are used to convey negative feelings of clumsiness or violence.

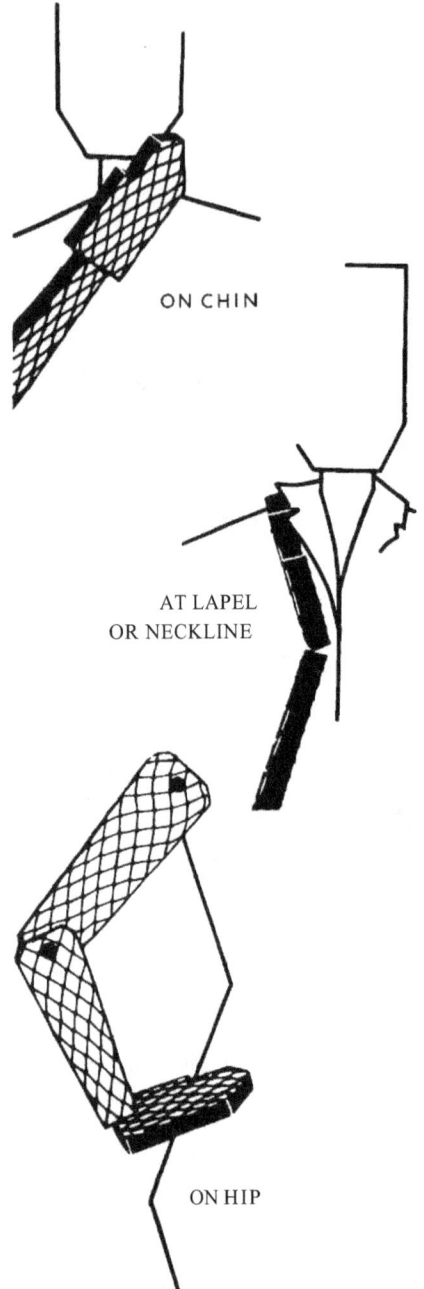

ON CHIN

AT LAPEL
OR NECKLINE

ON HIP

HAND-STOPS

are the places where hands normally stop. You should have used these ten *hand-stops* thousands of times without thinking of them... but can you remember them at the crucial moment?

Knowing a few hand-stops will provide you with a sound basis for interesting, relaxed, uncomplicated hand positions when you begin to wonder just what to do with a hand.

When a hand stops - creative effort should begin. Opportunity for origination presents itself at any given stop. No turn or movement, however slight, is insignificant. Never be afraid to explore all of the subtle differences that can be expressed with the hand.

Endless variations of actual positions at each of these stops can be originated by:

twisting the wrist
breaking the wrist
varying finger arrangements

Endless ideas for what the hand can do at each stop will stem from thinking about what you have seen and can do. For instance, a hand on top of the head might be pushing hair out of the eyes, scratching the head in puzzlement, holding a hat in the breeze, simply relaxing there, putting a pin in the hair, etc. If you'll form the habit of watching people do these things you'll soon discover that each of these actions can be done in many different ways ... with the hand remaining on top of the head!

Once the hand stops - start working with it to form bold or tapered positions which help communicate the idea of the picture accurately yet conform to the limitations of the camera.

68

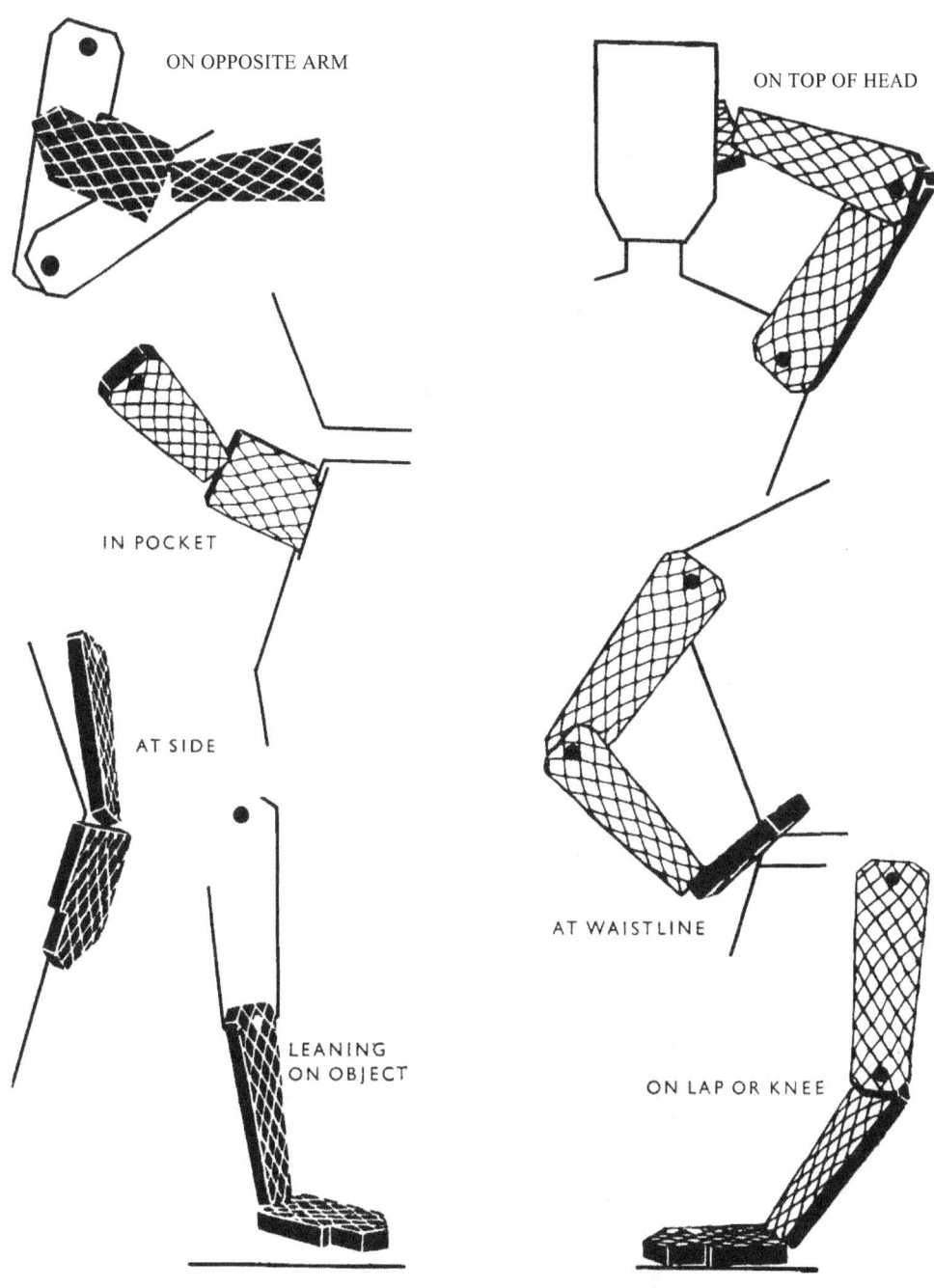

ON OPPOSITE ARM

ON TOP OF HEAD

IN POCKET

AT SIDE

AT WAISTLINE

LEANING
ON OBJECT

ON LAP OR KNEE

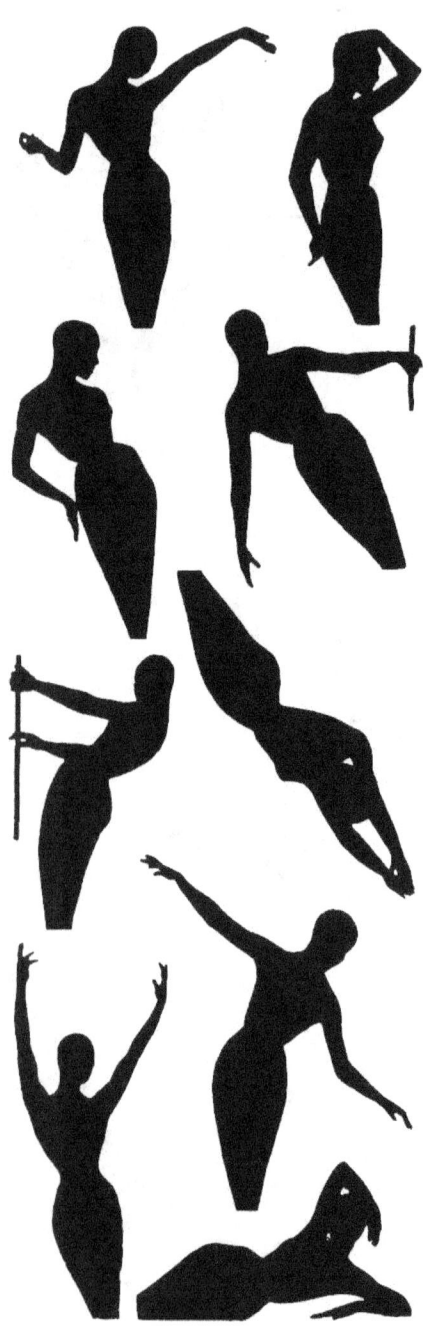

ARMS IN PICTURES

are the despair of countless directors and models. Some even resort to concealing the arms, reasoning that 'no arm movement is better than poor arm movement'. And, to an extent, they are right. You *can* keep your head above water - *but* you will never win any races that way!

Arms are essential to quality posing. Arms can be an asset or a liability and the only way to obtain effective results is to use them effectively.

If you are apprehensive about the problem - cut it in half. Work with one arm at a time. Remember that the camera is methodically collecting space and pressing it into a flat picture surface. You cannot ignore it.

The design in which the three segments of the arm reach this flat surface is of practical importance. Because the arm is fastened at one end and telescopes to the other, it seems sometimes to take on properties *of direction* in its flow of design. At other times it seems to encircle or bound areas - mentioned earlier as *traps*.

While some directors are sensitive to the excessive light these traps hold, all find them most useful in design.

When the arm makes a trap, its size, shape, location and position can be used to photographic advantage.

If the arm assumes direction and seems to go somewhere ... it does so in a *continuous line* or a *broken line*.

When you look closely at the arms on these pages you soon see that there are two kinds of continuous lines. One is absolutely straight: upper arm, forearm and hand in a line. The other is a flowing line composed of these same parts arranged in a curve.

When the line is broken it takes the eyes around right-angled corners, or down and back with acute angles at elbow and wrist.

The direction of the arm, from shoulder to finger tips, moves:

1) toward the body (up or down)
2) away from the body (up or down)
3) across the body (high or low)
4) parallel to the body (high or low)
5) or, relates itself to the horizontal, diagonal or vertical lines of props or to the page itself by crossing, becoming parallel to or striking it at an angle.

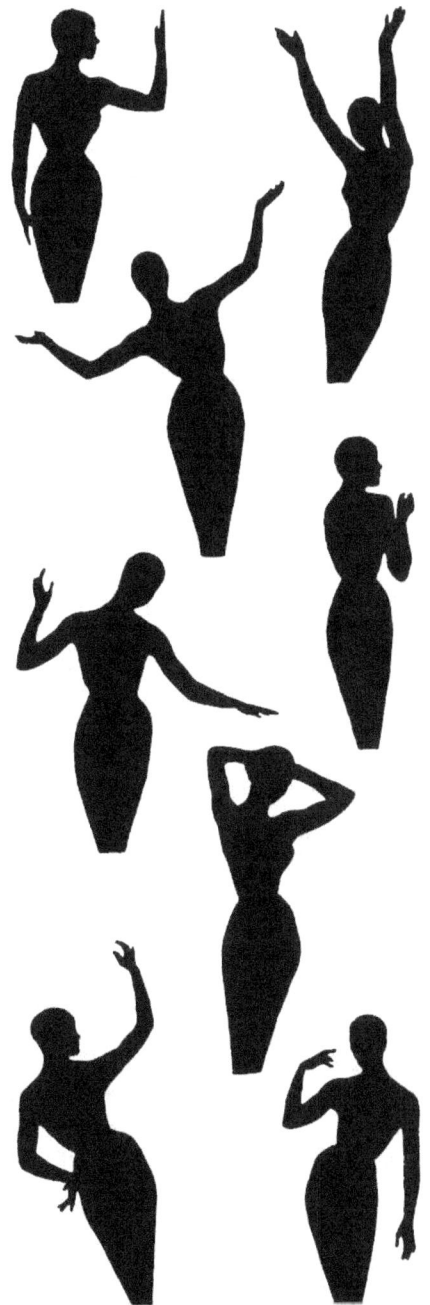

Whether you use dynamic symmetry, a special formula or your inborn sense of balance to arrange them - one thing is sure: there is a myriad of excellent positions to choose from.

Can you

... recognize the general design of each arm? Does it make a trap, a continuous or a broken line?

... spot and identify any rectangular traps? Many sizes of triangular ones?

... state quickly the general direction of each line? (Up, parallel to the body; out, at a right angle to the support, etc.)

... direct yourself or someone else in the specific position of each upper arm illustrated? (Use basic positions and sectors on page 60)

... recognize each forearm position illustrated (page 63)

... recognize each hand position illustrated? (Use pages 66 and 67)

BUILDING THE POSE
- D I R E C T O R

Arms pose no problems...
If you remember the following points:

1. All final instruction must come from you, the director, who can see what the camera is doing to the arms.

2. Keep the model's arms and hands from reaching toward or away from the camera to any great degree.

3. Tapered positions of the hand add length to the arm and bold positions shorten it.

4. Both arms do not have to show in every picture. In fact, in some positions, placing one arm behind the body often gives clean delineation to the body's outline. But if the forearm does not show, it is best not to let the hand pop out of the outline unexpectedly. It is quite distracting to a viewer to see a hand appearing from nowhere at the waistline or to notice a strange bump in a pocket.

5. Sharp angles at the elbow can be soften ed, if desired, by moving the elbow slightly toward or away from the camera and a right angle (from the camera's viewpoint) can be made obtuse by the same action.

6. An arm can always be made to appear more slender by diverting the wide inner elbow and flat forearm away from the cam era. There is a popular misconception that the full width of the elbow cannot be turned away from the camera without turn ing the hand also. Nevertheless, it is possible and most models can do it naturally or with a little practice ... whether the hand is sup porting the body or not.

7. Keep the elbow away from the waistline. If the arms must cross a standing figure, they should do so above or below the waist line. An elbow at the waistline makes the body appear thick, heavy and masculine unless an air space or contrast of tone pre vents the arms from attaching themselves to the silhouette and adding weight and bulk to the outline.

8. Soft flesh is distorted by pressure. When the soft part of the arm presses into a hard er surface it may lose its smooth outline. Pressure can be eased by leaning lightly, or when possible, carrying most of the weight on the hard parts of the arm such as the shoulder bone, elbow, wrist or hand.

9. An arm supporting the weight of the body, should not reveal too much rigidity or tension. Strain can be eased by better weight distribution or a momentary shift to ease it just before the picture is taken.

10. When thought is put into the proper loc ation of the elbow, no additional adjust ment of the upper arm is necessary. Also, with the capricious forearm secure at one end, all creative effort can be concentrated on the location of the other end of the fore arm and the position of the hand.

Have you ever had the perfect picture -except that the arms didn't look like mates? One was too thick while the other was too thin? Did you ever have a hand look like a stump? If you did, distortion and fore-shortening are not new to you. You know the havoc they can play with important pictures. But HOW can you communicate this to your model without going into complicated or technical detail?

It's simple if we take a tip from stage directors and chalk guide lines right on the floor. Make two lines parallel to each other and at right angles to your lens. Place your model between them and explain that she is standing between two larges panes of glass that have been set upon those lines. (The space between the glass depends upon the distance from which you are shooting and shouldn't be more than 14 or 16 inches apart if you are working fairly close.) Show her that the glass will limit her movements to positions acceptable to the camera.

Help her adapt the idea by letting her move her arms between the imaginary boundaries. Stop her when she strays out of bounds! A few minutes of experimenting will give her confidence.

While she is still mentally between the glass, ask her to turn her body to a J or side position and move her arms again ... reminding her that the glass has not moved.

Then explain to her that although the glass sandwich does not move when she moves . . . it does move when the camera moves. If you move your camera to one side the sandwich base revolves to face the lens. If your camera moves low and tilts up, the sandwich tilts forward. If the camera goes high and tilts down, the sandwich tilts back. (The model remains free to turn within the sandwich, regardless of which way it tilts or turns.)

In addition to briefing her on perspective you might also give her a quick review of hand-stops (five or more) to show her how many natural places there are in which to put each hand. The few minutes you spend explaining the rules of the game puts the model at ease, so working as a member of your team. The actual practice you receive while indoctrinating her will clarify your own thinking and help you to formulate a method of clear-cut and simple instruction.

Thus you'll soon turn a stilted subject into a sympathetic and creative model.

Fortunate is the director who works with a creative model. More fortunate the creative director who can guide his subject into preconceived or inspired attitudes. But most fortunate is the creative director who knows how to exploit a model's creativity!

When your model suggests poses by initiating action and you select what you want, a casual or candid type picture usually results. In order to save great amounts of time, you would do well to give your model a quick summary of key points in arm movement related to the camera as a basis for making more of her suggestions photographically useful.

If, on the other hand, you have a predetermined position that you want the model to assume as naturally as possible, you must be able to give simple and precise direction to bring it about.

Close your eyes, think of an arm position down to its smallest detail. Direct some model in the position of which you have been thinking. Ask yourself this question: Does it fit the mental image? Teach your mind's eye to see a picture first... then all you have to do is direct it. Practise until you have a bag full of tricks; pet phrases, subtle suggestions, key words, gestures, etc. that form and transform your model's position quickly and easily to the positions you want.

When these two methods of arriving at a pose are combined and you have a talented model who is able to create arm positions; when you have become a skillful director, able to select and correct, the basis for the third method of arriving at natural and interesting arm positions has been established. Pictures resulting from such a set-up invariably rate high.

Self evaluation . . .

will show you in which departments you need to develop more skill.

Go back to those old prints of yours (the good and the bad ones) and look through them for examples of:

1) Arms that flow in the right direction.

2) Arms that stop the eye when you want it stopped.

3) Positions of the arm that parallel the body, the page, a prop.

4) Arms that seem to balance the body nicely.

5) Mismatched hand sizes, excessive fore shortening or distortion.

6) Variety of arm angles. Do you seem to have any favorites?

7) The upper arm in positions other than the *out and down* sector.

8) Soft flesh pressured out of its natural position.

9) The elbow touching the waistline. (Is there separation ... either through a change of tone or through a trap?)

10) Arms crossing the body and not inter fering with waistline definition.

11) Bulky hand positions used to advantage.

12) Right angles at elbow or wrist used un intentionally (combined with acute or obtuse angles).

13) Right angles put to dramatic use.

14) Foreshortening of the forearm.

15) Elbows too near or too far away from the camera.

In other words, does your use of arms show variation, creativity, ease and natural-ness? Have you leaned too heavily upon one or two hand-stops without suggesting others? Are any positions masculine that should have been feminine? Any feminine that should have been masculine? Are any sophisticated that should have been ado-lescent or naive? Are any candid and loose that should contain dignity and formality?

Further your self-evaluation by doing a little research into the methods of current photographers who are having their work more frequently published than you. From several different magazines (in order to get a good cross section of work) clip all the hand positions you can find.

Separate them into the hand-stops we have illustrated and make separate piles for the extra hand-stops you will undoubt-edly run across.

Now start evaluating the pictures in each pile. For instance: hand on the hip. Are some hands placed lower than others? Do some use the thumb in front of the body instead of the fingers? Do others, with the fingers in front, use a different break of the wrist? Can you see more of the back of the hand in some? Note the most effective va-riations in each stack and try to determine what they add to the picture as a whole. Did you find any new ideas?

Try to imagine each picture at its incep-tion and what direction must have been necessary to attain the result.

In order to evaluate further your ability as a director, clip a picture from a maga-zine, study it (body, legs and arms) and lay it aside. Now, without looking at it again or letting the model see it, try to *move her with words.* Face away from your model, direct her from your mental image of the pose studied. When you have finished, turn around and see how closely your verbal direction reflects what you want!

BUILDING THE POSE
- MODEL

Adding to your many charms,
You posses two lovely arms.
They must be properly used,
So their worth is not abused;
For assets of utility
Can prove a liability.

So, our best advice to you, whenever you are modeling for a picture ... come armed with a working knowledge of what you can do with your arms!

Physically, arms . . .

... support the body in whole or in part,
... support an object,
... touch an object supported by other means, ... may be concealed to give prominence
   to other parts of the body, ...
balance the body.

Artistically, arms . . .

... express emotion,
... add design or balance to the composition,
... direct attention where desired, ... add interest or story to the picture, ... add character or color to the model.

Remember, also, that a pre-requisite of appropriate arm movement for the camera is a general knowledge of how the lens appraises arms. In order to appreciate its viewpoint - go to your mirror. Put your face ten inches away from the glass. Hold each hand up beside your face, palms toward the glass, thumbs touching the lobe of each ear. Compare the length of your hands, from the wrist to finger tips, with the length of your face, from the bottom of your chin up to your hairline. They are approximately the same size.

Now, move your right hand about five inches toward the mirror and your left hand about five inches away. Close one eye and compare the difference in the apparent size of your hands. With but few inches difference, the hand that moved toward the mirror will appear much larger than your face, while the hand that moved away will appear much smaller. The hands, in comparison to each other, will show even a greater difference.

The camera sees things in relatively the same manner. Movement to or away from the camera can play havoc with your proportions, or if you know how to use it, can help you.

Your natural question then is, 'what can I do when I can't actually see myself, and I don't know just how far I can move without distortion?' The answer is easy. First, listen to your director and think before you respond. Secondly, when you are expected to suggest poses yourself, mentally set your boundaries and keep parts from straying to or away from the camera.

Feel yourself sandwiched between two parallel panes of glass. (Illustrated and explained on page 58.) These panes of glass will enable you to move your arms sideways as your body faces the camera, or forward and back as your body is in a side view.

To familiarize yourself with this movement and establish an indelible awareness that will serve you well, take the time to make your own cardboard and cotter-pin figure as shown on page 148.

The arm will consist of three parts; the

upper arm, the forearm and the hand. In fact, make two versions of the hand... the broad flat hand like the one illustrated on page 64 and a taper-thin hand on page 149. Start manipulating the elbow first, then the wrist. Reproduce the arrangements you have originated before your mirror, or in silhouette practise.

Suggesting poses . . .

with ease and assurance, before the camera, results from concentrated observation and actual practice. Observation can be started by clipping forty to fifty full length pictures from magazines and spreading them before you on a large table. Get ready to separate them several times. The first time into two stacks,

1) *Continued-line arms*
   (straight and flowing) lines
2) *Broken-line arms*
   (acute, obtuse and right angles)

Where the arms are in different positions, cut the figure in half so that you can put each arm in its correct pile. While you are sorting them notice ...

... how long the arms look in the continued-line pile,
... the masculine look of those at right angles, ... the graceful obtuse-angled arms,
... how every forearm reaching toward the camera is foreshortened,
... the position of the elbow in relation to the waistline,
... how the arm becomes shorter when the forearm meets the upper arm at a very acute angle,
... the expressive qualities of the arms in each pose,
... the different patterns of the traps formed by the arms in relation to each other and the body; triangles, rectangles, squares, trapezoids, etc.

Now, shuffle your pictures and separate them into another two piles, this time according to the position of the wrist.

1) Straight wrist
2) Broken wrist

Further separate the broken wrists into those that are broken *in* (toward the body), *out, up, down, toward* and *away* from the camera.

Look closely at the last two; broken *toward* and broken *away* from the camera. Can you detect the wrist movement or combinations of movement that produced these positions? (Look for the thumb and palm of the hand to key the identity of their movement.)

Notice in all of the wrist pictures how some make a slight break, while others make an extreme break.

Do the straight wrist pictures seem athletic, crisp and strong to you? Do they depict assurance?

Do the broken wrist pictures give you a feeling of grace, of relaxation or flexibility?

Now, reshuffle your pictures a third time into examples of:

1) Bold hands
2) Tapered hands

Do you notice that tapered hands of women are used frequently? And that bold hands rival the expression and importance of the face?

Can you detect any picture in which either hand is displayed poorly but could have been improved by a simple movement of the wrist?

Fourth step is hand-stops. Reshuffle and separate your illustrations again into hand-stops (some of which appear on pages 68 and 69).

Which pile has the most variations of hand positions? (Do not count positions as different that are duplicates in reverse.)

Get in front of your mirror and see if you can originate at least five different hand positions at each hand-stop for which you found an example.

In your collection of pictures, have you noticed...

... any display of the broad inner elbow that could have been made more attractive by bending the elbow slightly and rotating it so that the narrow side faces the camera?

... any display of unnecessary tension, *sprung* joints or distorted flesh when the arm supports the weight of the body? (Double joints at the elbow or on the fingers also appear to be *sprung* in a picture unless arranged to look normal.)

... how the majority of arms and hands crossing the body are usually in a contrasting tone or color so they do not appear as part of the body?

... the casual, yet expert placement of hands and elbow to preserve waistline profile?

... any picture of the arms crossing the body at the waistline? If so, do they seem to cut the silhouette in half and make it appear heavier than if they crossed above or below the waistline?

... that a hand extended toward the camera looks like a stub at first glance?

... how much faster you can detect what a figure is doing when the hands and arms are separated from the body with air spaces?

Taking direction...

is an important phase of your being useful before the camera - particularly where arms are concerned. You, as a model, are composed of many individual parts. However, you also must be composed when given direction as to which part to move. Becoming flustered may result in the loss of a perfectly wonderful picture, should you change a whole arm when all the director asked you to do was to break a wrist or twist a forearm.

Therefore, complying with direction accurately is of utmost importance. You must know how every part of you is capable of moving camera-wise. When given a correction, of arm or hand placement, think before you move, 'Does he want me to move my whole arm or just part of it?' 'Should I twist it completely or just slightly?' Then move that part naturally into position *without looking at it*. And one other thing, so simple we hesitate to mention it, but it is also so important, that we must ... do learn to tell your *right* from your *left*. When the director says *right* he means *your right*. If he says *left*, do not move your right!

A very worthwhile way of learning to take direction is to practise giving direction. Pretend you are the director. Take your pile of pictures, with a friend for a model, and one by one, see if you can give directions for reproducing the arm positions of the subject to the finest detail.

BASIC
HEAD
TECHNIQUE

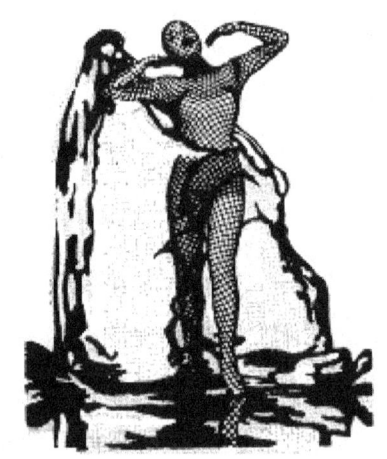

THE HEAD

must be considered photographically from two completely different aspects: i. its general form and 2. its specific expression.

First, let us consider the physical form of the head in the completed picture. It is a result, not only of the actual form of the head, but its particular view from the camera.

The least movement of the head produces marked changes in its countless planes. For this reason, complete and mutual understanding must be established between director and model as to the exact position meant by the commonly used terms, *full-face, profile* and *three-quarter head.*

> **Full-face** - means a full-faced view of the head. Other terms used *are: front-view, full-face angle* and *full front-view.*

> **Three-quarter head** - is called a 3/4 *turn, 3/4 view, '3/4 angle, :3/4 face, 3/4 face position;* or sometimes a *forty-five degree head.* These terms are generally applied to all intermediate positions between *full-face* and *profile.* However, those who like to split hairs designate the positions between 3/4 *head* and *profile* as 1/4 *profile, 1/2 profile, split profile* and 7/8 *turn.* Those who make this distinction, usually call the position to the front of the 3/4 *head* a 5/8 **turn.**

> **Profile** - or full side view of the face is also called *side position, side view, full profile, full turn,* 90 *turn, 1/2, view* or 1/2 *face view.*

A change from one basic view to another may be accomplished by moving the camera station, but most frequently it is the model who is required to move into position. Since the terms are established in relation to the model's movement, let us look at the movements that make these positions and subsequent views possible.

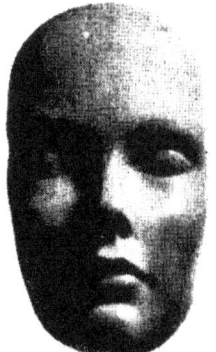

FULL FACE
(FRONT VIEW)

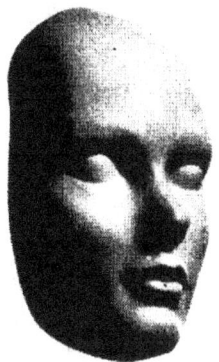

3 4 HEAD
(3/4 FACE VIEW)

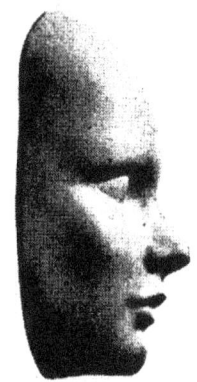

PROFILE
(FULL SIDE-VIEW)

THREE BASIC HEAD MOVEMENTS

bring the head into almost any desired position. When the camera is stationary, the model can move to a slight or great degree in three directions. These movements are familiar to all of us. By establishing key terms for these movements, we set the stage for understanding and team work between director and model. The terms are *horizontal turn, vertical lift* (or *drop*) and *diagonal tilt.* These movements may be used singly or in a combination of two, and, perhaps, all three.

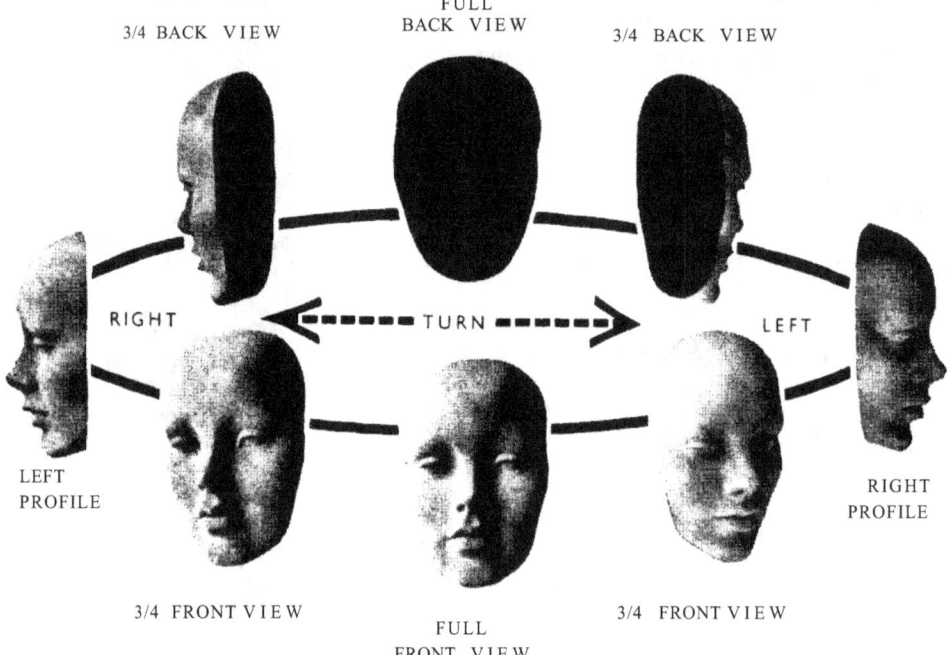

FULL BACK VIEW

3/4 BACK VIEW   3/4 BACK VIEW

RIGHT   ◄ ----- TURN ----- ►   LEFT

LEFT PROFILE

RIGHT PROFILE

3/4 FRONT VIEW   3/4 FRONT VIEW

FULL FRONT VIEW

The horizontal turn

When the body faces the camera, the head can turn from one shoulder to the other presenting many views: right profile; 3/4 right view, full face, 3/4 left view and left profile.

As one shoulder moves away from the camera, some views drop off, while others become possible - such as 3/4 back and back-view. These back views are used to display hairstyles, back detail or to draw the viewer's attention to something other than the face.

A horizontal turn of the head may be asked for in two ways by the director. He may say, 'Turn your head to the right', or 'I want your left profile', both of which requests would bring the *left side of the model's face* to the camera's view.

Vertical lift or drop...

is the upward or downward movement of the tip of the nose on an imaginary line perpendicular to the shoulder track.

Diagonal tilt...

is the slant of the head that puts the chin on one side of this perpendicular line and the top of the head on the other.

Notice how the shape of our mask is altered by the vertical lift, by the vertical drop and, to a lesser degree, by the horizontal turn. Also note the appearance of ease and interest added to the face by the tilt.

Head placement can be the basis for exaggerating or normalizing head structure and facial characteristics.

A round face looks oval to the camera in a 3/4 view. A long face can look round in full-face view when the chin is lifted.

An unconventional feature, such as a prominent chin or forehead can be minimized by tilting it away from the camera. A receding chin appears normal when it is extended toward the camera. The slightest movement makes a difference!

The comparative length and width of a face become unimportant in profile which accentuates only the features that appear in its side silhouette. Although the profile is good for hiding faults of structure, it loses impact when it comes to expression. It can project mood, esthetic qualities or serve as a means of directing the viewer's eye.

The full face view offers the best position for establishing direct personal contact, but requires symmetry of features that are hard to find. The 3/4 head can be used most effectively to both physical and dramatic advantage of the model.

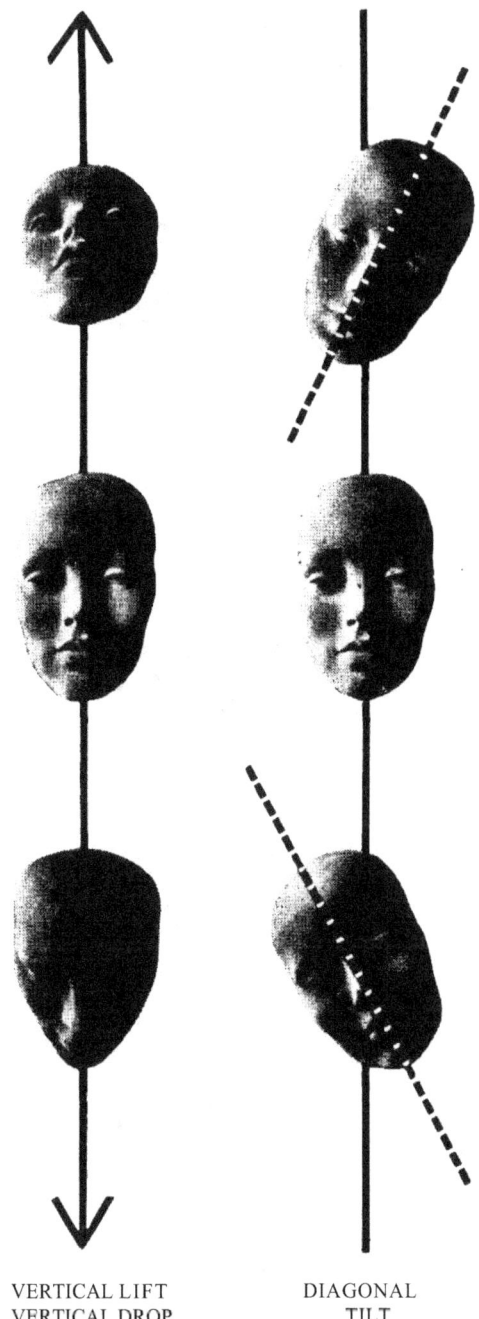

VERTICAL LIFT
VERTICAL DROP

DIAGONAL
TILT

81

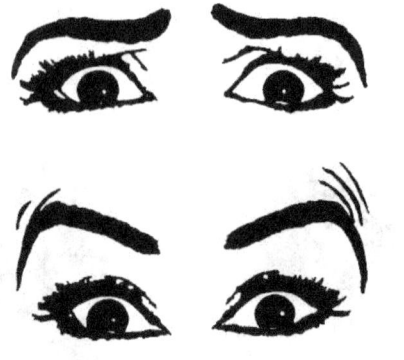

FLEXING THE BROWS

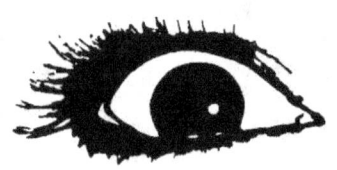

WIDE SEPARATION

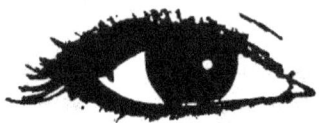

NORMAL SEPARATION

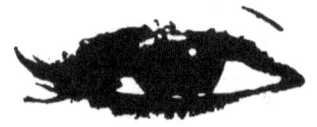

SLIGHT SEPARATION

SEPARATING THE EYELIDS

MOVABLE PARTS
OF THE FACE

are called upon to express or project emotions that the camera can record.

Each feature works independently or collectively with a network of muscles capable of controlling its physical shape. A model must be able to effect natural and smooth co-ordination of the muscles that bring the various parts of the face into play.

Eyebrows...

are controlled by a set of competent muscles at each end. The brows can move simultaneously or individually, guided by the message they must relay. The inner brows can be brought together and downward to express anger; together and upward for sorrow; upward and apart for fear; and upward in the middle to depict surprise.

Eyelids...

also respond to control and can range from slightly-parted to normal or widely separated positions. For normal effects each set of eyelids should be parted equally in slight or exaggerated variance.

Uncontrolled squinting is most often caused by bad smiling habits or glaring lights. The habit of squinting while smiling can be corrected by practice before the mirror. When bright lights cause the eyelids to misbehave, it is important to remember: *keep eyes open.* Get them used to glaring light! Focus them on the brightest spot they can comfortably endure. Eyelids will then remain unstrained and will respond, for the short duration of the exposure with an *open eye* expression.

The pupil...

of the eye is capable of rotating in a complete circle. Without moving the head, the pupil can move upward or downward, from side to side or to any points in between.

Care should be taken in If views and profile positions that the pupil of the eye nearest the camera remains visible to the lens. Otherwise the resulting picture appears to have a blank eyeball!

The mouth...

is as elastic as a rubber band and yields to a thousand and one shapes. It can open or close; its corners can be drawn together or stretched apart. The ends can be lifted or dropped. The mouth is capable of minute and extreme alteration.

We find certain words and sounds very useful for shaping the mouth. They not only help in setting a predetermined position of the mouth for the camera but they add realism and spontaneity to its appearance.

Notice how the mouth must be parted wide to release the sound of *Ah!*

This position can be attained by the use of any word or words ending in the *Ah* sound such as *New car!, Hurrah!,* etc.

The humming sound of *Mmmmm* closes the lips lightly, *Oooo* puckers the lips and a long *Eeee* spreads corners wide.

Lip make-up shapes the mouth. It is useful, not only for following fashionable style trends and for correcting irregularities in the original shape of the mouth, but in helping to increase specific expression. The corners of the mouth can be given an extra *lift* to depict happiness or can be discreetly painted downward to give the impression of hate, sorrow, petulance, etc.

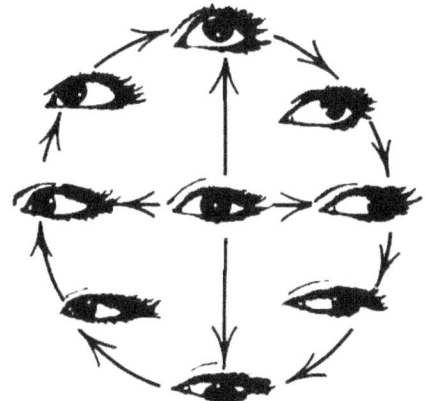

ROTATING THE PUPIL

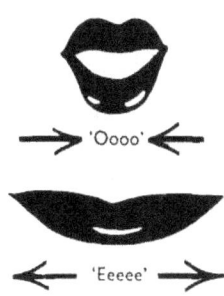

IN AND OUT

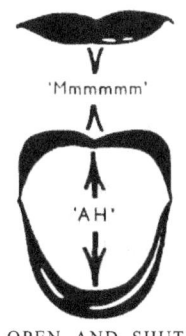

OPEN AND SHUT

SHAPING THE MOUTH

FACIAL EXPRESSION

is the movement of the features that tells us what is being felt by the model. With the right expression, her thoughts and emotions are projected through the camera to the viewer.

Many times, however, a model may think she is feeling something - even think she is showing it - but her facial mask has not moved or changed.

An experiment to prove this point was carried out recently in a photography class. A student was put in a chair and photographed gazing into the camera. In a second picture he was asked to feel extreme weight throughout his body. 'You are completely exhausted' he was told ... and the picture was snapped. When the two resulting prints were compared, no one could tell the difference between the *feeling* and *non-feeling* picture!

The answer, therefore, is, not only to feel an emotion, but to move the muscles of the face that will best express and project that feeling. A pout must bring the bottom lip forward. A sneer must curl the corners of the mouth downward or flare the nostrils outward. Hate must tense the jaw muscles, drop the corners of the mouth or perhaps close the eyelids to mere slits that contemplate revenge.

The motivation must be felt to the degree necessary by the model and portrayed in a manner that can be understood by the viewer. The muscles of the face are used in proportion to the intensity of the feeling, but never exaggerated (unless for comic or grotesque impressions) to the point of over-acting.

A picture tells a story, and the face, by its expression, becomes part of that story.

It may be of prime importance and tell the whole story; of secondary importance and add validity to the story or of minor importance and lend atmosphere to the story.

When the face is of prime importance, (usually true when the head fills a large part of the picture) the expression must depict character or situation. If the picture is a portrait, the expression must embody the key facet of the personality of the individual. If dramatic depth is to be recorded, the emotion must carry the picture.

When the face is of secondary importance, expression must add to the story. It must coincide with the emotion suggested by the action of the body. The fashion model executes many of these secondary expressions because the garment she wears is of first importance. Her expression calls attention to the dress by showing how happy, proud or self-possessed she is in wearing it.

When expression is of minor importance and is expected to do little more than lend atmosphere, it must be just as explicit as though it were the prime factor. It must not distract the viewer's eye away from the main point of interest. The emotion must balance delicately between expression and subordination. It must support the main point of interest in feeling and mood, yet possess no obvious characteristics that would call attention to itself.

In order to grasp elusive emotions, let us classify them into four basic groups: HAPPINESS, ANGER, SORROW and FEAR. Each has a means of communicating its feeling through facial movement. The immediate impression of each of these emotions is established by the eyebrows. Upon closer inspection the eyes tell the deeper story.

FOUR BASIC EMOTIONS

Happiness...

leaves the brows in their
natural position. It is the
eyes that project the emotion.
They must sparkle, brimming over with the inner
reason for the outward expression. The glow of
happiness extends from a feeling of comfortable
pleasure to ecstatic joy.

Anger...

draws the brows together
and downward. The eyes
flare with rebellion against
the action or situation that has caused this violent
emotion. The degree of anger ranges from a feeling
of slight irritation to one of rage and fury.

Sorrow...

draws the brows together
and upward. Eyes fill with
sympathy and longing to be
relieved of the burden of this emotion. There is a
pressing and twisting from within. The intensity
of sorrow can vary from disappointment to utter
tragedy.

Fear...

lifts and separates the brows.
Eyes reflect disbelief in what
they see. There is a cold
gripping sensation in the pit of the stomach. Fear
has many degrees and its emotion graduates all
the way from worry to horror.

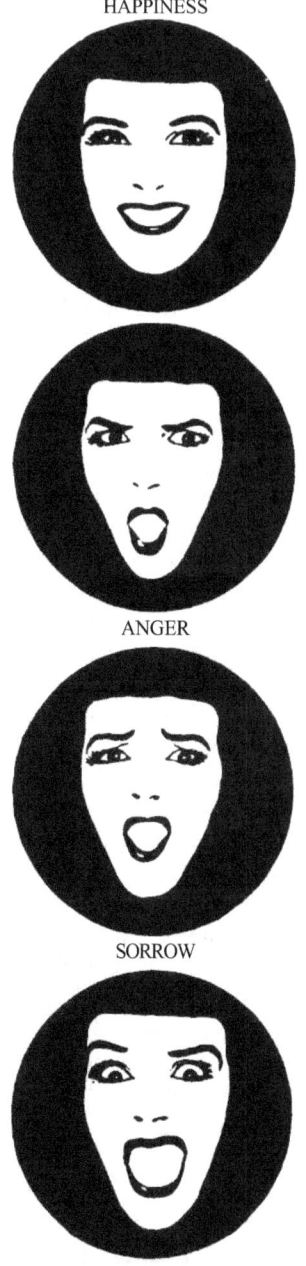

HAPPINESS

ANGER

SORROW

FEAR

BUILDING THE POSE
-DIRECTOR

No director need be given a list of reasons why a head is invaluable in a picture. Some directors do, however, welcome ideas on how to bring the model's best face forward - whether it is one of beauty, character and/or expression.

Before we come to our views of the subject, however, we would like to acknowledge the presence of the controversy existing over the *candid* versus the *controlled* pose.

Some directors contend they *never* direct their subject. 'To place a head or a mouth in a pre-determined position,' they say, 'would destroy all of the spontaneity and naturalness of the picture.'

Others, just as vehemently, contend that 'In a business that calls for consistent results, *lucky mood* and coincidence are not enough. They are not reliable and cannot be depended upon.'

We feel that when both director and model have a working knowledge of technique, each individual job will determine whether the pose requires *controlled, candid* or *controlled-candid* treatment.

Experienced directors practice many ways of getting a model to act and react *realistically* before the camera. Each has developed ways of controlling a model without having literally to push her into position. Adroit use of words, exemplary action, strategic suggestion and psychological motivation all bring forth expression that is dependable as well as spontaneous. At the same time most directors have found in actual practice, that with intelligent direction from behind the camera, any

capable model can accept correction and rearrange parts naturally without showing strain and losing spontaneity!

In photography we lean heavily upon the model's capabilities, yes, and in many instances even upon her ability to inspire us by doing something *her way* from which we can select or perfect a pose.

So, part of a director's success lies in his ability to keep a model suggesting ideas within the scope of the camera's ability to record them.

Many models feel they have exhausted the possibilities for different head positions when they have turned their head slowly from the left of the camera to the right of the camera! This can be most exasperating to a director (especially if you believe that you get the fullest creative contribution from a model by allowing her to move freely instead of placing her). Try a suggestion that will take her into several other positions from which you might select a pose. You might ask her to repeat the horizontal turn - this time with her chin up a little higher. This gives you at least six additional positions to choose from. Then ask her to lower her chin and repeat the horizontal turn - six more positions! By repeating each of these eighteen positions with her head *tilted right* and then with her head *tilted left,* you've added another thirty-six possibilities without yet *putting* her in any exact position.

If your model has trouble with the *tilt,* which is the most difficult direction to understand, you might try this. Hold a pencil vertically in front of your model's face. Let the tip of her nose touch the pencil and divide it equally lengthwise. Ask her to put her chin on one side of the pencil and her forehead on the other as you repeat the word *tilt*. With encouragement, let her try a few combined movements such as, 'Turn your head slightly to the right... that's good ... now tilt the top of your head right (or tilt your chin left).' If she loses her conception of tilt, hold the pencil before her again and she will usually remember it for the remainder of the sitting.

The head and its capability for arrangement of form and its ability to produce expression, is one means of getting your pictures to talk. If you can give direction, you hold the master key to it all.

As you become more adept at posing the head you will mentally fit certain types of faces into the positions that normalize or dramatize them. When you can anticipate changes that will take place with each movement, you can mentally arrange the pose before you ask your subject to try it. Thus, you can steer her into movements that result in suggestions (from her) you can use.

Study the features of each face to see whether the corrective positions we mention on page 81 are necessary. Many craftsmen welcome opportunity to dramatize disproportionate features. They find the results more gratifying than compliance with conventional ideas.

By persistent concentration on the varying shapes of the face and the impressions relayed to the viewer by each change of position, you soon begin to grasp qualities that otherwise escape your attention. The curious fact is, that once you begin detecting these subtleties you find yourself injecting a certain amount of atmosphere into a picture even before you call upon your subject for facial expression. When you find these additional means at your command for infusing a picture with meaning (over and above the use of expression) you can emphasize any given emotion dramatically and make any picture remarkably effective in its transmission of feeling.

Completely undirected movement by a model seldom transmits exactly the feeling desired, especially as far as a head is concerned. So most directors prefer to keep inherent control.

Built-in guide marks on the model's face tell you quickly just what position her head is in from the camera's viewpoint, and give you a clue as to the probable impression forthcoming.

When she faces the camera, the tip of her nose in direct line with the bottom of each ear, you know the position is centered. When her mouth or chin appear in the line of her ear lobes, her head is lifted, the mouth is emphasized and the mood of the picture will probably intimate sensuousness in some degree.

If the eyes or the bridge of the nose line up with the lobes of the ears, the head is tilted downward, the emphasis will be on the eyes and forehead and an impression of intellect will be stressed or implied.

Sometimes obtaining the exact expression may depend to a great extent on how well you can produce it instead of how well you can explain the mental process that goes into producing it. The most direct approach to obtaining expression when your model cannot understand motivation is to let her imitate it. When that becomes necessary, you are probably the one she will imitate. Therefore it is not stepping outside your realm to practise the expressions that communicate ideas you might want to put across. Thus you can sometimes set the mood and features of your model for camera presentation.

In order to familiarize yourself with the physical movements of the parts of the face shown on pages 82 and 83, get a model to sit for you and see if you can direct her into the variations of each part shown (or suggested). Try them yourself. Notice how much easier it is to shape the mouth by using positions necessary to make certain sounds and words with emotional content.

One reason for this is that the mind has begun to coordinate each of the different movable parts of the face when you use words and sounds with meaning. Experiment ; see if you can get a better expression by asking your model to use the word *Hurrah!* than you can by asking her to say the word *thaw*. Can you go a little further with this idea and give your model a thought upon which to build an expression encompassing each of these pictures?

For years it has been a half-joke for photographers to ask for the words *cheese* and *prunes* in order to get a smile; this was the only way they knew to relax grim jaws and lips. Now we know that they were partially right and that sounds can relax the mouth position. We have also discovered that the right sound can give us accurate control of the actual position of the mouth, and that the right word can also provide meaning that ties the mind in with the expression.

Thoughts can be introduced either by you or the model to augment physical expression and help coordinate the parts of the face with an appropriate photogenic expression. However, you must have a model with a flexible face. Her ability to express herself is limited by her ability to operate and control interrelationship of parts.

Broaden your own ability to direct by teaching yourself to observe and remember expressions you see every day so that you can use them.

Write down at least five situations you have seen in the last twenty-four hours that brought forth one of the four basic emotions. (Watch children for uninhibited and true expression.) Can you visualize the position of the mouth? What did the eyes say? Can you imagine a thought that would help you get that particular expression from a model?

Choose, from magazines, twenty different expressions that you like and might sometime want to use.

Divide all the pictures you have cut out into groups of the four basic emotions, *happiness, anger, sorrow* and *fear*. Under each picture write a sentence that would help motivate such an expression. For instance : some of your pictures might say, 'Won't he be surprised when he gets this gift!', 'Mmmmm, that smells *so* good!',

Direct a model in each of the expressions you have cut out.

Be ready to evaluate and correct ineffectual expressions as they appear.

Here is an exercise that will require more time to do than is apparent at first glance, but your efforts will be rewarded with something that can be of great use to you later:

Terminate at least five of the sentences you wrote under the facial expressions with a single word or simple phrase that: 1) sets the position of the mouth correctly and 2) holds, for the model, some meaning related to the sentence or expression.

When you have found these words, save them to try on at least three different models.

BUILDING THE POSE
- MODEL

Gone are the days when a beautiful face was the only requisite for still and moving pictures. Pretty features do not always make a good picture nor do irregular features necessarily produce a bad one.

Today, a face is deemed photogenic if it is flawlessly beautiful, or if it is interesting, or if it is expressive. The model with perfect features has increasing competition from the model who may not have as much to start with, but can use what she has.

Intelligent movement of the head can often hide or transform undesirable features. But all movement, due to the intricacies of lighting and camera technicalities, should be adjusted from the camera's viewpoint. You must have confidence that your director will see and modify anything that might detract from the kind of picture he wants.

It is necessary for you to know and understand the movements of the head so that you can suggest positions when called upon to do so, or comply with any changes he may ask for.

The flexibility of the head must be great, but your control of that flexibility must be positive. For the slightest movement of the head changes camerawise every aspect of its features. You must not only know how to move your head in any direction, but know how to move it to the exact degree needed.

A limber neck determines how much you can move your head without disturbing other parts of your body such as your shoulders or arms. Practice this neck-limbering exercise before your mirror...

1) Roll your head slowly in a complete circle first to the front. Drop your chin as far as you can.
2) Relax and shake your head. Drop it lower.
3) Then roll it, still relaxed, to your left shoulder, then to the back (with your chin stretched high).
4) Lower the chin again as the head comes over your right shoulder and to the front again.
5) Do this very slowly... three times to the right and then three times to the left. Every time you can see yourself in the mirror, check to be sure that you do not raise your shoulders especially while the head is passing over them.

Be sure that your shoulders remain stationary. In the words of a famous director, 'Get your neck out of your shoulders and your head out of your neck!'

The above exercise frees the head for two major movements: the horizontal *turn* and the vertical lift (or drop). Do you think you can combine these two movements at command?

Turn your head to the right and then lift it.' Turn your head slightly to the left and drop your chin.' 'Lift your head and turn it to the left.'

Try them!

Then you might try this simple exercise which will limber the muscles used to tilt the head - muscles which are seldom limber enough for creative posing.

1) Tilt your head to the right; your right ear toward your right shoulder.
2) Strain three times, relaxing between each try, to get more space between your left ear and your left shoulder.
3) Do only a few of these the first day but continue doing a few on each side every day.

The tilt of the head is something all of us do many times a day unconsciously, but few of us can execute it consciously upon command. Try tilting the top of your head to the right (your right ear toward your right shoulder). Now tilt the top of your head to the left. With shoulders remaining stationary wag your head like a pendulum -the top of your head making a greater arc than your chin.

Now do you think you could combine any two of the three movements, *turn, lift* and *tilt* upon command? Try it:

Turn your head to the right and tilt the top of your head to the left.'
'Lift your head and tilt the top of it to the left.'
'Drop your head and tilt the top of it to the right (chin to the left).'

Now combine all three movements with this command:

'Turn your head to the left, drop it slightly and then tilt left.'

Can you mix these commands further and still not become confused? Learn to listen to the exact command given by your director and think in two terms: direction and degree.

A mobile face is your next goal, it is an absolute necessity for the projection of e-motions. It is your means of communicating feeling to the viewer, for only by reading the signs of emotion upon your face can he get your message.

On the other hand, facial expression without feeling is as empty as feeling without facial expression ... one can go nowhere without the other.

Whether the action of the face is pronounced or subdued, control of all muscles must be maintained. A model, like an actress, must know what her face looks like at all times. She should be so familiar with it that she can visualize every change in expression accurately without having to look in the mirror.

Before practicing expression, see if you can move your face - feature by feature.

Eyebrows may be moved together and downward. Together and upward. When you find that you have no apparent control, use a fingertip to move them into place until the muscle can take on its duties a-lone. Move them up and down. Try to lift one while dropping the other. If one doesn't work ... try the other. (Raising one brow is excellent for a quizzical or tongue-in-cheek expression.)

Eyelids prove quite interesting when you experiment with them. Think of them as shades that can be pulled up or down over the eyes. Close them and try to open them very slowly, stopping with each infinitesimal movement. Close them the same way.

Can you raise your upper lid so that it no longer touches the top of the pupil of the eye? Try it by parting the lids as wide as possible in surprise or by raising your chin slightly while looking down and at the same time lifting the upper lids as high as possible.

Can you lower your upper lid until it covers the iris in your pupil without moving the lower lid? (This provocative movement should not be confused with the *squint* which raises the lower lid to get the same spacing - but not the same effect.)

Pupils of the eyes should not be confined to any one position. Are yours? Practice looking at the rim of a huge clock very close to your face. With your face to the front (do not move your head) stop your eyes momentarily at each of the twelve numbers. Focus your eyes on the distance and see if you can get the same degree of movement.

Turn your face to a 'I' view in your mirror and practice rotating the pupils of your eyes to the numbers on the same clock. Now try the exercise in profile. Note how you can use only about half of the numbers if you keep the pupil in view of the camera.

Mouth flexibility, though easy, must be channeled in the right direction. Mumblers will find these exercises more difficult than the enunciators for they have become lip-lazy. A good exercise to get those muscles working (and this will improve your speech too) is to:

Hold a cork the size of a quarter, between your teeth and enunciate these vowels out loud: A-E-I-O-U-and repeat them 3 times distinctly. Next, open your mouth to accommodate three of your fingers (one over the other) between your teeth and enunciate the vowels *Ah-Aw, Ah-A\\\ Ah-Aw, Ah-Aw*. With one finger: *ee-oo, ee-oo, ee-oo*.

Can you make the corners of your mouth go down in a sneer or a pout? Can you make them go up in happiness?

Before you start assembling the movements of these separate parts into actual facial expressions take a few minutes to arrange two mirrors in a special *book-fashion*. If you will open it about 75^0 at the *hinge* and put your head up close, you will learn much about the action of your face ... especially in J and profile views which you would otherwise never have an opportunity to see.

When you bring the various parts of your face to bear upon a single expression you must first consider your feelings and emotions. Consider the four basic emotions *fear, sorrow, anger* and *happiness*. Think of the thoughts and situations that go into creating those emotions.

What produces such reactions within you personally?

Start a scrapbook of expressions. Gather pictures that express the four basic emotions from magazines. Paste them in a book under their appropriate headings with others of like emotion for comparison. Keep adding to your collection at every possible opportunity. Then go before your double mirror and think of the thought the model in the picture must be expressing ... the word her lips must be forming ... say it aloud as you imitate the illustration. Lose your self-consciousness before the mirror and you are on the road to losing your self-consciousness before the camera.

Cover the lower half of your face with a sheet of paper (so it cannot assist with the expression) and project the emotions of *fear, sorrow* and *anger*. Do your eyebrows show the marked difference in each? Practice, and after you feel they are flexible see if someone else can correctly read the emotion you are expressing with your eyes and brows.

Imagination is essential to the creation of expression. Exercise your imagination along with your face. Give yourself vivid pictures that make you feel the emotion you must express.

The ability to suspend or hold an expression is an invaluable asset to any model and it, too, can be yours with a little well-aimed practice.

Repeat all the basic expressions again and this time see how long you can *hold it* or suspend the expression without letting it sag or fade away.

Seriously practice projecting emotion physically (to the right degree) and you will be rewarded with sparkling spontaneity in all of your pictures!

THE TIME HAS COME

to weigh anchor! By now you have perused or used the basic elements set forth in section one of this book.

You know how the body mechanically performs and the camera transforms ... how, together, they create a tangible image, visually and psychologically impressive.

Inspiration is always at your fingertips -if you but reach for it. You will find some *points of departure* for creative ideas in the advanced section of this book. As you hold to your course and increase your sensitivity, other ideas will reinforce your ability and speed you in new directions

When you go beyond the boundaries of this book, revitalize your creative thinking from time to time, by observing significant movement in the human beings near you.

You are now ready to set sail into a sea of creativity, impelled by your enthusiasm, directed by your goals and sped by your knowledge.

All aboard ... the best is yet to come!

ADVANCED POSING
TECHNIQUE

The mind loves to smoulder in familiar patterns. A single creative spark may set it aflame with ideas.

You, the advanced worker have developed discernment. You know that there is nothing new, nothing unusual, except in its presentation - a different twist or an unusual flair. That *why-didni't-I-think-of-it* change that makes some work outstanding. Therefore, whether you personally prefer to discover or devise poses ... whether you like to determine them experimentally, diagramatically or mathematically; whether you are trying to project a feeling of symbolic elegance, charm and dignity, or present a static, chiseled, stylized, inscrutable or enigmatic distortion, you know that a source of inspiration is invaluable to you. You are always looking for new *points of departure.*

This advanced section of the book is concerned with the photographic potential of the human body. It seeks to develop insight into the interplay of shapes and lines through arrangement of the photographic figure. Our aim is to examine this figure and its parts in an organized manner, to present possibilities for variation of each, and to inspire exploration along these, or your own ideas. What follows then, is not a discussion of individual poses, but a significant cross-section of possibilities.

The illustrations and their accompanying notes will not say to you, *Do this!* or *Do that!* They will merely serve as mental contacts for associating fresh principles of creation with work or situations you have already experienced.

We hope to thread your individual preferences for posing in orderly progression so that one tug at your memory will bring forth a string of consecutive ideas faster than the shutter can click!

At this point, the astute observer will wonder if this book is going to remain oblivious to poses in space - poses that occupy depth. He will also wonder if all posing, throughout the book, is to be represented in the light of a two-dimensional shadow. Yes, actually it is ... and for several very good reasons.

In art, principles of foreshortening *'may be enlarged upon, modified, or discarded as the artist desires'* as Burne Hogarth states in his *Dynamic Anatomy.*

In photography, principles of foreshortening may also be enlarged upon or modified, but they *cannot be discarded.* The camera optically determines every proportion of the transposed image. For this reason, a director ordinarily limits his model to the area of minimum perspective (unless utilizing lenses of abnormal long focal length that permit the camera to work at the extensive distances required to present realistic proportions regardless of the depth of the pose).

No photograph of a girl, is like the real thing. She just cannot be pinned down on paper as she is. However, once her image has been transferred to a two-dimensional surface, either by a silhouette or a photograph, you are free to consider it in terms of flat lines, angles and shapes. You can cope directly with its basic movement as well as arrange it sensibly and sensitively.

In this light it is possible to compare the silhouette with the photograph, and when necessary, it becomes relatively simple to substitute one for the other by adding or subtracting tone. (Although we recognize and respect the importance of textures, complex form, lighting and other technical considerations, many books have been written on those subjects. We wish to keep our sights focused on the figure, its simplicities and intricacies.)

For analytical study or actual arrangement of the body, the silhouette simplifies and eliminates all distracting trivia and brings you directly to the things that matter camera wise.

Impact, or immediate impression, which is so primary a requirement today, is gained through the figure's outline as it pushes through space and background. Thus, primary action and feeling must be expressed in the basic silhouette. All other things fall into being as the camera automatically records the tone, texture and line (within the outline) necessary to amplify the reality of the subject.

All the subtle surface textures and planes (that define change within this outline) are of interest to you, but need not preoccupy you, as they do the artist.

This does not mean that you can go to the other extreme and ignore lighting (which, after all, is the essence of the photographic image) but at this point, keep yourself free to do more creative thinking about the outline of the body than about its complex surface form.

Nor does the fact that you are free to concentrate on the silhouette mean that the subject must be cut out like a gingerbread man. The rim of the subject (even though brought into a flat surface by the camera) can still twine through space ... advance and recede as its edges are lost and found against the background... if you want it to.

It does mean that a director ordinarily likes to exercise control over the depth of the pose and prefers to establish the illusion of depth on the two-dimensional surface by interrelated arrangement of...

color,
texture,
tone (lighting),
overlapping shapes,
and/or line.

No director can afford *to* release his model recklessly into the deforming third plane.

Thus, we too will continue, in our illustrations and references, to restrict the body (as much as possible) to an area bounded by two parallel panes of glass perpendicular to the camera's lens axis.

The artist's work, with charcoal, pen or brush, unlike that of the photo-director, is a one-man operation. With only tools and technique he can paint a picture of a model with or without a model. His results come directly from palette to page.

The director with a camera, on the other hand, cannot make a picture of a girl -without the girl. On the other hand, neither can the model produce an illustriously eminent photograph of herself without some photo-direction. Neither one can function effectively without the camera and the other.

Thus by necessity, we have a two-person team with the camera as the referee. A hit is made only when both recognize the camera's authority and the fact that it is going to do its duty in a certain methodical way, recording what it sees while the shutter remains open.

The model's job is to present the most perfect position and expression possible. The director's job is to co-ordinate, recognize and record this decisive moment of perfection. Both work together with the camera and through the camera to attain the same end result - the right picture.

Hence, from here on, all references to posing will be made to both the model and the director, for at this stage you are a team and all information relates to you both.

As this book turns from basic mechanics for the beginner to creative variations for the advanced, it aims to stimulate posing ideas and so to move you to creation. There are unlimited physical and psychological possibilities of each part of the body.

It's true that no masterpiece was ever created by concentrating on the arrangement of the separate parts of the subject without first considering the whole. Thus, as you examine the movements of each part of the body, you might reasonably wonder if you are becoming too involved with minute detail and losing sight of the whole. *Do* not concern yourself. Absorb detail after detail. Study each part as though it were a subject in itself. Explore it. Exhaust its last possibility and then forget about it.

When you eventually concentrate on assembling the whole, each part will naturally fall into correct and even creative positions. For when you probe curiously into each basal root of the potential pose you unearth ever-increasing aspects of variation with which to create whatever your need demands. A unity will result that combines static parts and blends them in a symphony of right movements and meanings - recorded at the right moment.

Use each deviation as a springboard or point of departure through which transformation of the whole comes about. All nuances made possible through assorted positions, through the physical balance and action of parts of - the mechanical figure.

95

ADVANCED POSING TECHNIQUE

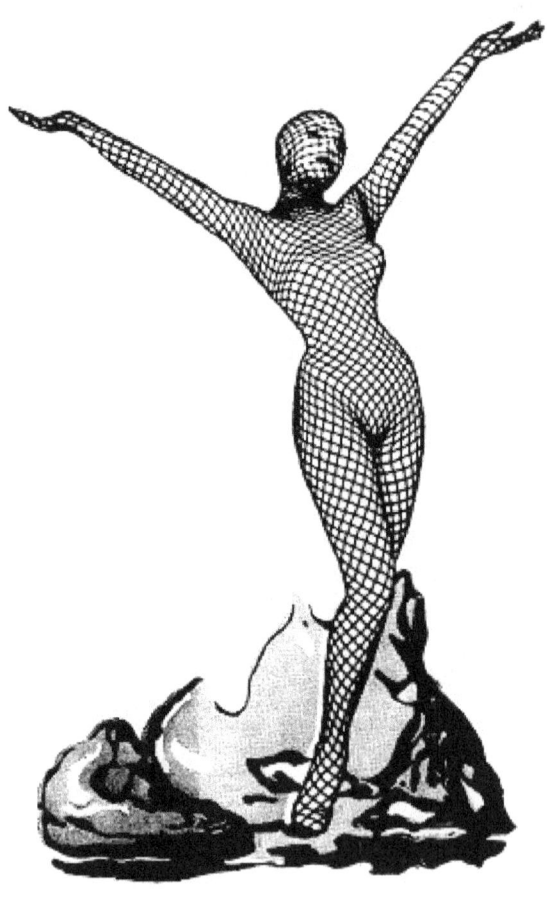

CREATIVE VARIATIONS

of the body do not stem from thinking only in terms of being drastically different. True creativity is the art of doing the usual in an unusually effective fashion ... with a shade of distinction.

When this is accomplished your work has an intangible *rightness* and no one but a fellow creator can detect what has made it so.

A creative body position is enchanting. You do not stop with a critical eye at any one part. It is a fresh interpretation of a position you know is possible, but haven't seen very often. It is just right and right up to the last detail.

You, who have already delved into creative posing, have you ever stopped to wonder at what point something ceases to be ordinary and takes on the qualities of the craftsman? If you are like most creators, you have been too busy producing results to understand how you arrived at that point. But if you are among those who probe the *hows* and the *whys,* you have probably found that creativity stems from digging deeper and deeper into a subject. Curiosity seeks out basics and their potentials for change down to minutiae and then - not by luck, accident or happenstance -you have achieved great sensitivity and can sense every subtle change that makes the big difference. For when you can recognize wisps of attitudes and can see variances through detail they become yours to use.

The body-line is the first and most prominent stroke on the page. It is the theme-line of your picture. It is established with a specific purpose in mind and serves as a basis of creative departure for other parts of the body. It can be a long-line, a zigzag

or perhaps a borderline combination of the two.

Have you noticed that all of these theme-lines create both physical and mental impressions? To a fine degree, you sense attitudes, character and vitality in each. For that reason we say that the body *talks.* It is much more than a trunk to which the limbs are attached, it is the stem through which design and story must flow smoothly ... enhanced rather than hindered.

To the discerning eye (and most eyes that read a picture are more discerning than we realize) every mood and expression is evident in the body.

Every movement made by a model is *read* by the way it relates (in conformity or opposition) to ...

other parts of the body, elements
surrounding the body, story or
purpose of the picture, picture
mood and feeling and
composition of the page.

As you carefully study or scan our diagramatic illustrations, you find that even in silhouette, you do sense attitudes and can feel life within and throughout the body, and when necessary, you can complete the details from your heightened imagination.

So, whether you prefer orthodox or *offbeat* attitudes, you find, of necessity, that you must be a kind of photographic physician with the ability to examine a pose, diagnose it quickly, and prescribe correction without disturbing its unity.

Let us expand our original T, C and 'S' concepts of body-lines and examine the mental attitudes each reflects as well as their possibilities for physical change.

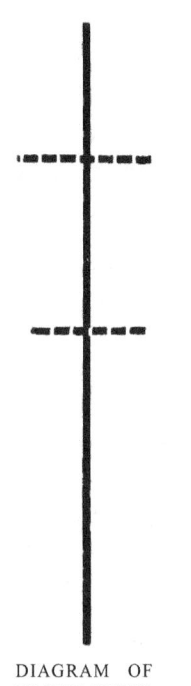

FRONT VIEW

DIAGRAM OF
FRONT VIEW

**VERTICAL 'I'
SILHOUETTE**

THE LONG-LINE
OF THE BODY

to the inexperienced eye, offers but little opportunity for change or variation. The reason being, that those who cannot recognize what is basic, cannot measure change. Basic long-lines of the body, as we have mentioned in the first section of the book, conform to three symbols the body can duplicate: an 'I', a 'C' or an 'S'

Each symbol can assume a vertical, horizontal or diagonal position in relation to the frame of the picture. Thus, basic long-line potentials for body position are nine:

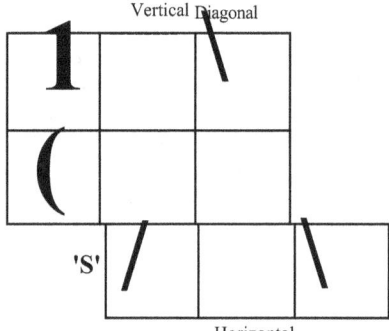

These nine basic long-line body positions have infinite possibilities for variation. Here is a list of five ideas for creative de parture which are easy to remember when you associate each variation to the number of parts of the body to be changed. Try this simple *count-down* before *shooting*.
5 .... 4 .... 3 .... 2 .... 1 .... click!

5 views which change the outline of the body as it turns (front, -J front, side, | back, back).
4 limbs (two arms, two legs) which vary the basic silhouette with their placement.
3 'p's - (P)urpose, (P)rops and (P)osition of the

Camera. Three external influences for change.

2 tracks (shoulder and hip) which affect subtle changes in proportion and meaning.

1 body-line which varies by how much the head and leg-line bend the basic silhouette.

For instance, here is the count-down applied to the first of the nine positions.

The vertical 'I' silhouette

The diagram itself has a feeling of formality and elegance. Our count down on this basic T gave us the following variations:

5. Front view used (others were possible).
4. Arms conform to the vertical and horizontal edges of the page. A few diagonals were used to spark interest. Legs were separated in different degree, used together or crossed.
3. Purpose... to maintain the feeling of formal elegance, high style design. Props... none.
Position of Camera... same for each pose.
2. Shoulder-hip movement... none.
1. Variation of body-line... none.

By varying only numbers 5, 4 and a part of 3 we created the panel of vertical 'I' positions to the right.

The long-line T silhouette is an interesting paradox; the novice can think of nothing else to do, while the experienced welcome its exciting possibilities.

Its appearance varies with the skill with which it is used. For a beginner it often comes out stolid, heavy or awkward, while those who handle it expertly bring out vibrancy, strength and assurance.

It is the oldest of all body positions; the long, vertical line has been associated with elegance, spirituality and grandeur down through the ages ... and yet, it is as ultra-modern, as timeless as tomorrow.

Vertical T silhouettes are quite adaptable when the body is to be part of a design, for their straight line can repeat the lines of columns, doorways or other properties.

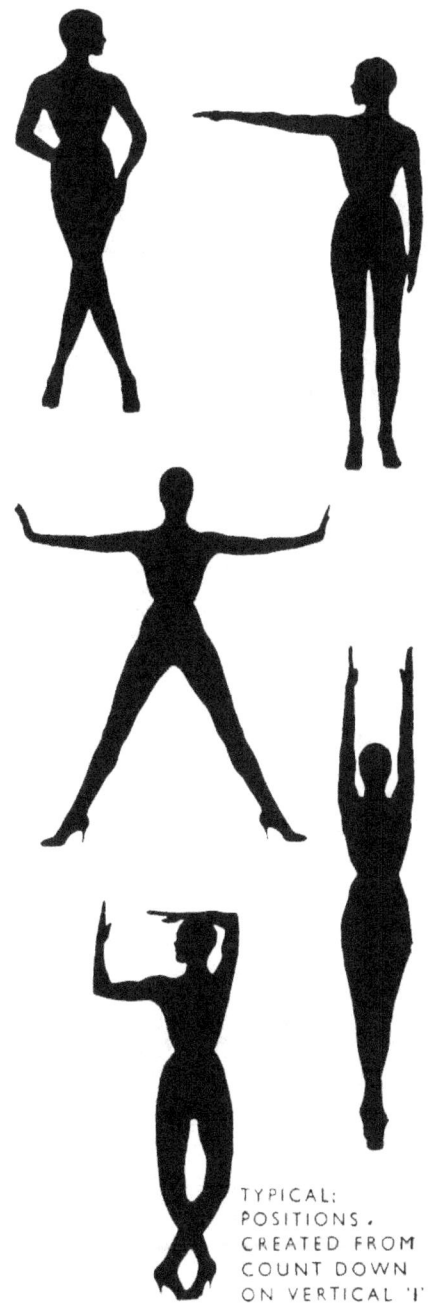

TYPICAL
POSITIONS,
CREATED FROM
COUNT DOWN
ON VERTICAL 'I'

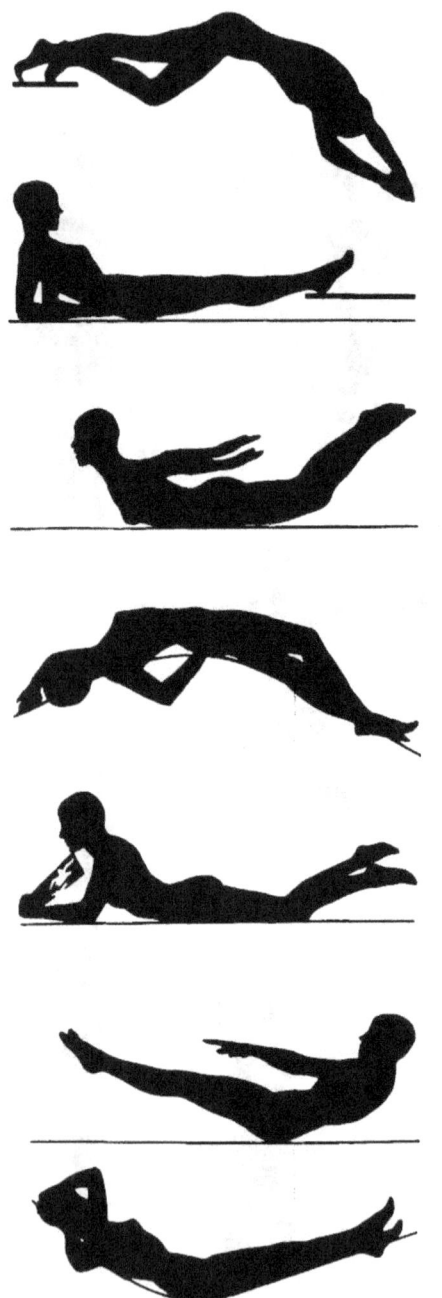

Before we apply a count-down to the

Horizontal 'C' Silhouette . . .

we should recognize the fact that it may appear (as illustrated to your left) with both ends up or with both ends down.

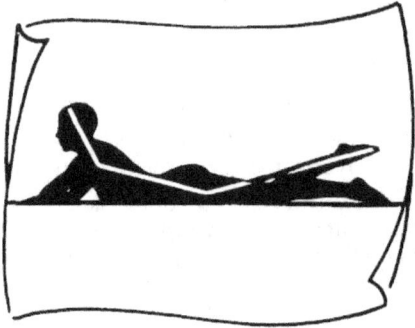

The count-down for varying the 'C long-line in these positions, produced the following variations:

5 views were possible. We restricted all positions to the side-view, relying upon other sources for variation.

4 limbs added much. Legs repeated each other to help complete the 'C'. Arms were varied to support objects or the body .. .some extended, some repeated the body's line while others added relaxation or expression.

3 important 'P's. Props included a rounded mound, a hammock, a springboard, a step and the floor. Position of the camera... raised, lowered. Purpose of the panel was to show the horizontal 'C' in side-view only.

2 tracks (show shoulder and hip change in the first illustration only).

1 body-line (curve remained approximately the same in each picture with the head and leg lines angled in inverse proportion to maintain it.)

The 'C' is an easy line to work with, for the body bends naturally at the waist with the head forming one end of the curve and the show-leg completing it. Its flowing line puts movement in a picture even when the action of the subject is restricted to repose.

100

Diagonal 'S' silhouette . . .

variations with the 'S' in a regular position or flowing backward.

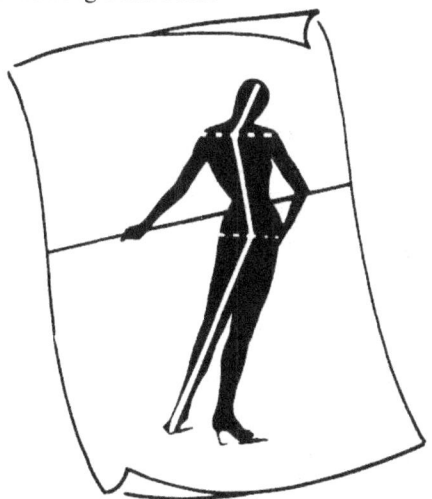

The diagonal 'S' silhouette is an artistic line in itself. Its set of reversed curves impart a feeling of variation even before other parts are placed. It has aesthetic grace and expresses fluid action (especially evident in the diagonal position).

Our count down (below) produced the sample variations to the right:

5. As the previous illustrations did not incorporate it we used a 3/4 *hack view*.

4. The show-leg, used on the opposite side of the body from the head balances it. The arms were used in some of the positions to elongate the 'S' curve, in others, to balance it both pictorially and physically. Some support the body ...one set of arms repeats two lines of the page while the body flows between them.

3. Props (a ladder and a cane) were used to support the stationary diagonal positions while the others, balanced in action, maintain themselves. Position of camera - raised, lowered.

2. Shoulder and hip tracks were varied to control body proportions and add flexibility.

1. The body-line was varied by tilting head and show-leg tilt for balance and action.

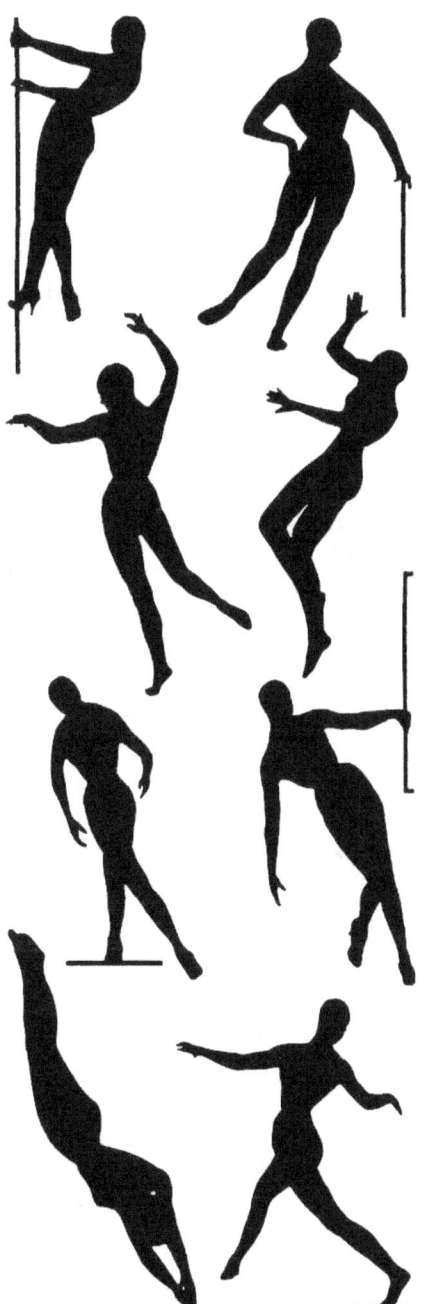

101

IDEAS FLOW FREELY FROM BASIC

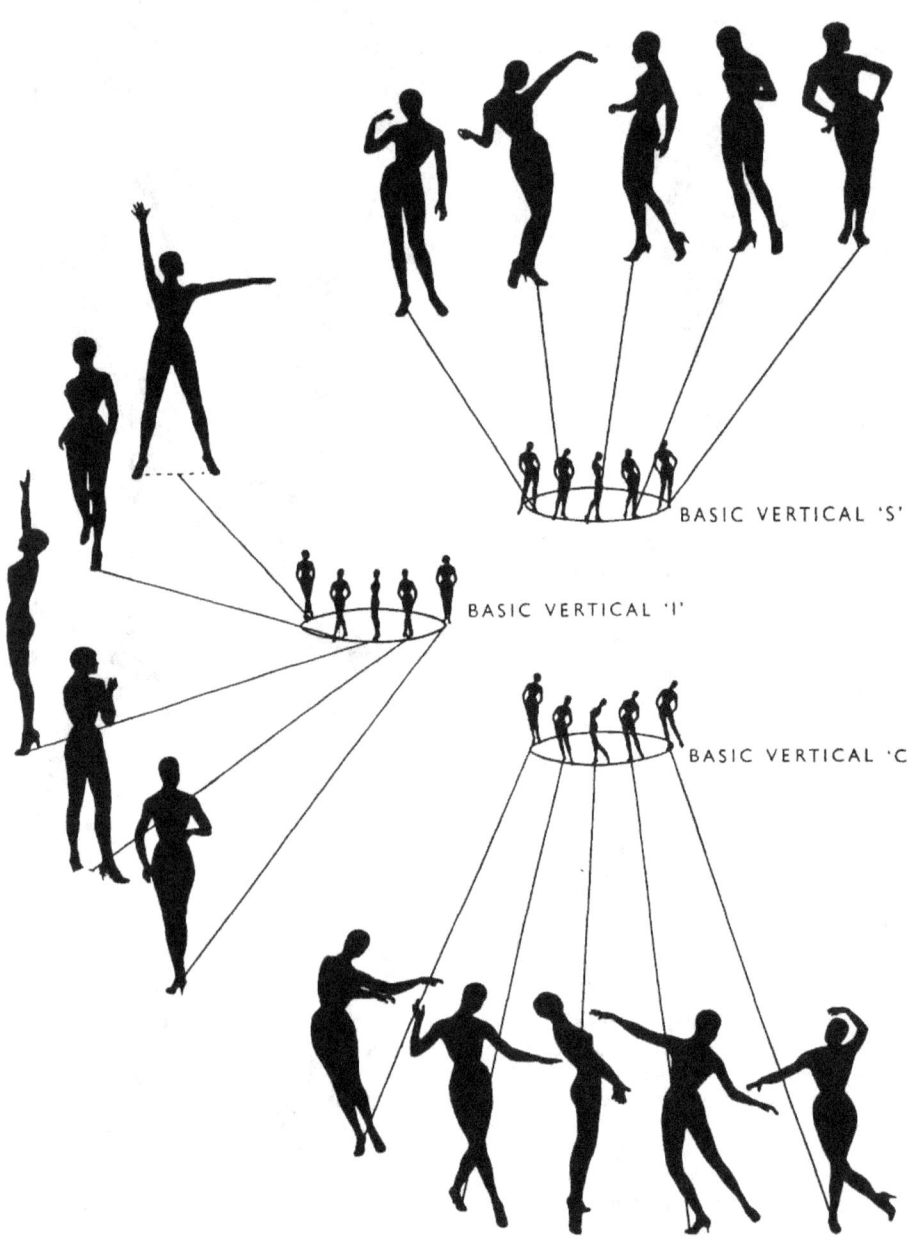

BASIC VERTICAL 'S'

BASIC VERTICAL 'I'

BASIC VERTICAL 'C'

VERTICAL OR DIAGONAL BODY-LINES

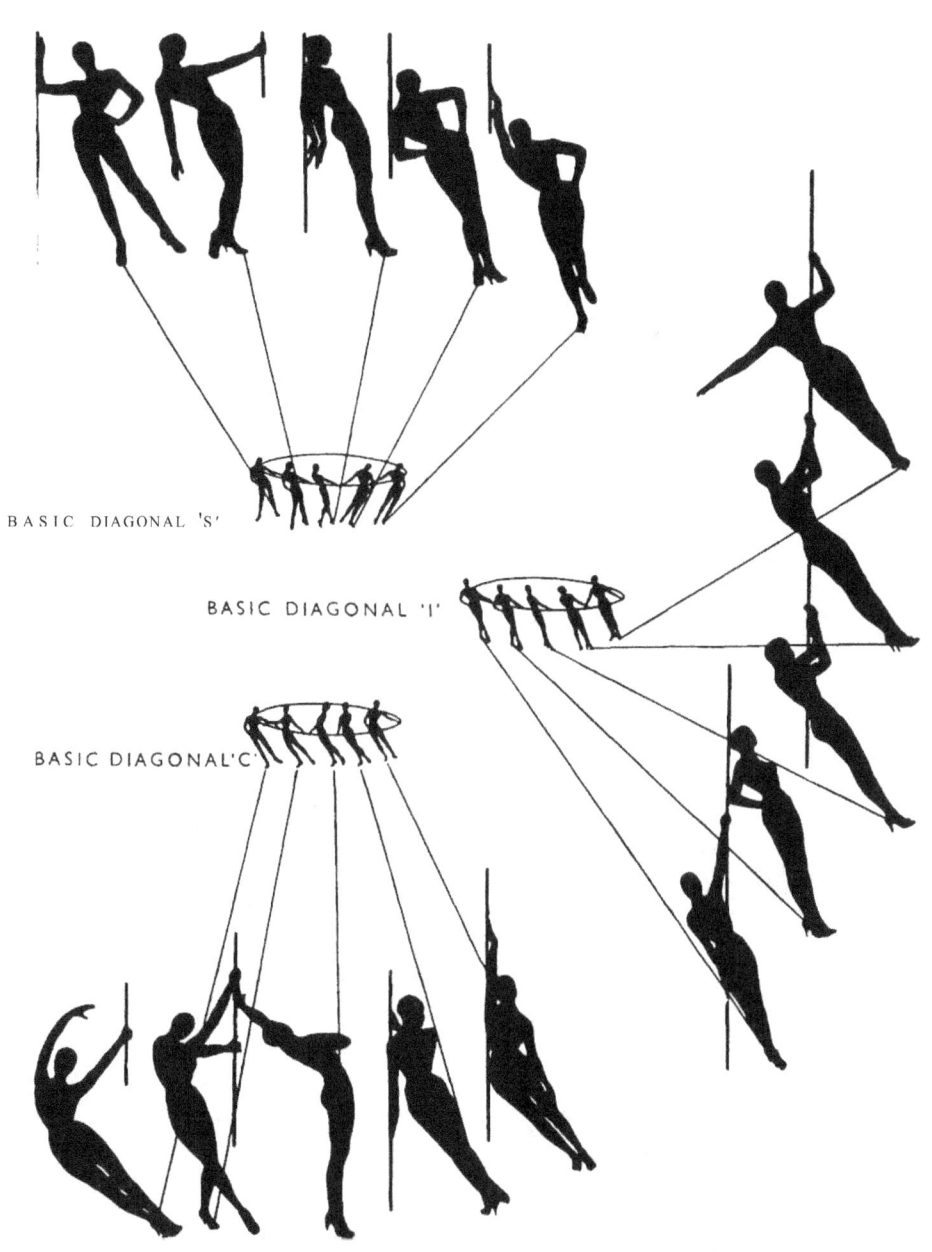

BASIC DIAGONAL 'S'

BASIC DIAGONAL 'I'

BASIC DIAGONAL 'C'

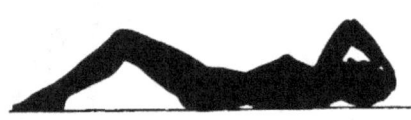

FRONT VIEW

3/4 FRONT VIEW

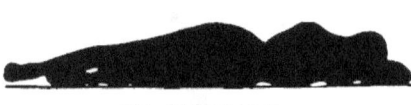

SIDE VIEW

3/4 BACK VIEW

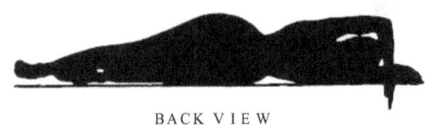

BACK VIEW

HORIZONTAL 'I' SILHOUETTES

IDEAS ALSO FLOW

from basic horizontal body-lines and can surpass the vertical and diagonal positions in variety since both the legs and the arms are free to multiply arrangements.

Every picture made is subject to limitations of many kinds; poor props, improper lighting, lack of time, wrong equipment, problem backgrounds, client, layout, etc. Whatever the conditions may be, however, that impose restrictions and close the door on any one position of the human body, several variations will always be available when you try the count down ...

5 views (through which the contour of the body can be changed as it turns by degrees from its slender side view to its broadest full-front or back view).

4 limbs (which can conform to the attitude or line the body has established or can oppose that line and add emphasis or interest. Limbs can be used to correlate the body's relationship to other parts of the picture).

3 'p's (Purpose, Props and Position of Camera) which are the important external elements that add to the final appraisal of the picture. Purpose must be established - it's like taking aim. Props must be selected for utility or artistry or significance. Position of Camera must take advantage of all technical and physical considerations relevant to a good picture.

2 tracks (shoulder and hip) offer subtle and vast opportunity for body change. Explore them!

1 body-line (which can be varied in any of its nine basic positions by increasing, decreasing or reversing its curves).

Remember, when one of the above suggestions becomes an invariable, it is time for another variation to enter your picture. Have you experimented with the changes that become possible through count down number 2, for example? Have you tried varying hip and shoulder tracks for different effects?

104

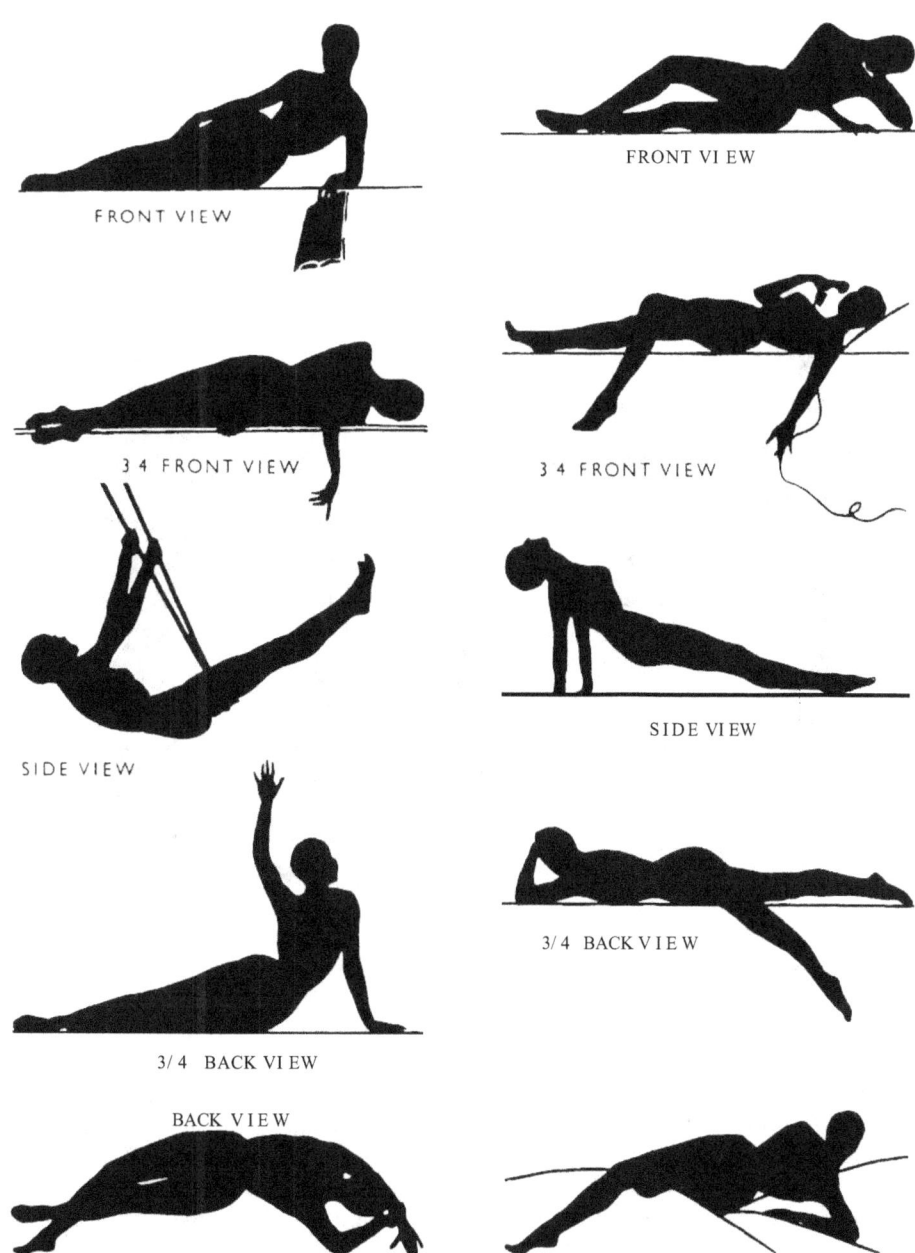

FRONT VIEW

FRONT VIEW

3 4 FRONT VIEW

3 4 FRONT VIEW

SIDE VIEW

SIDE VIEW

3/4 BACK VIEW

3/ 4 BACK VIEW

BACK VIEW

•C SILHOUETTES

BACK VIEW

'S' SILHOUETTES

SHOULDER AND HIP
TRACK VARIATIONS

add style to a picture. Only the expert suspects or knows the full extent of their elasticity. The pictures that reflect their adept use are seldom a result of lucky accident, but the distinct mark of *know-how* and *can-do*.

Their relationship to each other and to the horizontal edges of the finished picture warrants deliberate inspection. Let us examine the *turn, tilt, twist* movements which establish the positions of shoulder and hip tracks and vary their relationships.

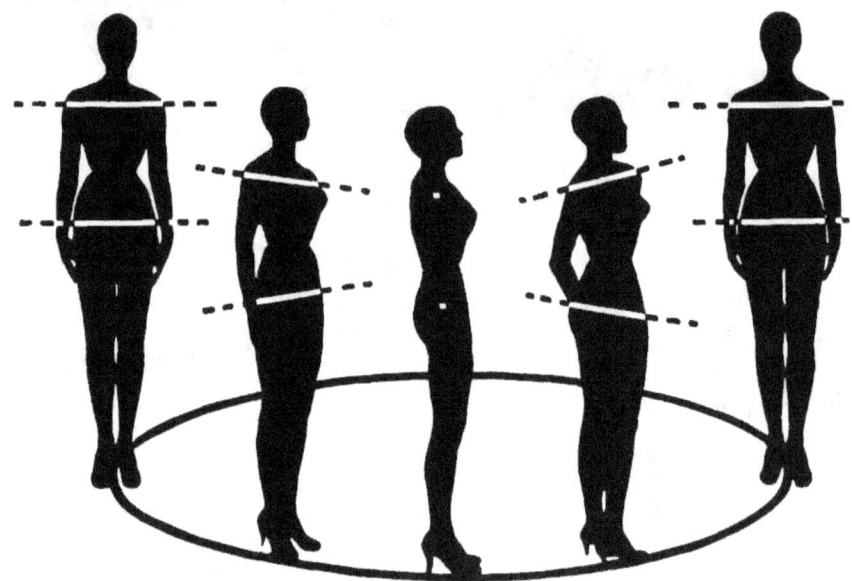

TURNING

Shoulder and hip tracks

remain in a single plane which revolves before the camera. If the body were a puppet or marionette, it would require but two strings to effect this simple turn.

One string would be attached to the left ends of the shoulder and hip tracks and the other connect the right ends of the tracks. A movement of either string, toward or away from the camera, would move the hip and shoulder on the same side in unison ... parallel to each other and the floor.

Even though the tracks remain parallel to each other as they turn, they appear to tilt toward each other as the body moves into any 3/4 position. The greater the turn of the model, the more noticeably the tracks tilt in the picture. If the lines were extended, they would meet each other at a *vanishing* point whose location would depend upon the amount of turn and the proximity of the camera. The camera is busy flattening the third plane into two dimensions. Perspective can alter shoulder and hip tracks that have not actually changed.

When a puppeteer has but few strings on a doll it can walk, bend, turn in jerky stilted movements which repeat frequently; the lack of strings limits its action. The more strings the more independently and smoothly the parts move.

If, in arranging a pose, we want to enjoy greater freedom of movement, more variety of positions and have more control of the body in operation, we must also *attach more strings* and learn where they go and what they can do.

Let us attach four strings instead of two to our model, one to each end of the hip track and one to each end of the shoulder track - and see what we can do.

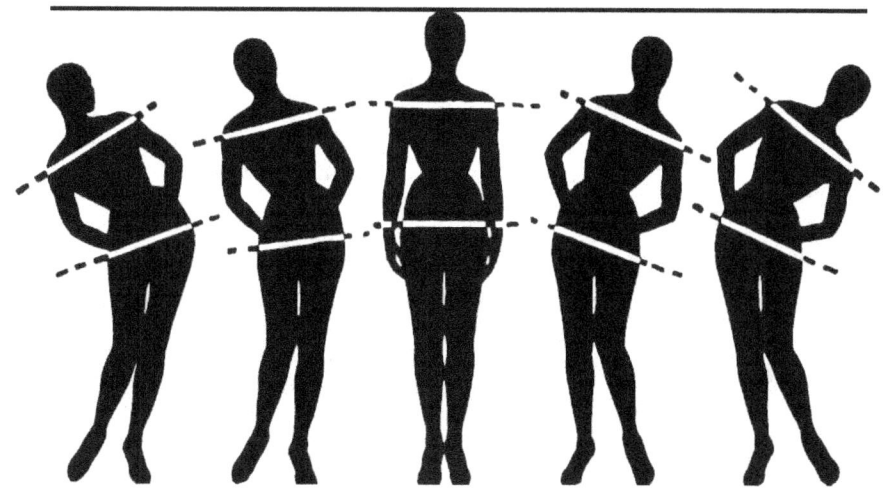

TILTIN G

Shoulder and hip tracks

Very interesting! We find that we can tilt them at an angle with the floor (yet keep them in the same plane and parallel to each other) with either end high.

They can be tilted toward each other (at either end) and remain one over the other or with one sliding out from under the other (still in the same plane).

For delicate differences, we can tilt the shoulder track and let the hip track remain parallel to the horizontal line of the page.

We can reverse this procedure and tilt the hip track and let the shoulder track remain horizontal to the page.

For even more variation, we can combine any of these positions with the turning body and let the camera add some variations of its own in the ? views. A great number of usable variations are at hand when your imagination or creativity pulls the strings.

Interesting effects also result when we move the shoulder in one plane and the hips in another ...

TWISTING SHOULDER
AND HIP TRACKS

independently puts fluidity into any body-line. The torso, in its elasticity, picks up a sense of action that makes the picture a living, vibrant thing.

We will not need to attach any new strings to our marionette to experiment with this twisting movement. In fact, we can simplify the manipulation of the strings by attaching a control-bar to the tops of each pair of strings.

One control-bar for the shoulder track and one for the hip track.

With our puppet, each control-bar would be capable of revolving in a complete circle. In humans, however, the degree of twisting done by the shoulders and hip tracks is limited by the flexibility of the model.

As each control-bar revolves, the hips or the shoulders revolve with it and the circumference of the imaginary circles (inscribed by the ends of the tracks) are parallel to each other, even though one track may turn to the right, the other to the left.

Use these bars parallel to each other as you explore the possibilities of this wonderful movement.

Remember that as one shoulder twists away from the camera, perspective will automatically make that shoulder appear tilted, while a reverse movement would make a tilted shoulder appear straight and parallel to the bottom of the picture.

When you arrange a pose, do you take advantage of the possibilities of this *twisting* movement and its effect on the body's attitude and outline?

108

With this twisting movement you can change the two-dimensional proportions of the body or the relationship of the parts to each other.

In a picture we think of the body not only in relation to external objects appearing with it, but in relation to its own proportions. We measure the size of the hips in relation to the size of the shoulders: the size of the waistline in relation to the hips, head or shoulders.

Notice the illustration on the left. The hip track is facing the camera and is parallel to the floor. The shoulder track has revolved, bringing one shoulder toward the camera and one away from the camera. Although the shoulder track on the subject remains parallel to the hip track they appear tilted toward each other in the silhouette because of the turn ... and something more important happens. The shoulders, that were at one time wider than the hips, now appear smaller in outline and proportion!

To the right, the illustration shows that the twist has been reversed; the shoulders face the camera and the hips are turned away. This again alters the proportions *of* the body. The shoulders now appear broader and the hips have been slenderized in turning away from the camera.

Some use the shoulders and hips to add fluidity to the body, some to correct defects in proportion, some to dramatize parts.

We all know that a man's shoulders should appear wider than his hips *(fashion's-fleeting-fancy* may demand that a woman be pictured this way). We also know that a voluptuous bustline and rounded-out hip puts forth that *fully-feminine-feeling.* We should never forget that the picture we want comes from pulling the right strings!

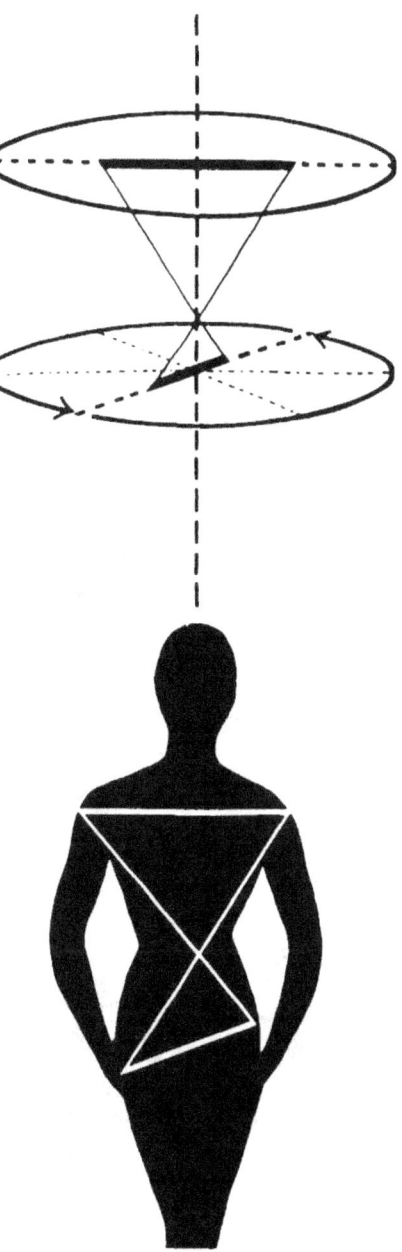

SHOULDERS FACING CAMERA
HIPS TURNED AWAY

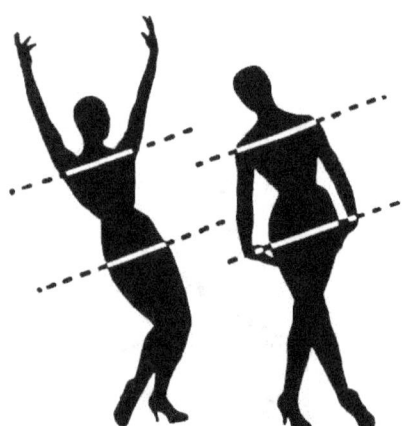

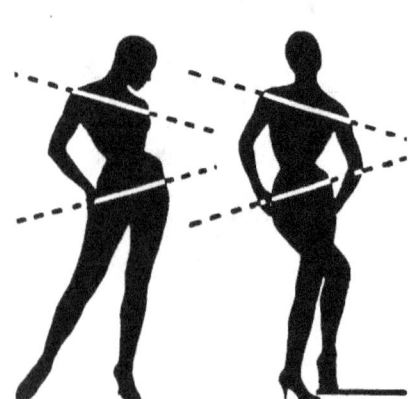

LEGS APART   LEGS CROSSED

TRACK VARIATIONS
(S H O U L D E R A N D H I P)

created upon a pre-determined pattern, provide a source of variation that can be unique. By setting up an imaginary problem we can illustrate with a very real solution.

The problem
To create twelve different 'S' body-positions.

Unique solution
Build each pose on a diagram of shoulder-hip track variation.

First, draw three pairs of lines to represent:

shoulder-hip tracks
parallel to each other
and to the horizon

shoulder-hip tracks
parallel to each other
but slanted up to the
right

shoulder-hip tracks
converging to the right.
neither line in a horizontal position.

These represent three very different positions for the shoulders and hips. If you thread a forward 'S' body-line and a backward S body-line through each pair of lines...

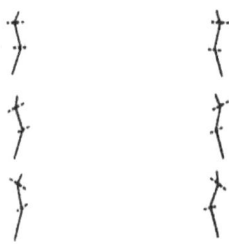

... you have doubled possibilities and now have ideas for six different poses.

110

At this point we decided to construct a pose on each diagram in which the girl's body faced in a certain direction. In the left panel each pose is directed left and in the right panel some look right and others are front-view. By adding the model's *right* and *left* stance we have arrived at the required twelve different basic ideas for the poses.

In order to follow these patterns, all three movements of the shoulder-hip tracks - *turn, tilt* and *twist* - were employed. (By setting the pattern on the flat picture surface it is easy to get what you want.)

Just for good measure, we decided to get further variety by letting all of the pictures on the left side of each panel have the feet apart and all of the pictures in the right of each panel have the feet crossed: then we fitted a pose into each pattern or diagram. Variety? Of course! They all have to be different. Perhaps you'd like to try some poses of your own on these same patterns. It's fun!

Also try:

shoulder-track slanting up
to the right,   _____
hip-track horizontal.

shoulder-track horizontal,   _____
hip-track slanting
up to the right.

Interlace a forward or a reverse 'S' body-line through each set of lines, decide what body view you want and in which direction the model is to face. Fit a pose into each one. Don't overlook the 'C and 'I' body-lines that might also be used.

Possibility for shoulder-hip track change can never be exhausted. Countless positions can be created by pre-determining shoulder-hip track patterns on the finished picture.

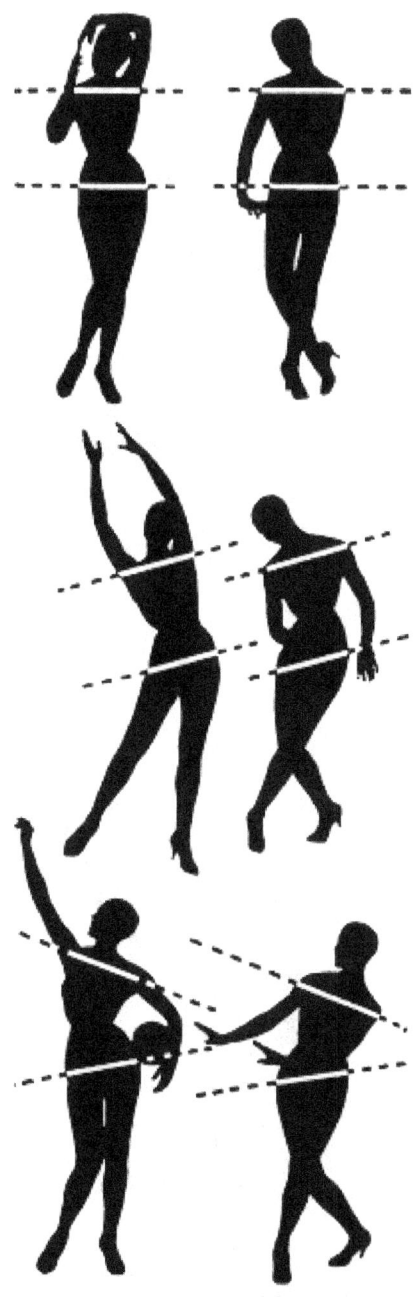

LEGS APART   LEGS CROSSED

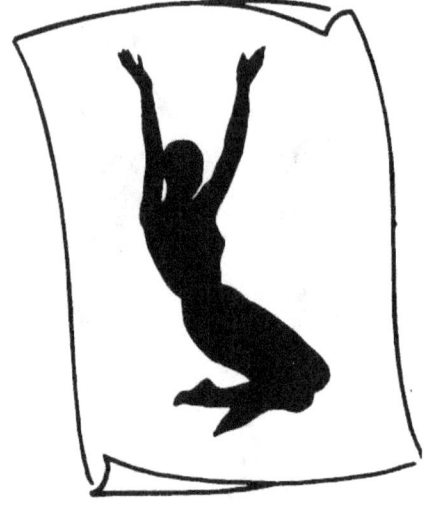

THE ZIGZAG BODY-LINE

found in sitting, kneeling and other contracted postures, offers a definite challenge
to a director's adroit manipulation of his
model and camera as well as to the model's
ability to create and visualize her position
from the camera's view.

Much has been written, and your own
experience has brought the knowledge to
you first-hand, on what can happen to the
body-lines (especially the leg-lines) in these
positions. You have watched distortion
dominate the picture as the feet come closer
to the camera and the head shrivels away.

You have seen how in response to slight
movement perspective (in the finished picture) has altered straight shoulder tracks
that were posed parallel to the floor. One
end appeared tilted or angled as the body
turned. Sometimes only a matter of inches,
away from the camera.

True, perspective problems decrease as
the distance increases between the subject
and the camera. But haven't you found that
it isn't always possible to work at a suffi-
cient distance to prevent distortion? Thus,
to help with the majority of your actual
sittings (in which you would like to position the body without distorted effects) let
us continue to confine our posing area,
as much as possible, between imaginary
panes of glass. Within this sandwich, we
will find ample opportunity to expand
posing ideas.

As you study these zigzag body positions
you see that their contracted postures can
no longer conform to the long-line body
symbols (I, C and S) but must be considered
and classified by the *angles* they form: the
degree of each and their relationship to
each other and to the page.

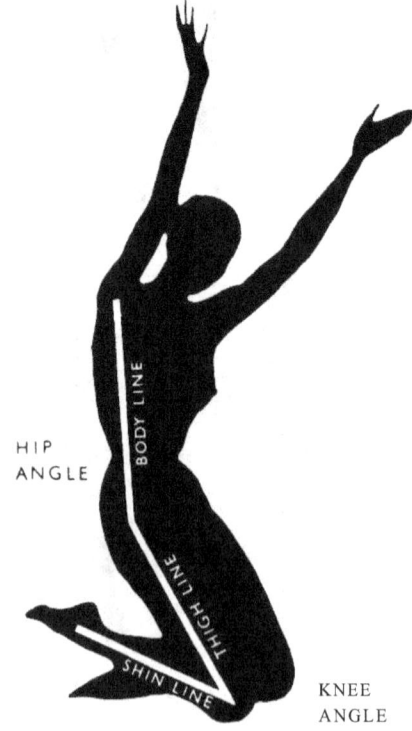

HIP
ANGLE

BODY LINE

THIGH LINE

SHIN LINE

KNEE
ANGLE

TWO KEY-ANCLES

in zigzag silhouettes are formed, one at the hip and one at the knee. These angles are evaluated either from the camera view or from the two dimensional picture surface. They cannot be determined by the degree at which a model bends her knee or hip (unless she is in a direct side view), because the camera changes these angles when it transposes her to the flat surface. There are nine primary combinations possible.

HIP ANGLES

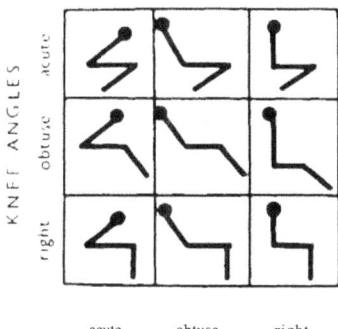

acute   obtuse   right

Each little figure can be tipped in any direction on the flat picture surface... effective departures for varying a pose!

THREE KEY-LINES

in zigzag silhouettes (controlled by the degree and position of the two key angles) vary visually in importance by their relationship to other elements in the picture. If at least two of these lines are parallel to the page or prop-lines (vertical, diagonal or horizontal) their position acquires significance and impact.

The length of any one (or all three) of the body lines is at its fullest when it is presented in a side-view to the camera. If a line is foreshortened, be sure the change is compatible with the rest of the picture.

FIVE KEY-VARIATIONS

in zigzag silhouettes are established by placing any primary angle combination on a point, or points of support and exploring the five considerations for change in numerical sequence. With emphasis now centered in different areas, let us review the count-down quickly, keeping the zigzag figure in mind:

5 views. The body must be changed gingerly from side to 3/4 or full-front and back views, as distortion can become quite a problem. While a front view causes the least problems in a long-line silhouette, you'll find the sideview presenting the fewest problems in the zigzag silhouette. (The direction the body faces is determined by the position of the upper part of the torso or *chest box.*)
4 limbs. Both the legs and the arms offer maximum advantages for variation in zigzag positions. Since the full length of the body is contracted, they usually take up a greater portion of the picture space also.
3 p's (all external elements). Purpose, Props and Position of the camera each assumes vital meaning, especially the last two. The support from which the position stems is the most important prop in the picture and we shall examine it more thoroughly in the next few pages. Camera station is also important and some of its variation of position are explored on page 141.
2 tracks. Shoulder-hip relationships are of utmost value in varying the zigzag figure.
1 body-line. Although the *body-line* in the zigzag silhouette is in another form it is still extended and contracted by varying the degree of the angles (hip and knee, in this instance).

In summarizing, it seems that in the zigzag, number 3 of the count-down becomes of foremost interest, numbers 2 and 4 hold their own and numbers 1 and 5 become more or less limited by the third dimension. Since *external elements are* of prime importance in zigzag positions, let us see how...

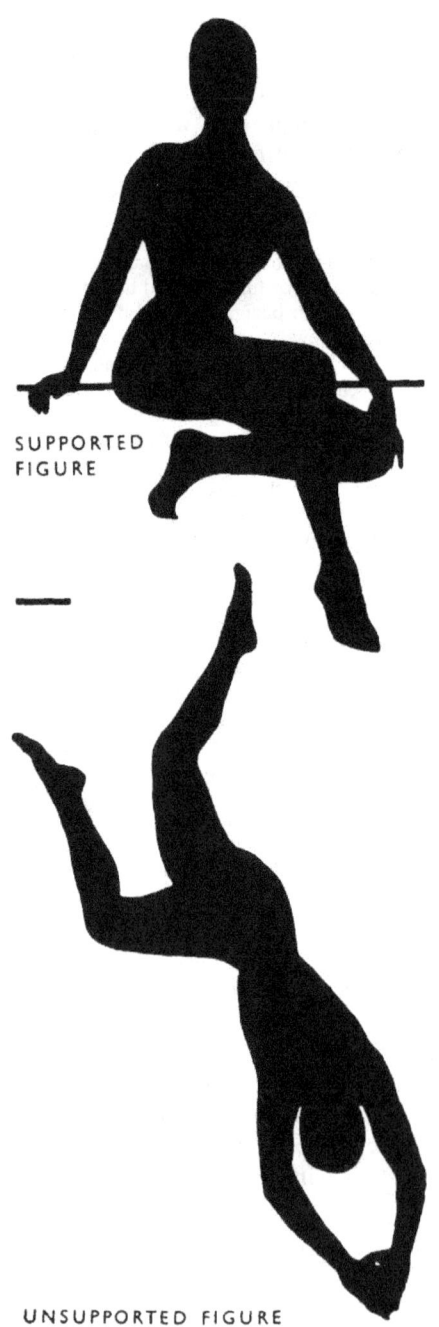

SUPPORTED
FIGURE

UNSUPPORTED FIGURE

ZIGZAG CHANGES
CAN EVOLVE

from a point of support. You can tip or tilt the zig-zag figure, with credibility, in many directions if you can imagine what would support the body in that position.

The supported figure uses a part (or parts) of the body to balance its weight upon a secure external object such as the floor, a chair, wall, etc. for a fleeting or indefinite period of time. The distribution of weight limits the duration of the pose.

The unsupported figure has no apparent means of support touching it... for the moment. It is in the process of leaving or arriving at a source of support, but at the instant the picture was taken it was in a state of isolation. Even if the support itself is not shown or used, its presence must be felt by the viewer. The viewer seeks understanding and must see or sense the point of support.

Two types of body surfaces support its weight for an interval of time. Bone creates the hard surfaces which maintain their shape under pressure, while flesh or muscle create the softer surfaces that conform (in different degree) to the object upon which they rest.

HARD BODY PARTS	SOFT BODY PARTS
feet and hands	buttocks
shoulders	thighs and calf
elbows and knees	stomach
head	forearm (fleshy part)
back	upper arm

Take the chart of the nine primary angle combinations (page 113) and turn the book so that a different part of the body supports the weight of each position. Can you see the difference the support makes? These *points of support* can become *points of departure.* They can make your zigzag positions different even before using a count-down. Let's examine the commonly used points of support and explore their variations.

THE SEAT

is the most natural and common point of support for the body. But that does not limit its possibilities for introducing change in any way.

In devising poses it is easy to get off the beaten path by arranging different combinations of zigzag angles with a body poised on the seat (hip angle). As these variations are combined with the count-down you find changes taking place similar to those in the panel to the right:

5. Three front views, two side views, and four J front views have changed the outline of the figure considerably. 3/4 back and full back views were also available but not used.

4. Arms were used to extend the line of the body, to support the legs, to support the body on the legs, to form patterns with the lines of the page, the body and even to depict a feeling of pleasure in one position.

    The legs have completed angles of the body-line or have formed patterns of their own, some have offered the body a secondary means of support which reduces strain and adds freedom and believability to the picture as a whole.

3. Props changed, as to the different heights upon which the body rests.

    Even the portion of the seat upon which the weight rests is varied. The bulk of the weight can rest on the side, back or front portion of the buttocks.

    Positions of the camera were varied to help keep these positions in pleasing proportions.

    The purpose and action of each picture is also different as you can see.

2. The shoulder-hip tracks were twisted in almost every picture to make the pose more effective and keep the parts of the body in reasonable proportion.

1. The body-line was changed greatly in its angles. A diagram of each of these illustrations will reveal their variation.

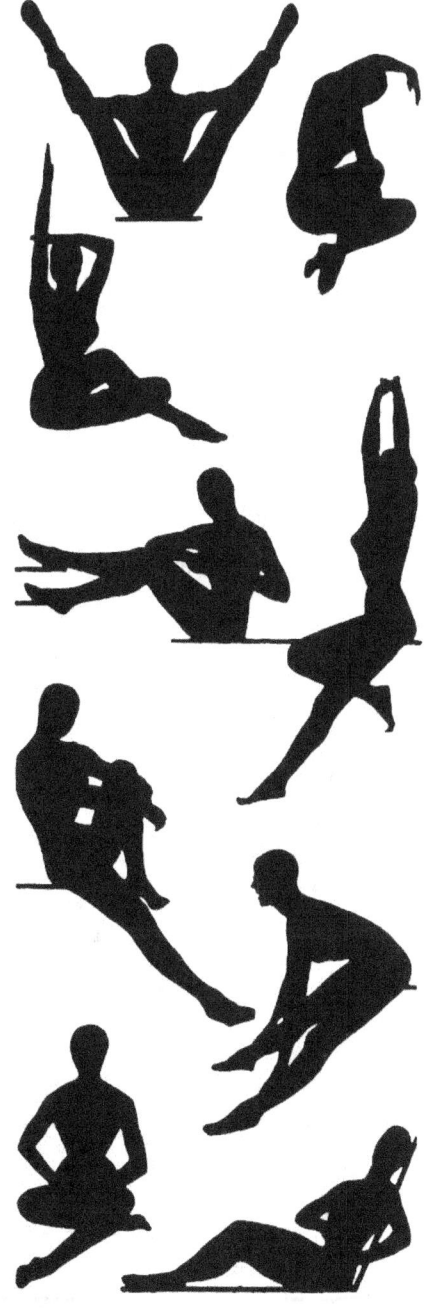

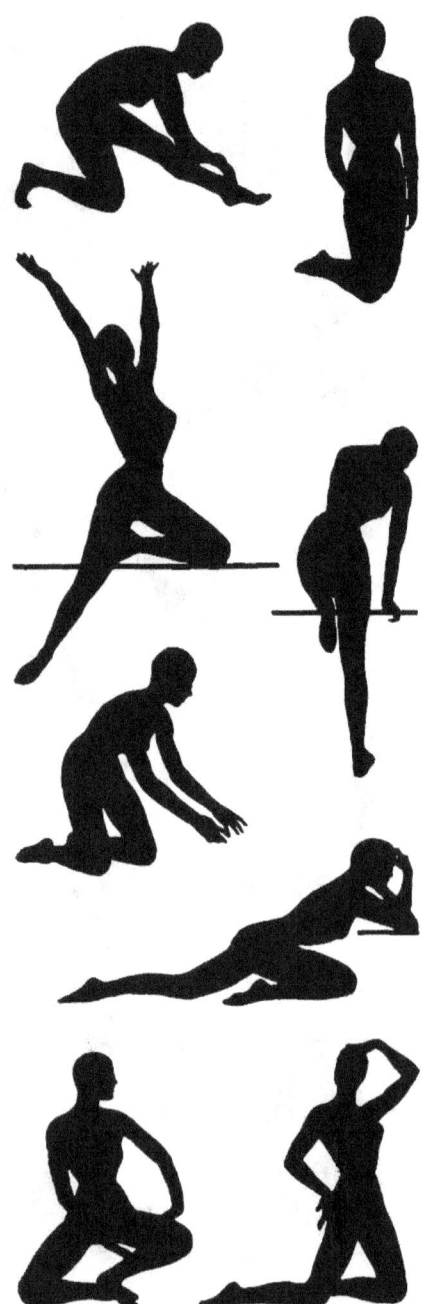

THE KNEES

(or knee) are also a very common point of support. Although they provide the body with a hard surface that is not distorted by pressure, they are an uncomfortable area upon which to place weight for any length of time, especially if the support is hard. First, you must decide if one or both knees are to be the body's point of support. From that point many variations of either become possible as you combine primary angles to establish position. Explore further with your count down.

5. All five views of the body are possible with the knee as the point of support, keeping in mind the distortion tendencies of some positions unless they are used for special effects.

4. One or both knees can be used to support the body at different heights, and using different angles. Arms are often used as a secondary means of support to take part of the weight from the sensitive knees.

    Legs can form interesting geometries, parallels and opposing angles.

    Both arms and at least one leg are usually free to be used in depicting story-telling action or for artistic arrangement.

3. Of the three external elements, the most important (next to the prop or support) is the position of the camera. It must be located carefully if parts of the body are not to lump themselves together and become distorted. Remember that as the camera moves, the juxtaposition of lines makes radical changes in the model's position. 'X'-plore the *Dutch angles* (where the camera is cocked sidewise) as well as the different split-level heights possible.

2. The shoulder and hip tracks are most flexible in kneeling positions because neither is used as a means of support (as when the body is resting on the seat or the back). Ingenious combinations of twist and tilt put movement into a position where action is otherwise impossible.

1. Body-line varies, in its combinations of angles, their position on the page, and by degree.

THE BACK

is another common point of support and is often used, for it leaves all four limbs free for artistic arrangement.

Positions on the back, which is a broad point of support, are usually comfortable and can be maintained for a long period of time. Where the model must remain almost completely relaxed, this horizontal position is often used, whether the pose (in the finished picture) appears in a horizontal, diagonal or vertical position.

With imaginative arrangement, a pose taken with the figure on its back and printed in a vertical position, achieves startling or unusual effects when neither the model nor her garments seem to be affected by the vertical pull of gravity.

In spite of the fact that purists criticize such manipulation and decry the practice, many glamorous and alluring 3/4 body and head views are taken every day with the subject resting on her back and the print then inverted for viewing.

After having established the back as the point of support for any pose (and determined the body's lines and angles) you can proceed with your count-down possibilities.

NOTE: If you have mentally diagrammed the figures in these panels, you will find a few long-line silhouettes along with the zigzags. This was done with the express purpose of having you consider a figure's potential from its point of support. For although most vertical long-line positions use their feet as their main point of support, the horizontal and diagonal long-line and the majority of zigzag silhouettes utilize other points. Some of them are very unusual and produce unusual results.

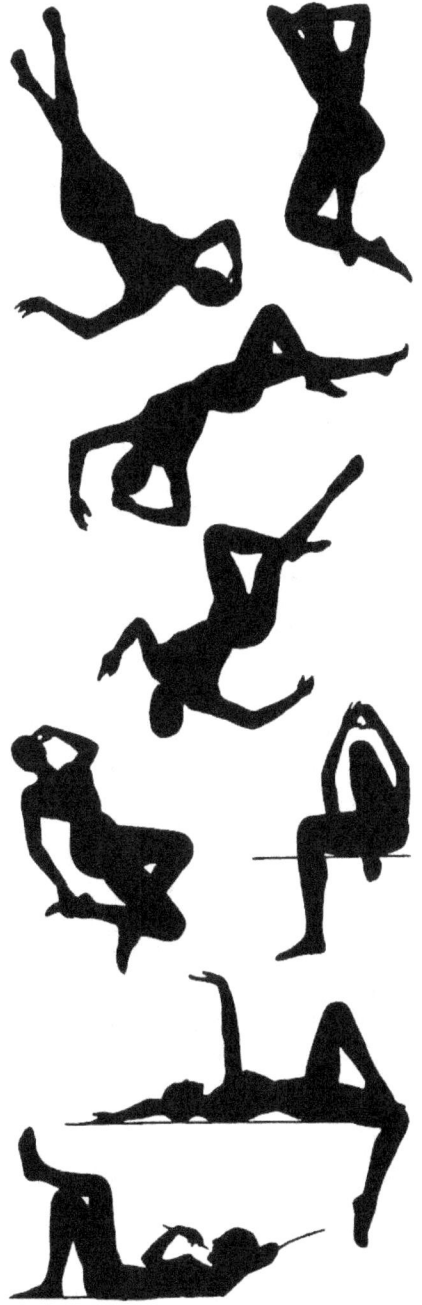

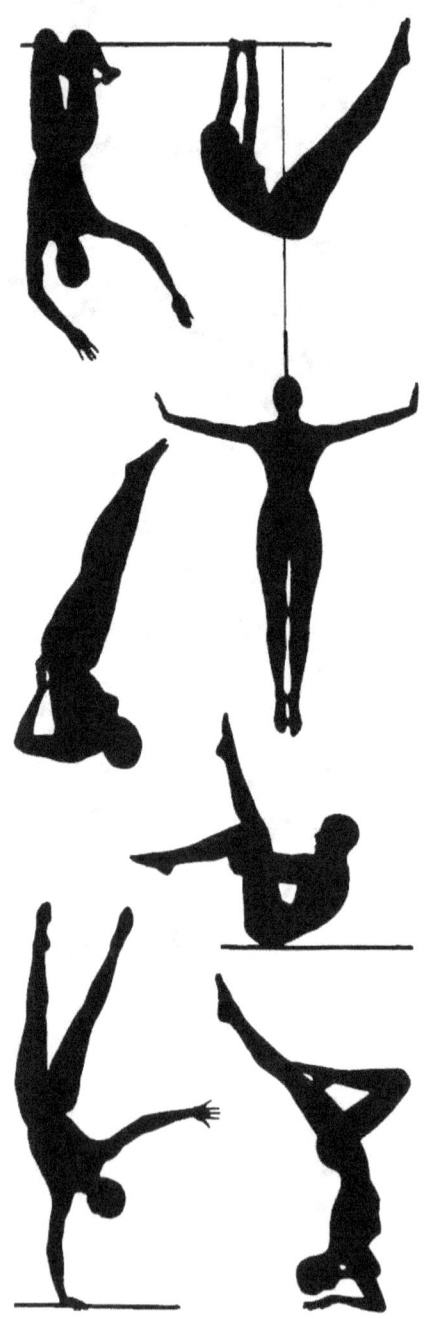

UNCOMMON
POINTS OF SUPPORT

upon which the body can balance or suspend itself for long intervals or for the decisive moment necessary to record a picture are:

lungs (on or under water)	hands	forearm
backs of knees	toes	stomach
	teeth	shoulders
back of hips	head	hair, etc.
finger tips		

Positions evolving from one or more of these points of support generally require physical co-ordination from the model, imagination from the director and result in pictures of striking impact.

While it is true that some of these pictures, stemming from an uncommon point of support, use highly-trained acrobats, dancers, swimmers and athletes, it is also true that others - just as effective - result from the use of a well co-ordinated model and a director with an eye for detail who knows how to utilize split-second timing, dramatic framing, judicious cropping, special lighting and perhaps temporary points of support, along with other artifices to produce results.

A well co-ordinated model who can perform an action once, can usually repeat the position with the necessary correction or variation while the director records it at a pre-determined point without loss of its *candid* qualities.

The fact that these positions of short duration must be snapped quickly, gives rise to the supposition that there is very little that can be varied. This is not so.

These positions of transitory or short duration can still be subjected to planning in connection with the count-down.

MULTIPLE
POINTS OF SUPPORT

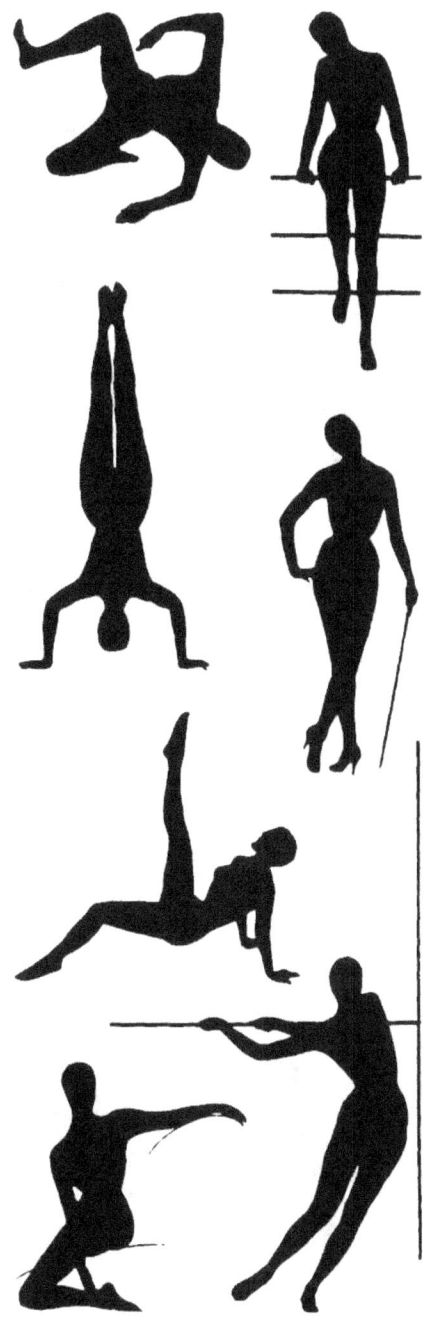

can distribute body weight to several related parts of the figure.

It is stimulating to begin thinking of unusual combinations of parts that might be used as multiple supports and then to stretch your imagination in visualizing positions that would result.

Let us look at some of the parts that can be used in combination to support the body:

shoulders		toes	thighs
	forearms	fist	hands
feet	fingers	calf	knees
back	stomach	side	heels
head	elbows	hip	teeth
arms			

seat It is astonishing how many ideas you can *pick out of a hat* if you will mentally juggle the above list. At random, select two or three points of support and arrange long-line or zigzag positions that would incorporate them. It is then you begin to realize the limitless possibilities of the body for dynamic expression.

Count-down will add to these positions, but when you consider the three important 'P's be sure you utilize your props to their fullest extent. A long object, held by the model can be used as an extra arm or leg, an additional point of support, to throw the equilibrium of the body into delightful and credible positions that would otherwise be impossible.

This *extra limb* can be many things ... an oar, stick, cane, golf club, skewer, pole, bat, parasol, etc. In advertising and pictorial photographs, it is often used to direct attention to specific areas as well as to help support the body's weight.

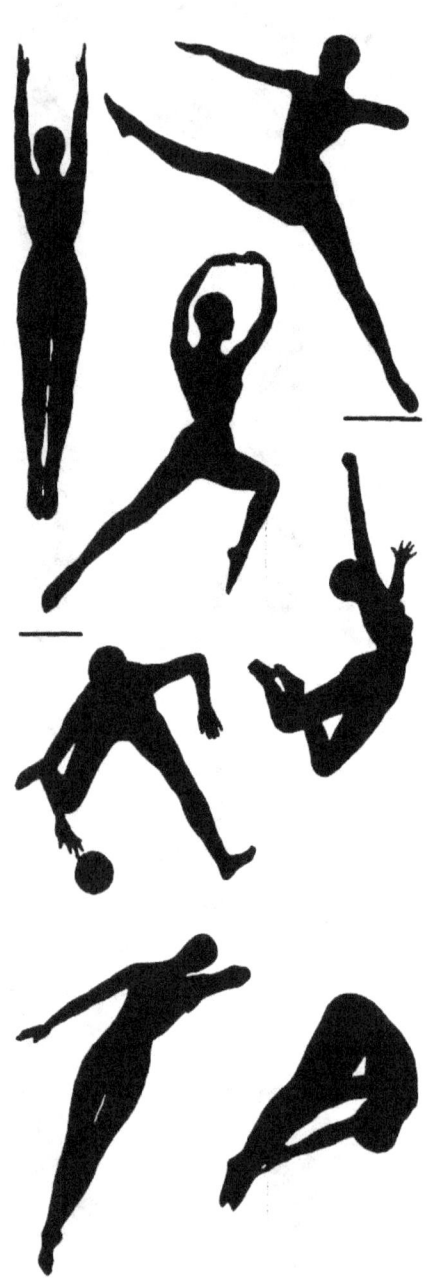

UNSUPPORTED FIGURES

appear to be rising to or falling from an object that would support their weight. The camera has seemingly *caught* the figure in this transitory state.

Unsupported figures can be separated and grouped according to recognizable differences, one is of action *under control* and the other is of action *out of control.*

Action under control . . .

does not give rise to a feeling of concern or alarm on the part of the viewer, for the primary feeling is that the position has been repeated over and over again without disastrous results.

These positions are readily associated with highly-trained and talented dancers, acrobats, trapeze artists, stunt men and athletes.

Some of the patterns for the body, while rising and falling, have an accepted standard of perfection such as difficult ballet leaps, swan dives, high jumps, etc. When this is the case, the control must be absolute, the position correct in every respect so as to satisfy the knowing critic. In these positions it is best to use a model experienced in the field of activity to be portrayed ... for one false action or minute detail will condemn the pose. However, great variation can still be achieved by planning. Oft-times directors underestimate the ability of their models and fail to ask for the variations and extra effort that would make the picture more outstanding.

The space-propelled feeling of the body in the air is usually increased by eliminating the point, from the finished picture, from which the action originated.

ACTION OUT OF CONTROL

astonishes a viewer and gives him a feeling of uneasiness and concern for the outcome of the action. Because these pictures are thrilling and urgent, they attract immediate attention and are, therefore, useful for comic or climatic effects.

In some of these unsupported figures a part of the body may actually touch the object that could support it, but the body itself is deprived of power (as a boxer collapsing or a woman slipping on ice) and the fall continues.

There are clowns, comedians and stunt men adept in credible and exaggerated falls. However, an adept model's fall can be photographed in its first disorganized stages, giving her time to right herself before touching the ground or being caught by an assistant or a net. The camera can also be angled to add a greater sense of lost balance.

A popular method for getting pictures of action apparently out of control is to let the model spring from a trampoline and station the camera low enough to eliminate the prop from view. Thus, a picture which seems to have the body falling with complete disorganization into space, can be repeated, with variation, over and over.

Extend your repertoire into the realm of *controlled-act ion* (under your control) pictures of unsupported figures, both those in which the action appears to be under the control of the model and those in which it appears to be out of the model's control. Pictures that were impossible only yesterday are now yours for the making. Take advantage of today's high speed film, fast lenses and knowledge of body-action!

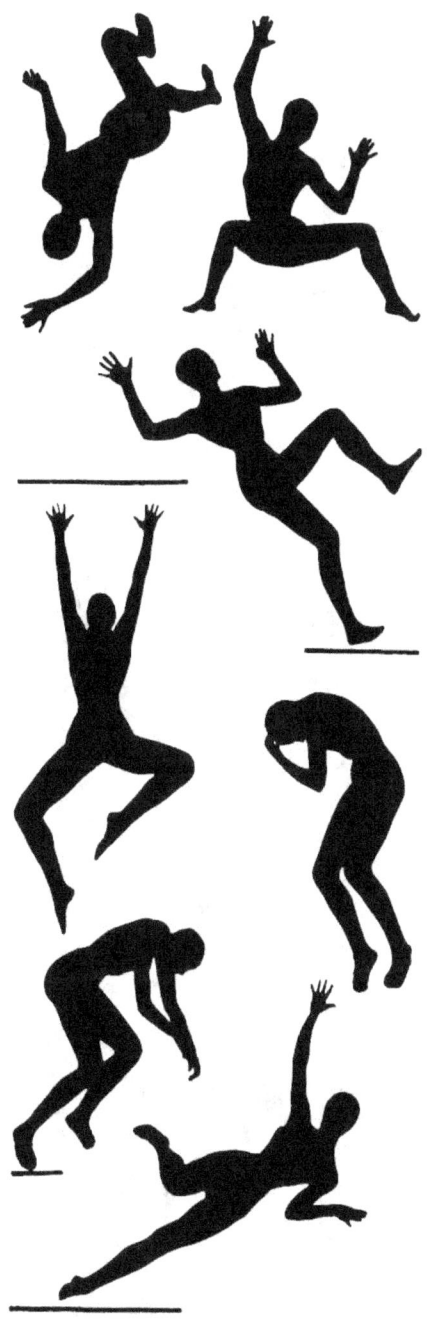

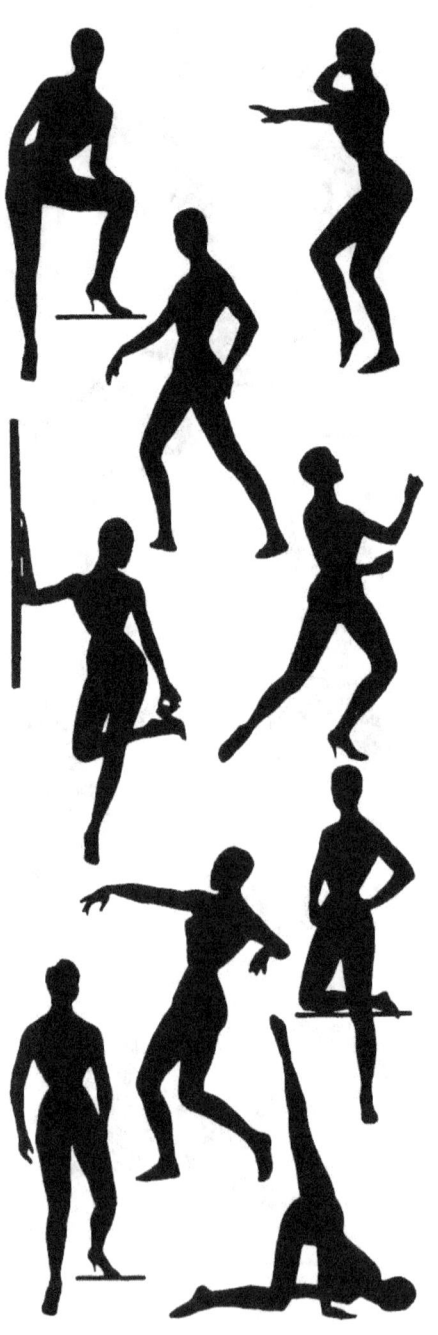

BORDERLINE SILHOUETTES

will catch your eye as you become super sensitive to the lines, angles and capabilities of the human figure for arrangement and variation.

Interesting to note, when you arrive at this point of great discernment, is that in addition to long-line silhouettes and zigzag silhouettes there seem to be some borderline silhouettes ... some that bear characteristics of each, but that fall predominantly into one group or the other.

Predominantly long-line ...

figures have the general appearance of the long-line silhouettes. The leg nearest the camera can almost always be used as the determining factor. If the hip and knees are not bent too much and the eye follows the body's long-line, the eye of the viewer will normally flow with it and the position is *predominantly long-line.*

Predominantly zigzag ...

figures generally give the appearance of a zigzag line with the leg nearest the camera considerably bent at either the hip or the knee (or both). Each person may make the distinction between predominantly long line or zigzag in a slightly different place, but it makes no great difference for ...

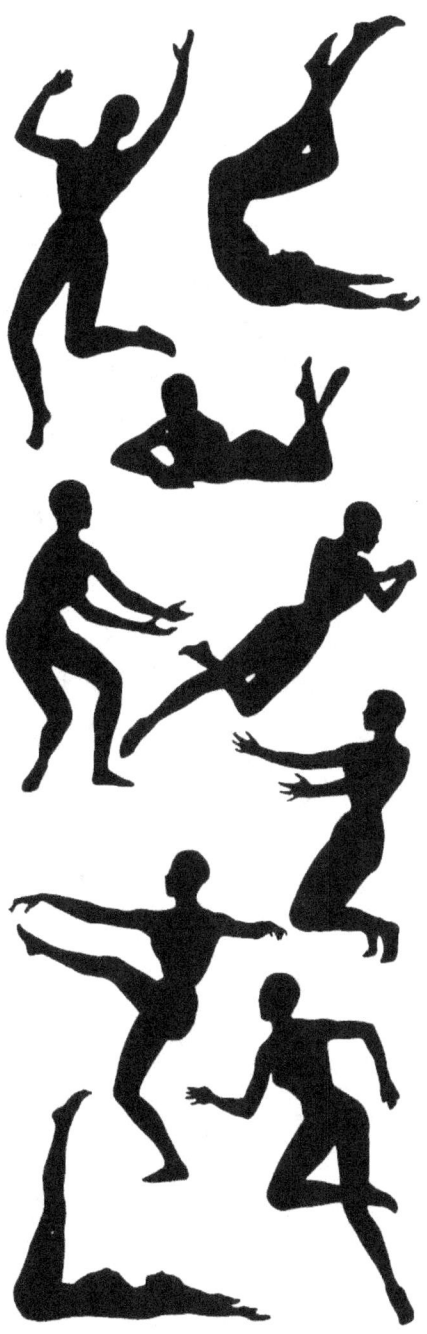

... when one of these fringe-silhouettes is to be duplicated before the camera, the mind's eye can compare either of the diagrams with the human figure and position its parts accordingly. If neither diagram gives you a completely satisfactory line to work from, use both lines, which together, form an unmistakable template and leave no doubt as to the position of any part of the figure being arranged.

HOW THE BODY TALKS

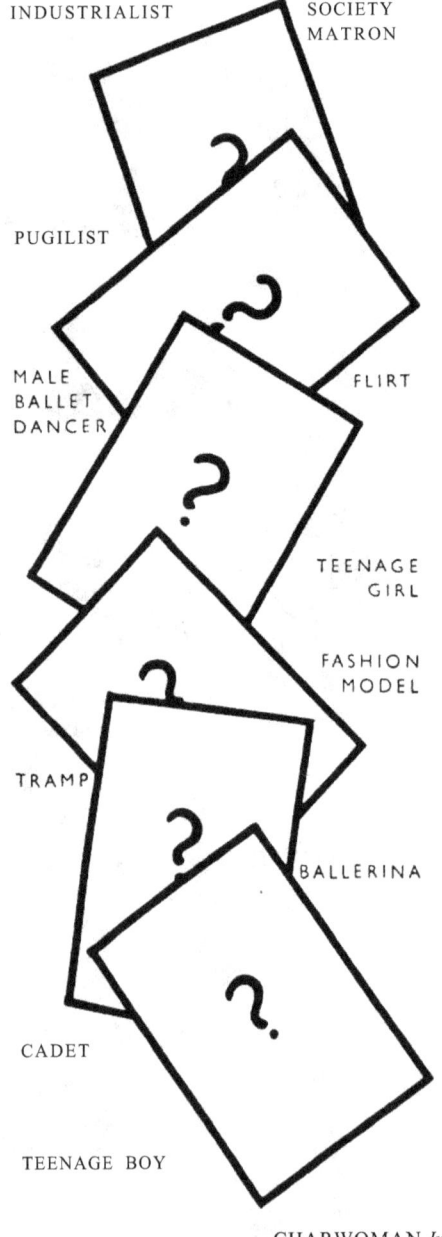

is no mystery. It speaks of character within, state of health, state of mind, age, station in life. It talks in attitudes that are universally understandable and are repeatable. When you seek to use the body as a means of communication, rather than as a physical assemblage of parts, you reach deep into the realm of its typical characteristics, feelings, psychological reactions and a myriad of intangible qualities. General impressions of types of people, their moods and station in life are pretty nearly the same the world over. The physical characteristics, or mental attitudes made evident by their stance sets each apart.

Visualize six male characters of approximately the same size and weight; a tramp, an industrialist, a cadet, a pugilist, a ballet dancer, a teenage boy. Mentally dress them all alike and face them toward the camera. Would anything in their body stance or bearing reveal differences in their character or occupation? What positions would you accentuate to set them even further apart from the other men?

Imagine six female characters such as those listed. Each is distinctly different in carriage and attitude. Reach into your memory for more and more details about these people, for the model and director who have developed an acute sensitivity to the people around them must have a rich storehouse from which to draw and can translate expressiveness into their work from memory. The keener the original observation the more exact the impression that can be created.

Did you know that a great deal of the responsibility for carrying these body messages falls upon the shoulders?

INDUSTRIALIST SOCIETY MATRON PUGILIST MALE BALLET DANCER FLIRT TEENAGE GIRL FASHION MODEL TRAMP BALLERINA CADET TEENAGE BOY

CHARWOMAN *In posing each of the above, what body attitude, action or stance could identify each for the viewer? Make each body talk... loud and clear!*

SHOULDERS
CREATE IMPRESSIONS

of mood and character. They, more than any other part of the torso reveal the spirit of the model and are considered a thermometer from which the temperature of the mood can be measured.

Although it takes but little physical force to move the shoulders, they are capable of exerting great mental force in the finished picture.

Neutral shoulders...
> have little expression of their own and are used as a starting point from which to measure how much expression you wish them to project. They need not move from this position at all if they are not to express anything.

Forward shoulders ...
> relay a feeling of weariness, weakness, sickness, shyness, etc.

Low shoulders...
> reflect studied poise, elegance, natural case, casualness, etc.

Back shoulders ...
> give the impression of physical vitality, pride, courage, strength, happiness, etc.

High shoulders ...
> may give the impression of lack of confidence, tension, strain, fright, etc.

Different combinations of these movements suggest complex feelings or mixed emotions such as:

Up and forward shoulders ...
indicate that the model is kittenish, flirtatious, coquettish, etc. **Low and forward shoulders** ...
> reveal age, defection, discouragement, weariness, etc.

These movements that bring the shoulders into expressive positions may be slight or great, depending upon the role they must play.

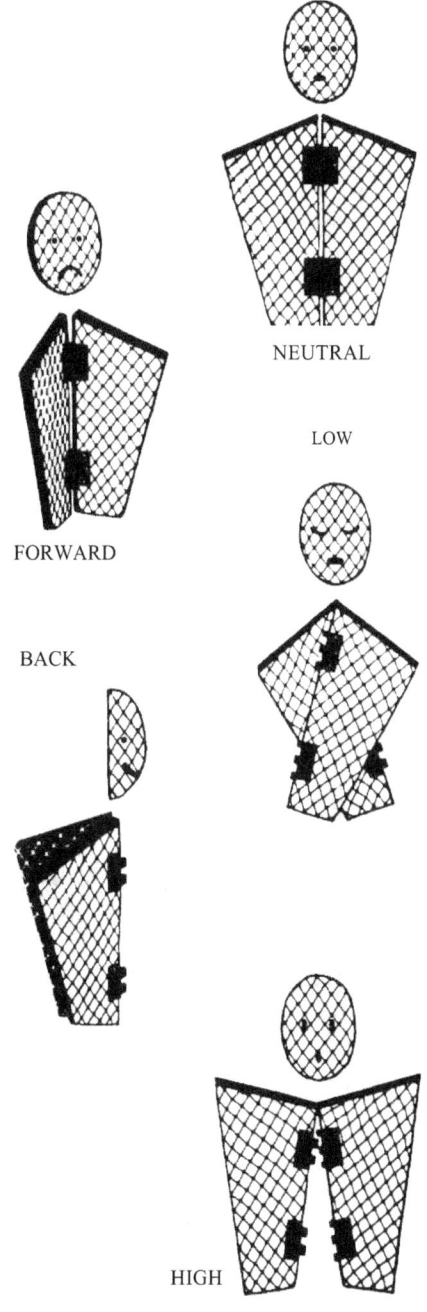

FORWARD

BACK

NEUTRAL

LOW

HIGH

125

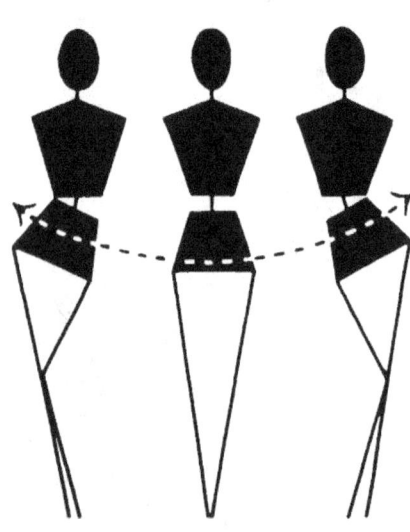

SHOULDER-TRACK SWINGS
HIP-TRACK PARALLEL TO BOTTOM OF PAGE

HIP-TRACK SWINGS
SHOULDER-TRACK PARALLEL TO PAGE

TORSO POSITIONS

can also delineate mental attitudes, depict character and convey moods.

Have you ever noticed how the relationship of the upper torso to the lower torso creates a definite impression? Would you believe that so slight a matter as the relationship of each part to the edges of the picture page could make a difference? It does.

Look at these simple block figures. If they, in their simplicity, can emit feeling, think of how much more can be projected by the human figure in a similar position.

When the model is facing the camera...
with her hip-track stationary (parallel to the bottom of the page) and her shoulder-track tipped to the side, you might get a feeling of curiosity, interest, concern, alertness, etc. as you do from the end figures in the group above, left.

A different impression is conveyed when the shoulder-track remains stationary and the hip-track swings sideways (although the waist is bent to the same degree as in the illustration above). A common reaction to the end figures below, would be an interpretation of flirtation (haughty above ... naughty below) or casualness. Do you sense these distinctions?

Positions of parts of the body in relation to the page, build feelings, even in the arrangement of groups. Notice how the group below, whose shoulders lean toward each other, appear more friendly than the three figures above, whose shoulders draw away from each other.

The position of each part of the body, on the picture page, makes a difference ... regardless of how the body faces.

When the model is in side view...
the same relative action and reaction takes place.

The straight central figures, parallel to the sides of the page, have a formal, regal or military bearing, their very lines have masculinity and solidity.

When the hip-block remains stationary and the chest-box tilts back, you get an impression of animation and youthfulness, or at the other extreme, one of contempt, disbelief, shock, fright or the feeling that the person is drawing away from something or some thought.

When the hips remain stationary and the chest-box tilts forward, its position connotes interest or attention. You visualize a building superintendent watching basement construction or a woman listening to a child or, you may picture something entirely different and feel that the person is old or tired.

If the chest-box remains stationary while the hip block swings (pendulum fashion) at the waist, our simple block and line figures take on different expressions, attitudes and meanings. For, as the hip-block swings back into a bustle it suggests a primitive conception of posture as well as an air of opinion or conceit. Yet when the hip-block swings forward all that is changed and you sense, instead, the poise associated with a socialite, a fashion model or an athlete.

These general conceptions of attitudes that we have defined from certain positions, do not constitute an attempt to interpret all figures in these terms. These positions serve only to show the possibility for interpretation (or misinterpretation) through body attitude. Once you are aware of these possibilities, you can explore them further.

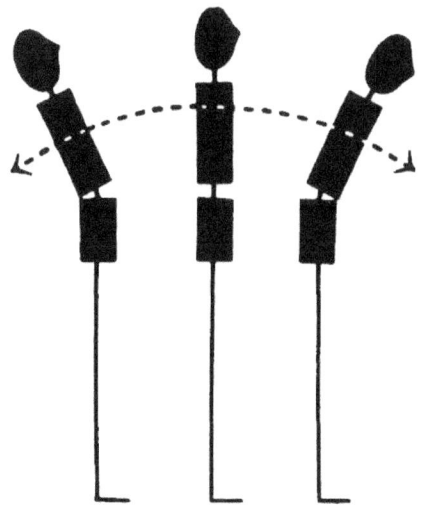

CHEST-BOX TILTS FORWARD OR BACK
HIP-BLOCK PARALLEL TO SIDES OF PAGE

HIP-BLOCK SWINGS FORWARD OR BACK

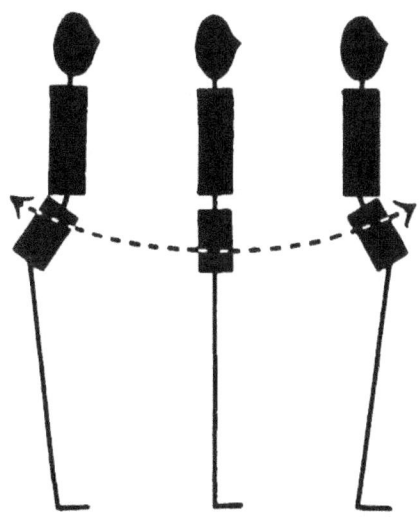

CHEST-BOX PARALLEL TO SIDES OF PAGE

MUSCULAR TENSION

of a body marks the sincerity of a picture. No matter how excellent a body attitude, how perfect the arrangement of parts may be, the body, from toe to fingertip, must be in complete muscular compatibility with the mood and message to be expressed.

Only too often the credibility of a model's serenity and ease in a picture has been destroyed not by the smile on her face but by the give-away tension in her hunched shoulders or rigid little finger!

It is wise to remember that still pictures remain at hand for constant scrutiny. The second or third glance may reveal insincere detail. Even the layman is sensitive to a false pose although he cannot always put his finger on what is causing that feeling.

To the last detail, the body and all its parts must state and reaffirm what the picture has set out to establish in impressional-impact or specific expression. All emotion travels through the body's complete nervous system split seconds before the face and body react. Although it is the mind that conceives the thought and emotion, it is the body that passes that feeling on to the parts that can help express it visually.

In anger, the body relays the message to the face bringing the muscles of the brows together and downward, tensing the lips. The message, hurrying along another series of nerve ends causes the hands to clench in defense. Further on, perhaps, the feet are set firmly on the ground while the diaphragm expands the lungs in readiness to explode into action. Emotion bristles in every gesture and exudes from every pore. Since the body is the instrument through which the mind communicates, it does not remain unaffected as it transmits these messages. Often a single part of the body in undesirable tension discredits the whole picture. The model may project an attitude perfectly ... except that:

The *muscles around her mouth* say, 'Why can't he hurry and take that picture?' An *index finger,* too straight at the last joint, screams, 'I look so pretty!' and of course -does not!
A little finger is curled in absurd tension and somehow reminds us of someone *playacting the lady.*
Uncalled for *tension in the neck* strains the whole bearing.
A big toe points too far downward and advertizes the effort of the model to look *just so...* unnatural!
Shoulders gradually sneak upward until by the time the picture is made anyone can sense she is ill at ease.
She forgot to pull her *tummy* in. *Back collapsed* and *shoulders slumped forward:* she *is* tired but her picture need not show it! *Mind sagged* and expression wandered away, as you can see by her face!

A model must co-ordinate each part of her body to the proper amount of tension demanded by the over-all picture. She must learn to *express* the message with all parts of her body so the director can evaluate it in the light of the viewer's point of command. The director must be ready to correct weak spots in the tell-tale areas or change any part that is not in keeping with the situation. He must be ready to arrest these tensions at their inception.

Tension is electricity that runs throughout pictures and the amount of voltage each pose contains depends upon the mood to be evoked or the impact to be gained. Though the degree of tension is modified to fit each character and situation, it can be observed, as it mounts ... in four distinct stages ...

NO-TENSION

lets the viewer find the body in a completely relaxed state. It denotes a complete lack of either mental or physical stimulus. It is serene and tranquil. Nothing is happening to disturb the model in her state of drowsiness or blissful dreaming.

LOW-TENSION

conveys the feeling to the viewer that the mind is working although the body has not yet been moved to noticeable action. It is a sort of pre-action picture in which one senses the stirring of the mind and that more movement will be forthcoming. Low-tension pictures include those of leisurely action in which you feel the body is moving with ease as the mind reflects upon direction and control. Current flows through the picture in soft waves.

TENSION

indicates to the viewer that the body has been brought into vibrant and alert action. The mind has stimulated and motivated the body so both are keyed to the same degree. Good models control mental and muscular tension balancing them so that the viewer looks at the action and is not conscious of the effort. *Tension* projects a feeling of reality in which action and energy are well directed.

HIGH-TENSION

makes the viewer conscious that the body is vibrating with energy that is (or almost is) out of control ... sparks are flying and the body is in a state of such strain, it cannot contain itself with the extreme mental or physical burden placed upon it. Violent emotion exudes from the entire body and is visible in every muscle.

When *pitching* an emotion ... think not only of the direction it is to be thrown but also, how far it must go!

The distance at which any of these tensions will be viewed also affects the degree to which they must be emphasized or underplayed.

Close up camera views require restraint -controlled but effective gestures and action. For when the audience is close it sees small details and can read *tight* movement.

Full length camera views of the body call for slightly stronger gestures to project the same reaction. Fine points of facial expression are no longer distinguishable as the head now shares the picture with the whole figure.

Distant views of the body require broad gestures and exaggerated tension as delicate expression is no longer visible.

PHYSICAL AND MENTAL TENSIONS

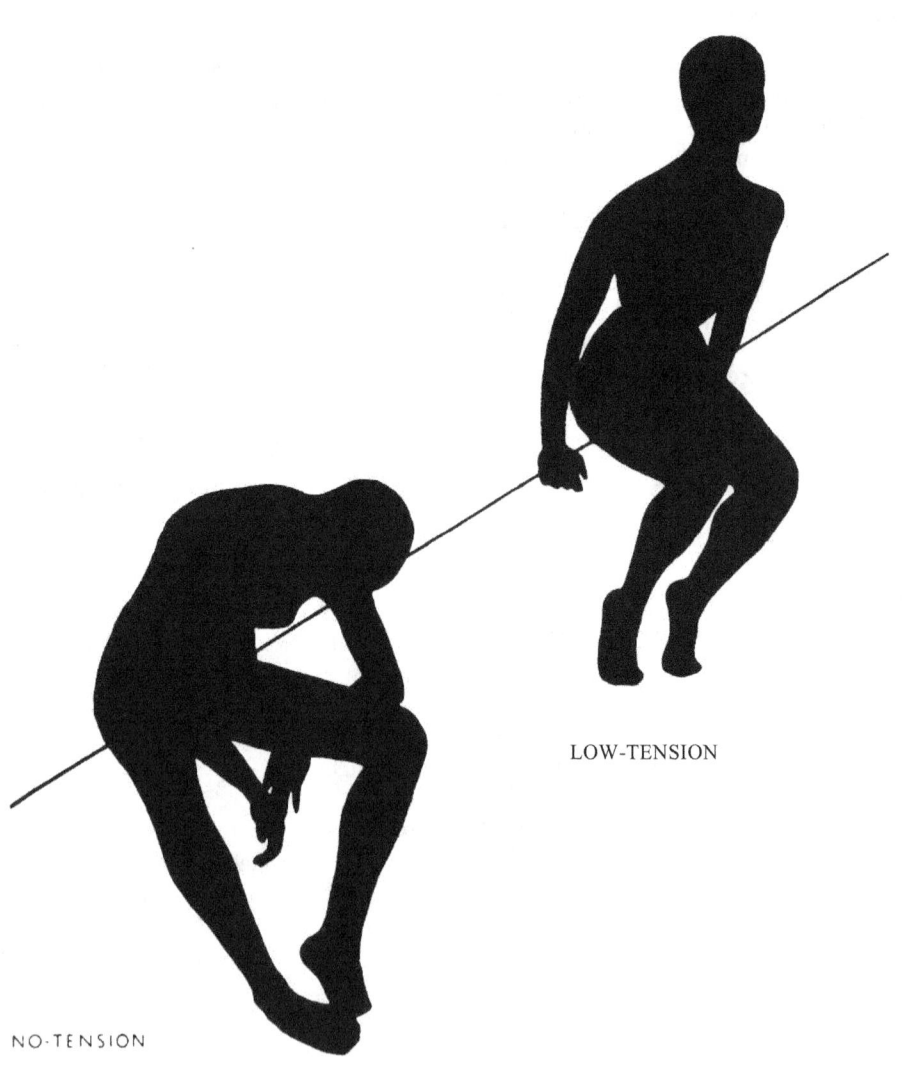

LOW-TENSION

NO-TENSION

MUST BALANCE TO LOOK RIGHT

TENSION

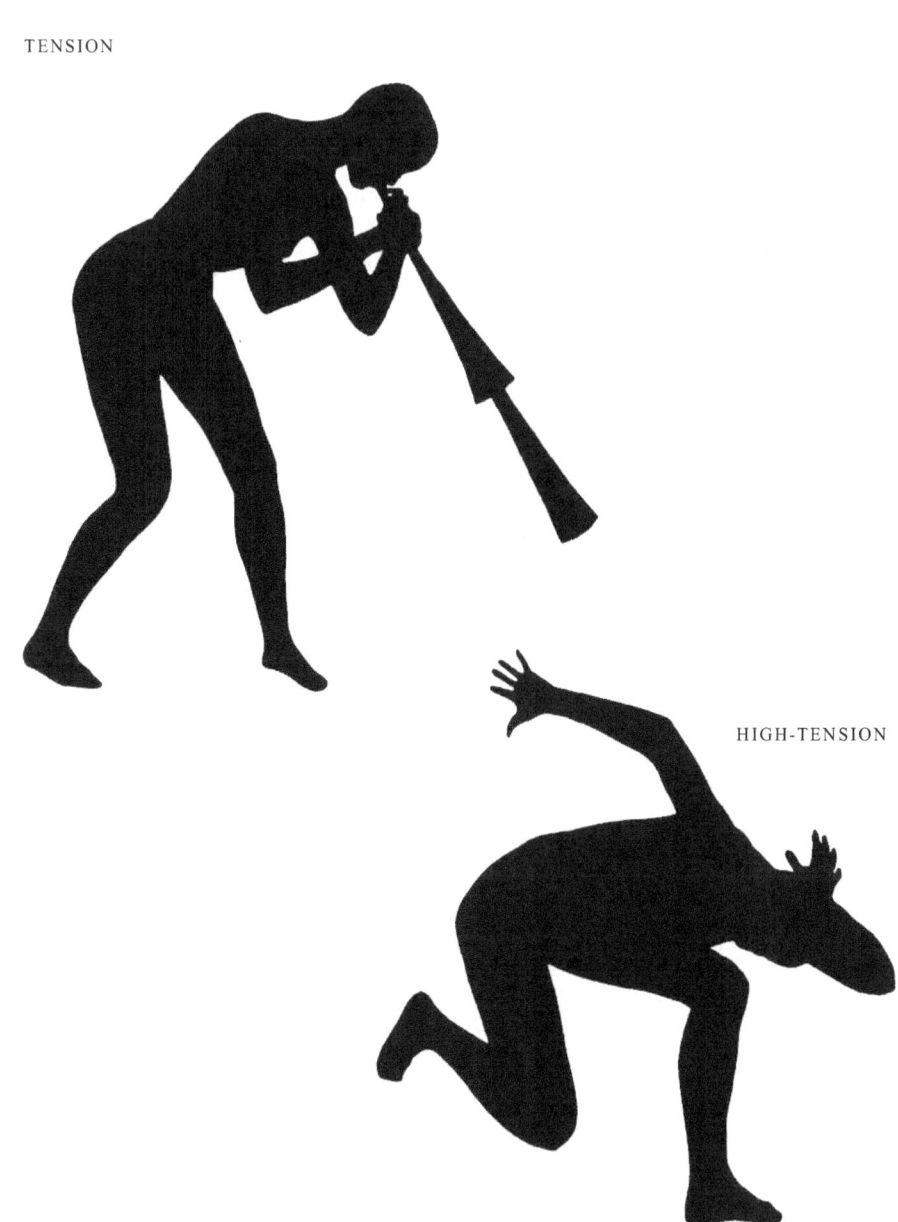

HIGH-TENSION

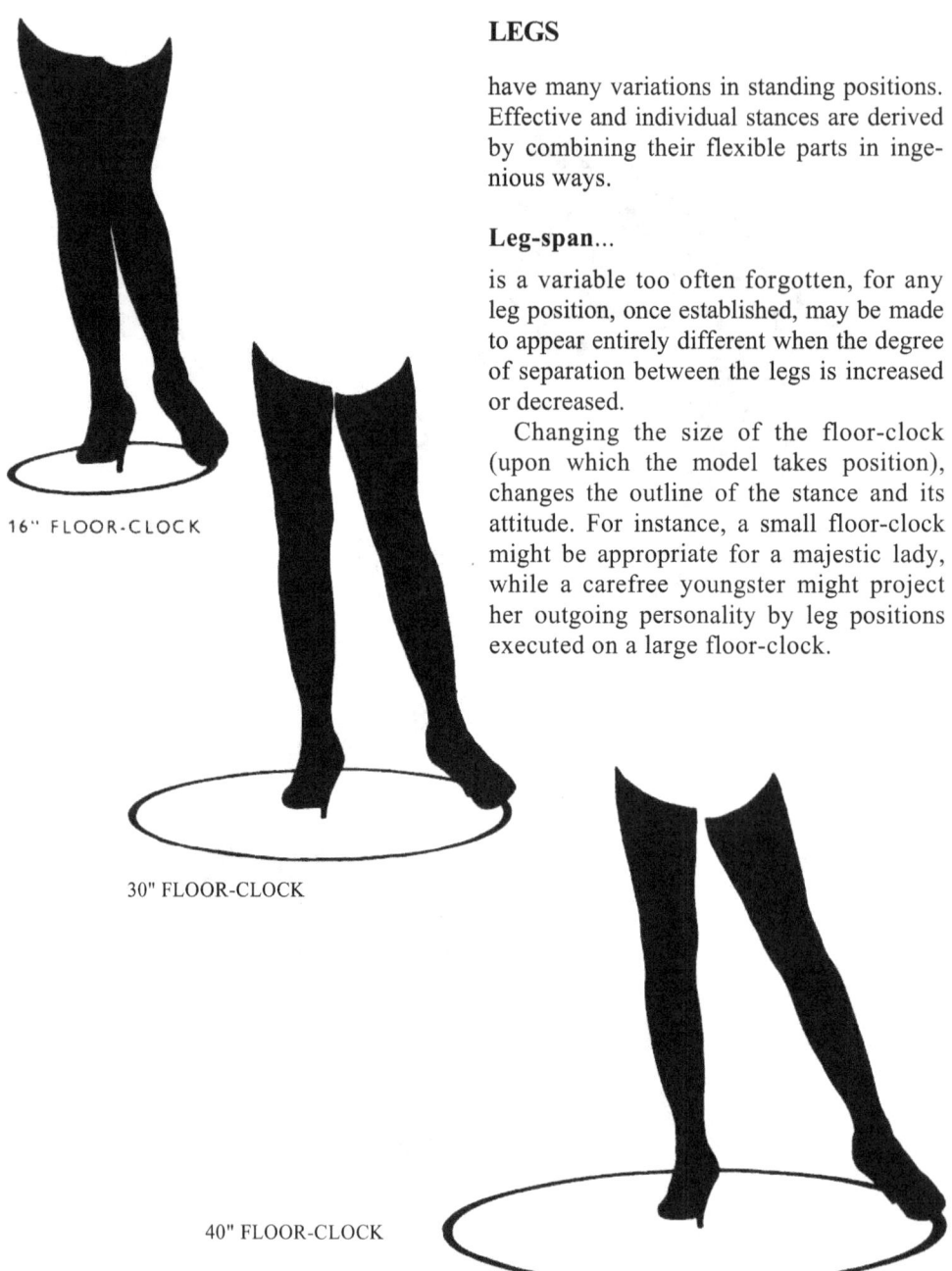

LEGS

have many variations in standing positions. Effective and individual stances are derived by combining their flexible parts in ingenious ways.

Leg-span...

is a variable too often forgotten, for any leg position, once established, may be made to appear entirely different when the degree of separation between the legs is increased or decreased.

Changing the size of the floor-clock (upon which the model takes position), changes the outline of the stance and its attitude. For instance, a small floor-clock might be appropriate for a majestic lady, while a carefree youngster might project her outgoing personality by leg positions executed on a large floor-clock.

16" FLOOR-CLOCK

30" FLOOR-CLOCK

40" FLOOR-CLOCK

TOE-HEEL
COMBINATIONS

provide natural as well as expressive sources for foot variation.

BOTH FEET FLAT ON CLOCK

BOTH FEET UP ON TOES.
(one on ball *one on* tip)

ONE FOOT FLAT ON CLOCK
ONE FOOT ON HEEL

ONE FOOT FLAT ON CLOCK
ONE FOOT UP ON TOE (ball)

ONE FOOT FLAT ON CLOCK
ONE FOOT UP ON TOE (tip)

ONE FOOT FLAT ON CLOCK
ONE FOOT rocked out

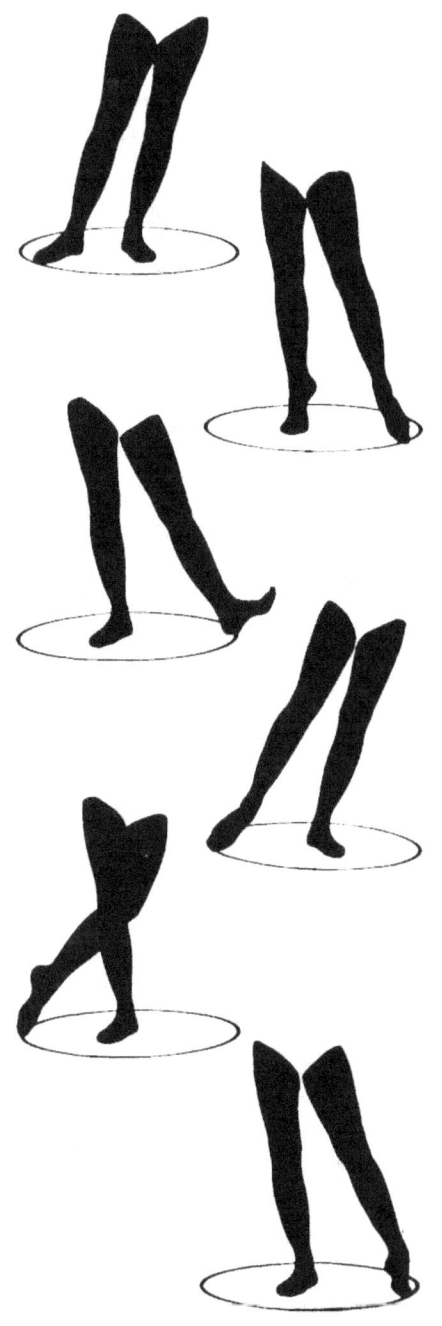

133

KNEE-BEND
COMBINATIONS

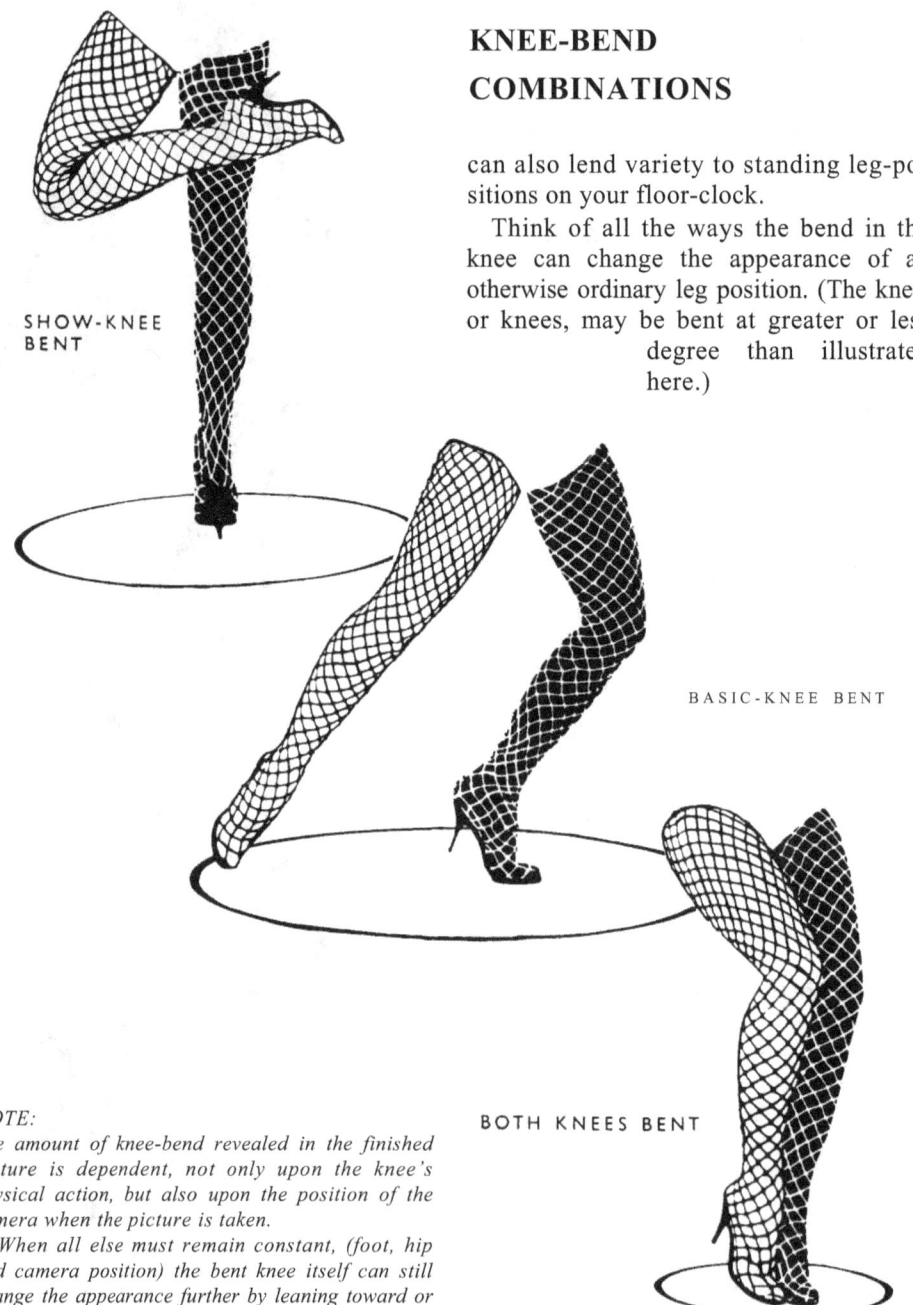

SHOW-KNEE
BENT

BASIC-KNEE BENT

BOTH KNEES BENT

can also lend variety to standing leg-positions on your floor-clock.

Think of all the ways the bend in the knee can change the appearance of an otherwise ordinary leg position. (The knee, or knees, may be bent at greater or less degree than illustrated here.)

NOTE:
The amount of knee-bend revealed in the finished picture is dependent, not only upon the knee's physical action, but also upon the position of the camera when the picture is taken.

When all else must remain constant, (foot, hip and camera position) the bent knee itself can still change the appearance further by leaning toward or swinging away from the camera.

134

LEG AND FOOT
VARIATIONS

such as *floor-clock-stops, leg-span, toe-heel placement* and *knee bend...* when explored to their fullest, or used in combinations with each other, reveal the leg's potential for an infinite number of positions.

In assuming or directing leg positions, you will notice that, whether the show-foot touches the floor or not, the numbers on the imaginary floor-clock can identify the direction the toe is pointing.

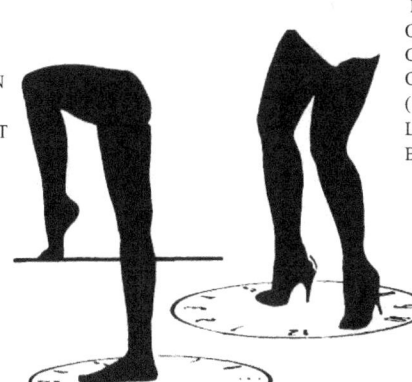

SHOW-KNEE BENT
ONE FOOT FLAT, ON
CLOCK ONE FOOT ON
TOE LEG-SPAN..
MEDIUM BASIC-FOOT
AT 3

BASIC-KNEE BENT
ONE FOOT FLAT ON
CLOCK
ONE "ROCKED IN"
(ON TOE)
LEG-SPAN.. MEDIUM
BASIC-FOOT AT 5

BASIC-KNEE BENT
ONE FOOT FLAT ON
CLOCK
ONE FOOT ONE TOE
(TIP)
LEG-SPAN., MEDIUM
BAS C-FOOT AT 2

BOTH KNEES BENT
BOTH FEET ON TOES
LEG-SPAN. MEDIUM
BASIC-FOOT AT 4

A twist of the hips . . .

after the leg position has been established, can reapportion the body's weight and balance. The hips can twist in either direction to make slight or radical changes in the appearance of the whole body.

135

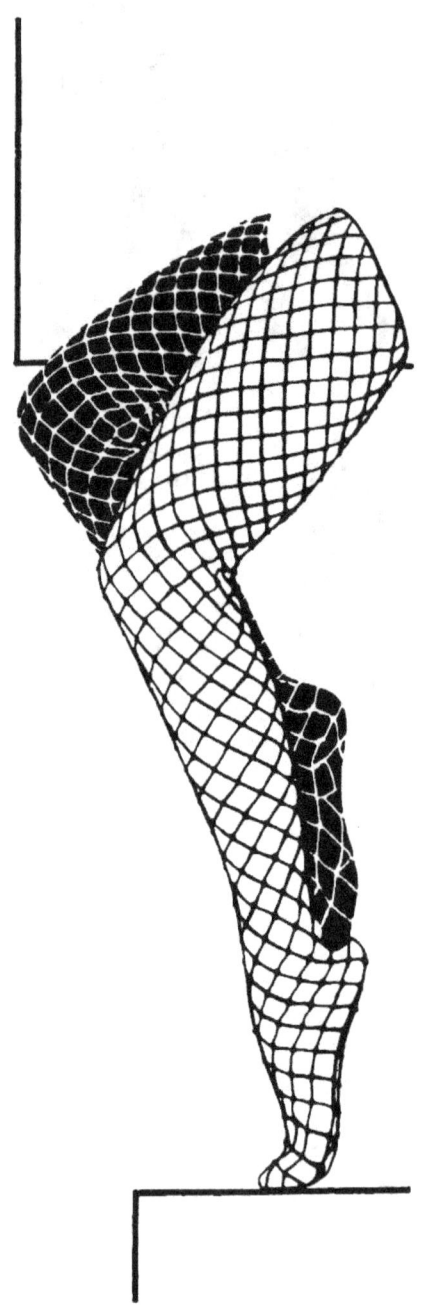

LEGS IN SITTING POSITIONS

play a completely different role in pictures than legs in standing positions. No longer needed to support the body's weight, they can now be used for design, compositional arrangement and expression; they may either compete or co-operate with the arms. In their new role they present an interesting challenge to both the model and the director.

In the pictures you have taken, observed or analyzed, you have no doubt noticed that generally one leg (the leg nearest the camera) appears to be more important than the other.

'First come ... first observed' is the law of legs in pictures and should guide directors and models posing them.

The most important leg is the *primary* leg, while the leg further from the camera, and of less importance, becomes the *secondary* leg. For easy identification of legs in sitting positions, we have illustrated the primary leg as light and the secondary leg as dark.

The secondary leg creates a background for the primary leg and usually adjusts itself to the scheme of things as an effective blend or counterpart.

When legs are equidistant from the camera and in exactly the same position they should be arranged with equal care.

Distortion of flesh...

in sitting or reclining positions becomes evident at the calf or thigh when too much pressure is applied. The disfigurement of the calf (be sure to watch for it) is easily eliminated, while thigh distortion requires a redistribution of body weight.

PROPORTIONS
OF LEGS

must be considered when the legs are re-
leased from the duty of supporting the
body's weight in sitting (or reclining) positions. Their new freedom creates problems
in perspective (through point of view) ordinarily never considered when the body is
standing upon them. When the legs are as
free as the arms, they too may extend too
far toward or too far away from the camera,
straying into danger zones that play havoc
with their proportions.

If the glass sandwich that restricted the
movement of the arms can now be used to
encompass the whole body and especially
to restrict the movement of the legs, your
problems in arranging them for sitting and
reclining positions become negligible.

Legs are not concealed by clothing...

in sitting (and reclining figures) because
their covering is generally pliant and re-
veals the mass that lies beneath.

Whether drapery accentuates the contour of the leg by folding around it or accentuates its position by radiating from the
angle of the knee makes no difference; the
viewer is still conscious of their proportions.
The outline and form revealed suggest the
entire position and make the correct arrangement of leg angles very pertinent to
the success of the picture as a whole.

Model and director...

'Keep your eye on the angles... as well as the curves !'

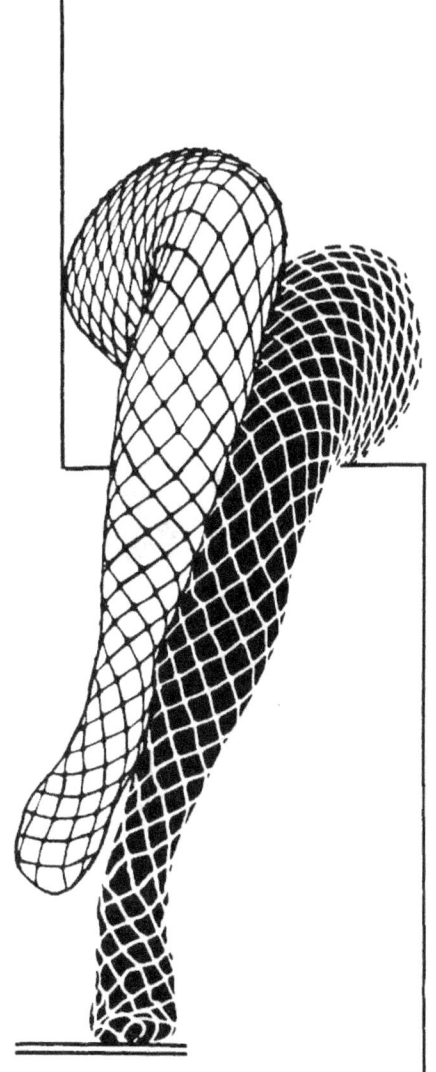

COMBINING
KNEE ANGELS

is one way of bringing variety into the leg
positions of sitting and reclining figures.
An immediate mental image of what the
(combined primary and secondary leg)
knee angles look like (on the finished picture's flat surface) can be an invaluable aid
in planning positions.

Remember, these angles result from:

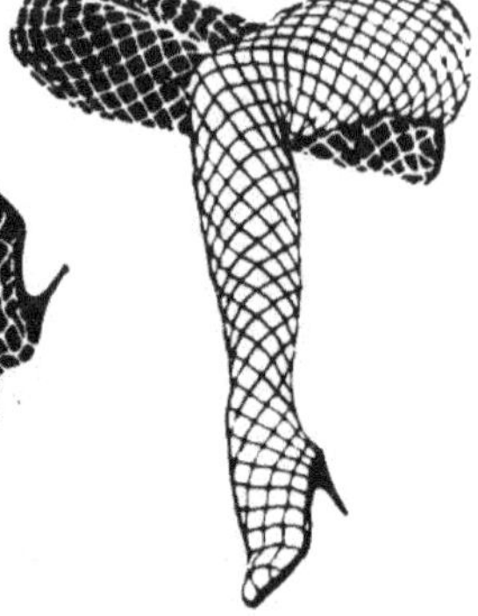

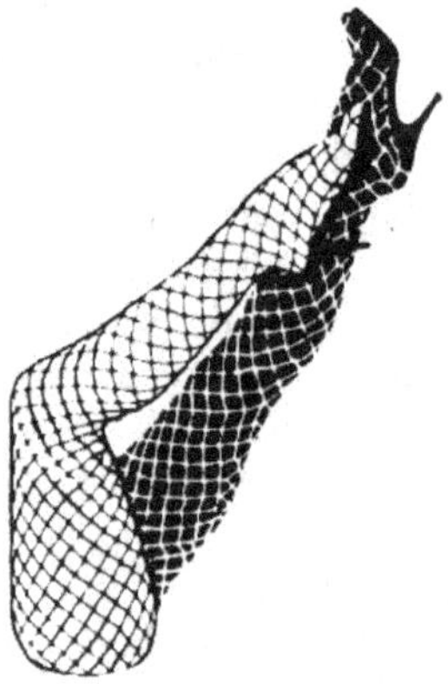

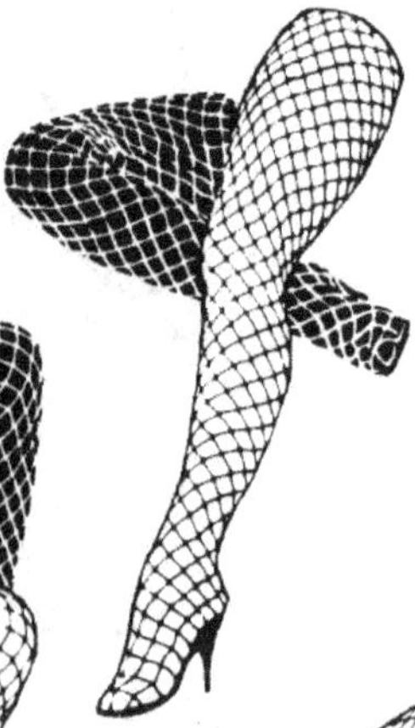

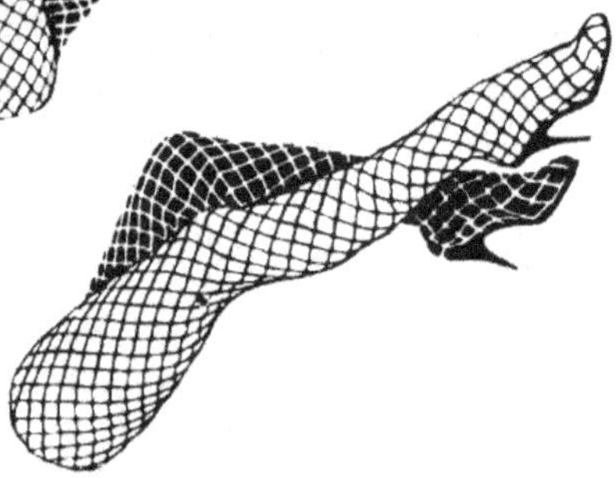

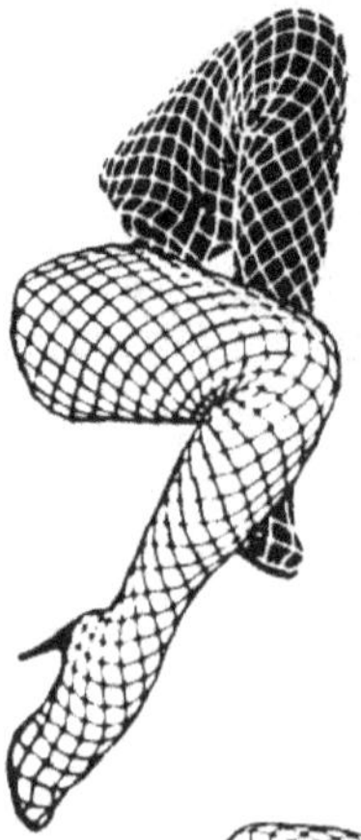

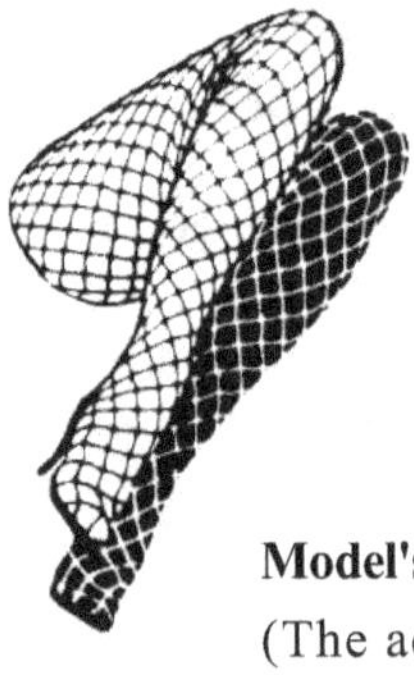

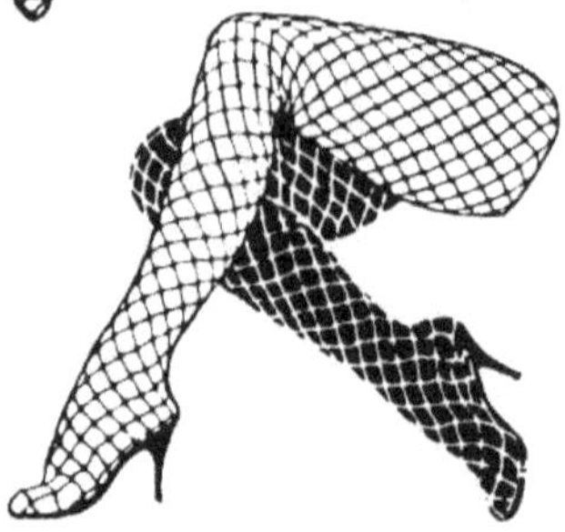

Model's leg-position and

(The actual angles the legs form in
dividually and in combination.)

Camera's Viewpoint

(Every angle not in profile to the
camera is subject to perspective
alteration in some degree.)

138

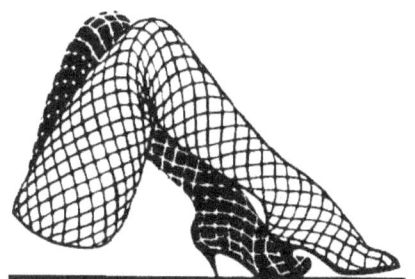

POSITION A

LEG ANGLES

can evolve into leg positions by progressing logically from one angle to the next. Watch the primary knee unfold from its high position in illustration A to the low level in position B and then contract in position C.

The secondary leg unfolded only at the hip to put the leg in position C.

Three very different leg positions originate from these simple movements and if you diagram each knee angle, you will find only two changes in the primary knee (none in the secondary knee).

POSITION B

**Can you
visualize**

...the change that would take place in the leg positions illustrated on this page if:

... the knee angle of each primary leg was increased? - decreased?

... the hip-tracks were turned toward the camera? - away from the camera?

... the knees leaned toward or away from the camera?

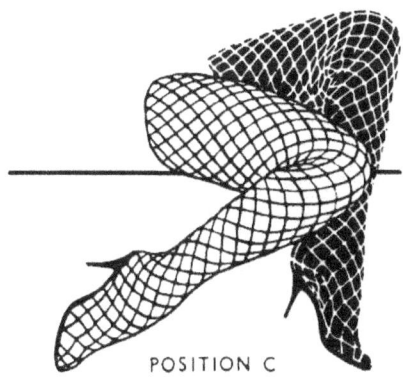

POSITION C

139

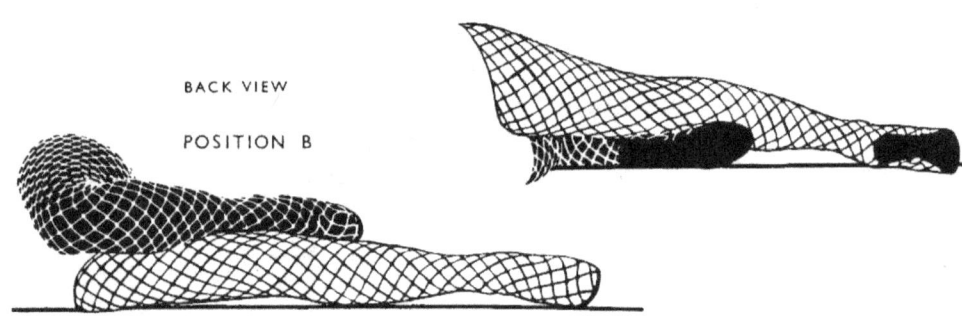

BACK VIEW

POSITION A

FRONT VIEW

THE MODEL ROTATES

and interesting changes take place even though the actual angles of her legs remain the same as they were in positions A, B and C of the preceding page.

Were you able to visualize this front and back view of position A as the model rotated her knees toward the camera or away from it? Did positions B and C rotate properly in your mind?

BACK VIEW

POSITION B

FRONT VIEW

Can you now visualize

... the changes that would take place in positions A, B and C on the preceding page if:

... the camera were moved to a higher or lower position?
... the camera were shifted to the extreme right?
... the camera were shifted to the extreme left?

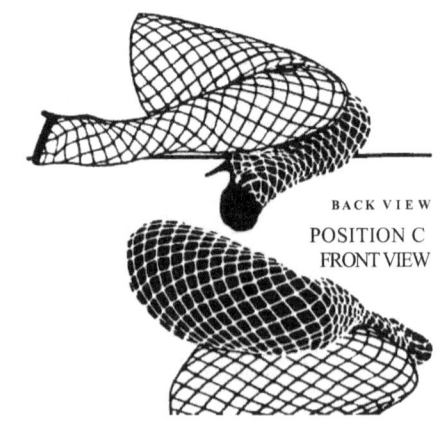

BACK VIEW

POSITION C
FRONT VIEW

THE CAMERA SHIFTS

and more variation is noted. In position B, notice how the appearance of the legs changes when the camera shifts either to the extreme right of the model, or to her

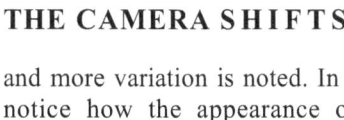

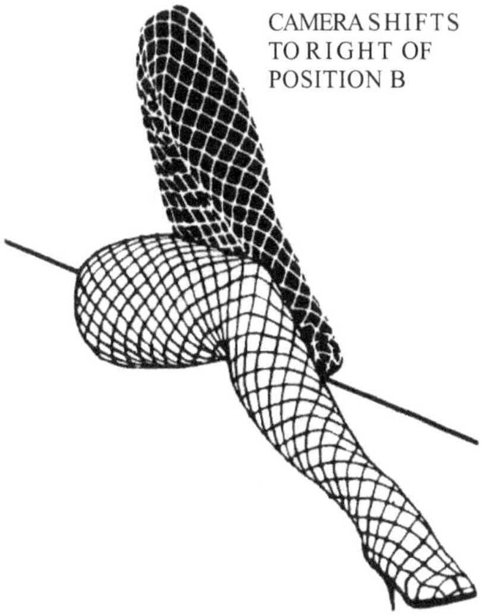

CAMERA SHIFTS
TO RIGHT OF
POSITION B

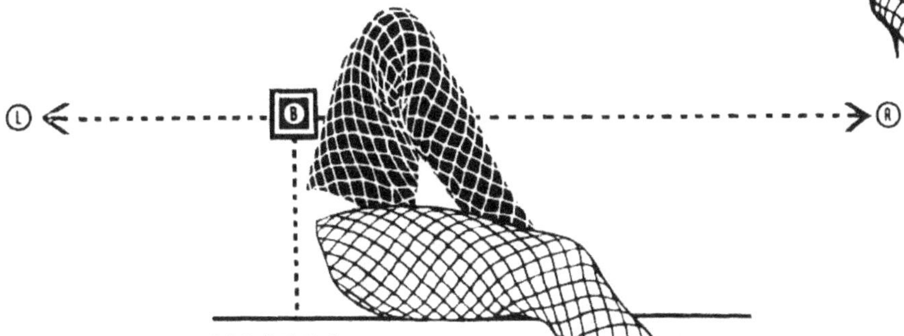

Ⓛ ← - - - - - - - - Ⓑ - - - - - - - - → Ⓡ

POSITION B

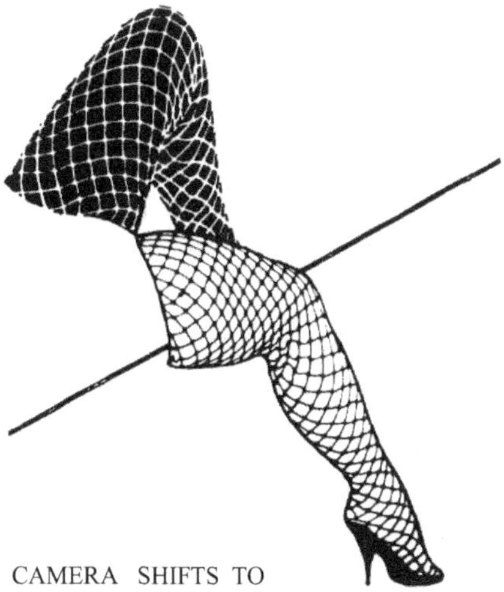

CAMERA SHIFTS TO
LEFT OF POSITION B
extreme left.

You, the director

... vary legs in sitting and reclining positions by command of both your model and your equipment. Your ability to visualize and anticipate the results of all major and minor changes is of paramount importance. It is you who must decide which moves -your model or your camera - and how much!

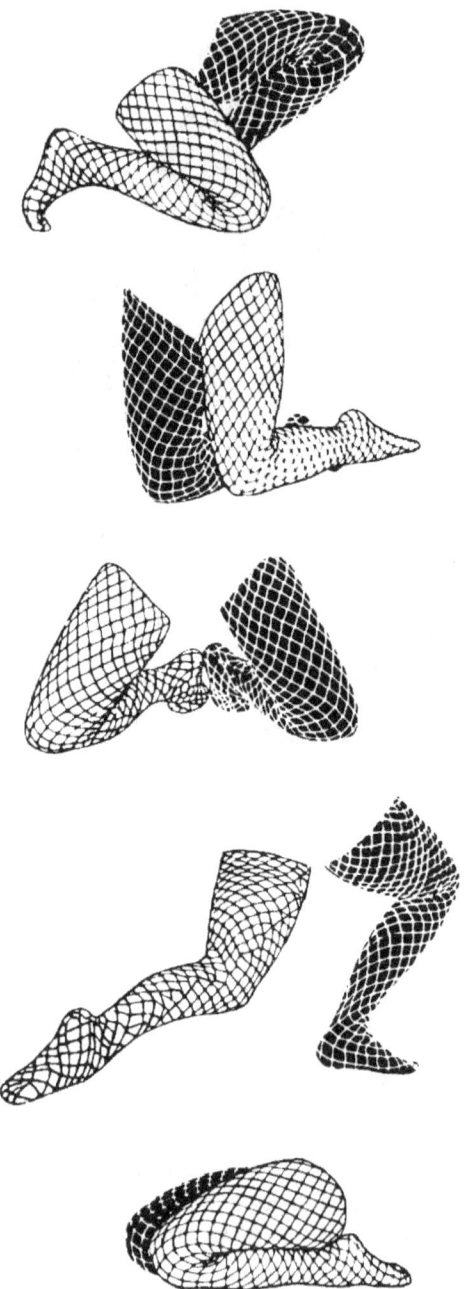

LEGS KNEELING
OR CROUCHING

are affected by the same variables as legs in sitting and reclining positions. You can gain variation by:

> changing the angles formed by the hip and knee of the primary leg.

> changing the angles formed by the hip and knee of the secondary leg.

> combining the angles to coincide with or counterpoint each other.

> making the legs of equal or unequal importance.

> using different degrees of tension.

> twisting the hip track slightly toward or away from the camera.

> changing the camera station from the front to either side.

> changing the camera's viewpoint from high to low, or low to high.

> tilting the camera to bring out different relationships of the leg angles to the page.

> rotating the knees toward or away from the camera.

> .combining different positions of the feet with the different leg positions.

IDEAS FOR UNUSUAL
LEG POSITIONS

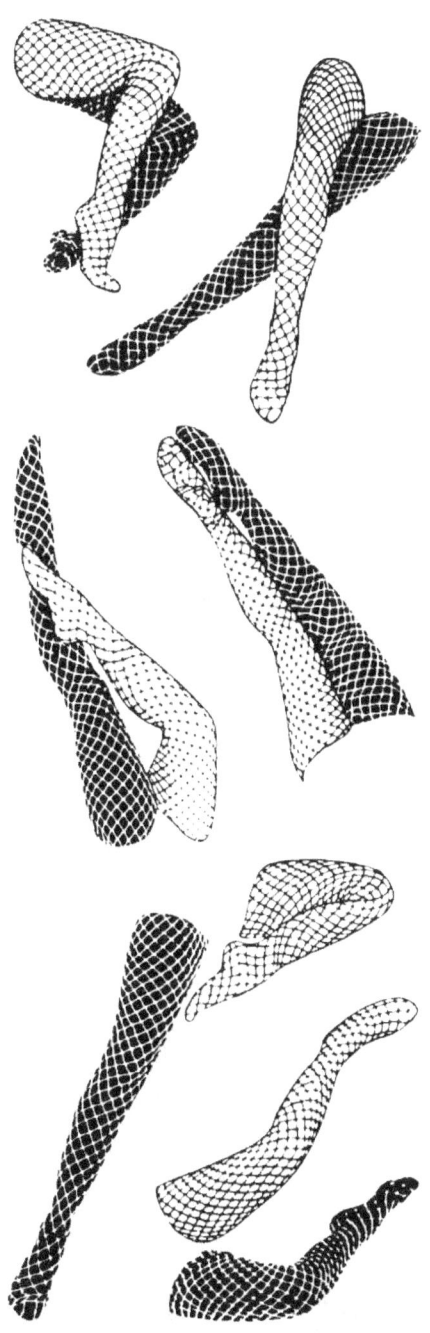

can come to you in many strange ways, some from the past and some from the present:

The past

... old cultures (Egyptian, Chinese, Aztec, etc.)

... dance patterns (ballet, modern, character, etc.)

... art (paintings, sculpture, sketches, etc.)

... characterizations (symbolic or typical)

The present

...research (magazines, books, TV, movies, newspapers, etc.)

... observation (of people around you in action -even yourself)

... talent (model or director, or both drawing on memory, association, coordination or imagination, etc.)

... through the photographie style of the picture, whether it is:
artistic (directs the eye in composition; repeats lines or props, or page; forms patterns or designs) *expressive* (expresses mood or message)

...mechanical aids: unique camera angles or cropping; using assorted heights and shapes of props or points of support; working from *points of departure* with variations of legs and feet.

Three of the ideas mentioned; *design, expression* and *tension* attract our deliberate attention as possibilities or sources for arriving at variations of leg position. Let's examine each of the three.

143

FORMAL LEG PATTERNS

appear almost exclusively in full-front and full-back views of the figure, (regardless of its position).

When the legs are doing the same thing at the same time and are equidistant from the camera, they begin to form designs or patterns. (It is interesting to note the similarity of the straight leg positions to the formal Roman numerals II, V and X.)

These formal leg patterns are generally used for their design and geometric possibilities. Their repetitive quality can emphasize and strengthen the message the face and body are expressing.

When you have in mind a picture that requires such emphasis and formality start with a formal leg position and develop the idea from there!

Formal legs blend well with the vertical 'I' silhouette and can be used with the diagonal and horizontal 'I's to great advantage.

If you use a position that approximates one of these formal positions close enough for a viewer to pick up the pattern, it is much better consciously to attempt its perfection than to *miss by a hair* and produce pointless nothings.

144

INFORMAL PATTERNS

are created by legs when their action or their position from the camera view are not identical.

These unconventional leg positions have a spontaneous, free or spirited air about them. They are interesting, expressive and casual.

For an entirely new approach to their arrangement, lift legs out of the realm of a human part and begin to think of them (and make them function) as folding sticks, parts of a jumping-jack or a pinwheel. Let them spin around an imaginary center point, make figure 4's, or letter K's. Any of the positions we show here could have been arranged on a tablecloth ... with toothpicks!

Such a train of thought, admittedly light-hearted, will take you away from hackneyed thinking and open vistas for leg positions you never dreamed possible.

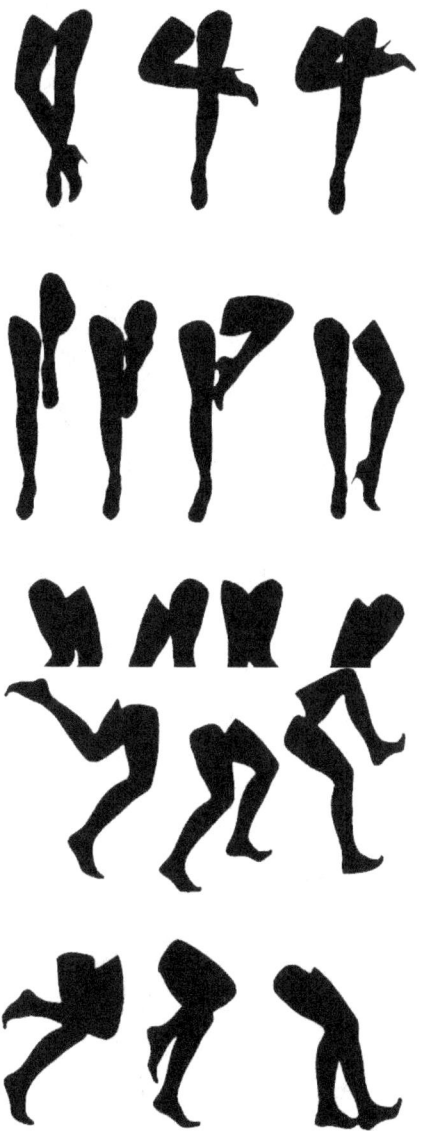

Study the legs illustrated on this page. Do they stir your imagination? Can you almost picture the position the rest of the body was in?

Once you start visualizing the missing pieces of this picture puzzle, you can go on from there and develop the position for the whole body.

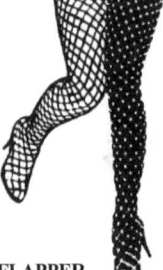

LEGS EXPRESS CHARACTER AND MOOD

CHEERLEADER

in their arrangements. Certain positions have gained recognition, through long association with the actions, attitudes, emotions and physical characteristics of people in various professions and walks of life. With each of the following characters in mind, think of a stance that could be associated (in a viewer's mind) with:

football hero,   fashion model,
can-can dancer,   policeman,
clown,   bathing beauty,
cowboy,   show girl, etc.
ballerina,
cadet,

COWBOY

BASHFULNESS

FLAPPER

(CHARLESTON)

BALLERINA

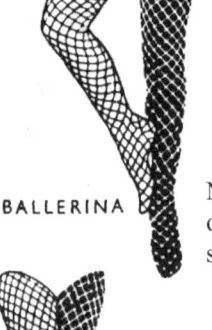

MODEL

SHOW GIRL

Now, think of positions for legs (either standing or sitting) that could intensify the mood or sharpen the impression of:

weariness.   coquetry.
anger,   ecstasy,
assurance,   defiance,
slovenliness,   pride,
awkwardness,   frenzy,
impatience,   pomposity,
shyness,   contentment,
nervousness,   pleasure,
energy,   etc.

146

LEGS INDICATE TENSION

in the mind and the body. They often prove or refute the sincerity of the pose as a whole. The mind and emotions control the leg and its parts. Thus, legs, like the body, are capable of displaying four degrees of tension. When . . .

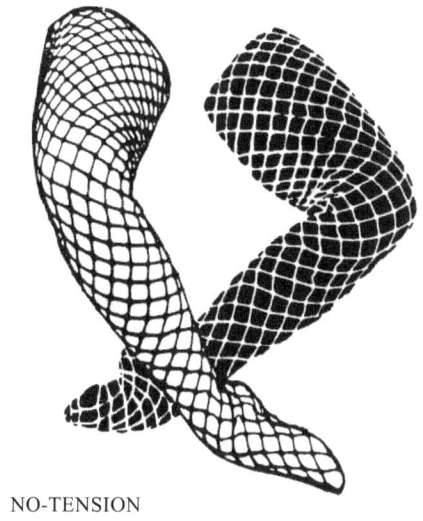

NO-TENSION

No-tension exists, leg muscles and joints are relaxed and denote complete ease. Legs cannot support the body in this condition.

Low-tension begins to appear, the legs may support the body in a simple standing position or, the muscle tone in sitting and reclining positions implies that action is imminent.

Tension rises, legs are called into specific operation to support the balanced physical and mental action taking place.

High-tension develops, leg muscles strain to denote extreme mental or physical exertion.

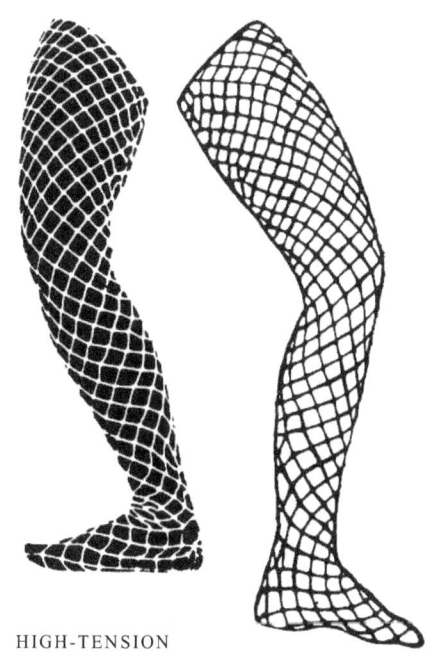

HIGH-TENSION

147

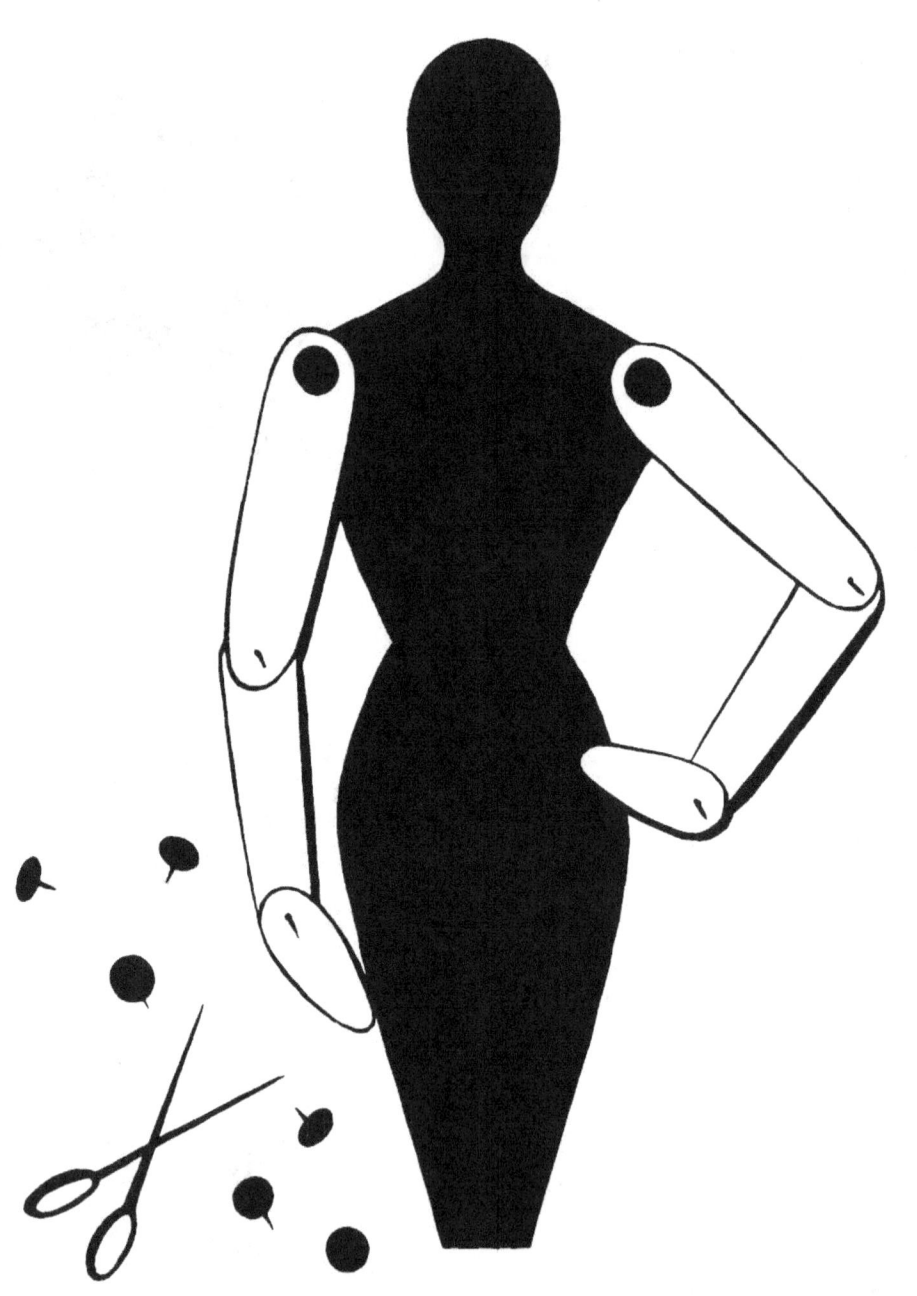

CREATE ARM POSITIONS WITH A CUT-OUT

ARM VARIATIONS

may be countless, but good photographic variations are limited both by the camera's station and the effect the picture is to produce upon the viewer.

Mentally to transpose real arms (which are free to move in three dimensions) into an image of arms (which appears on the two dimensional picture surface) is difficult - unless you think in terms of their limitations.

Arrangements inspired by cut-out figures (such as the one illustrated) incorporate all of these limitations by suggesting positions relatively unaffected by the camera's *flattening power* and by avoiding the danger zones in which the arms may *shrink* or *grow*.

Make your own cut-out. You will be amazed at the interesting variations and patterns you can create and then imitate.

Trace the outline of the body on the left and transfer it to cardboard. Next cut out two parts of each of the three arm segments illustrated here. With ordinary thumb tacks, assemble each arm at the elbow and wrist. Next, turn the arm over and tack it to the body at the shoulder joint.

Now move the arms about and see how they suggest ideas from which you may work!

This figure has proved so graphic in illustrating the limitations placed by the camera upon arm movement in pictures that many photographers have put large-scale versions upon their studio walls and use them to direct inexperienced models into positions they want. Before an important sitting they may even experiment with it themselves - create useful informal and formal variations.

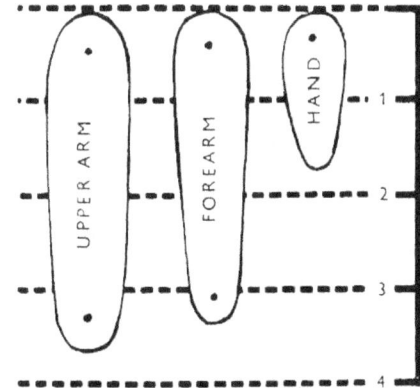

TRACE AND CUT TWO OF EACH OF THE THREE SECTIONS SHOWN ABOVE

ASSEMBLE THESE THREE PARTS BY PUTTING A THUMB TACK THROUGH EACH ELBOW AND WRIST JOINT

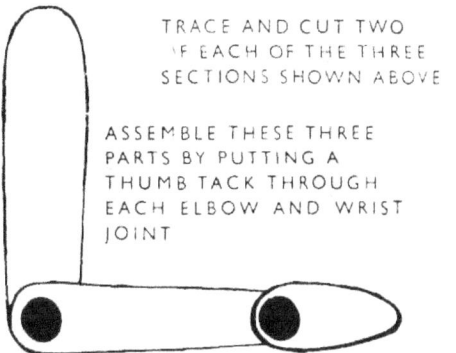

TURN EACH ARM OVER AND ATTACH AT THE SHOULDER JOINT WITH A THUMB TACK

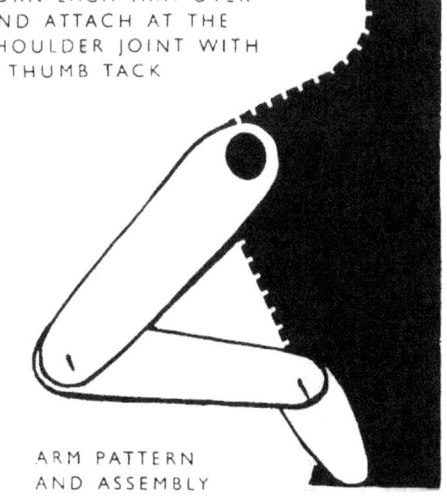

ARM PATTERN AND ASSEMBLY

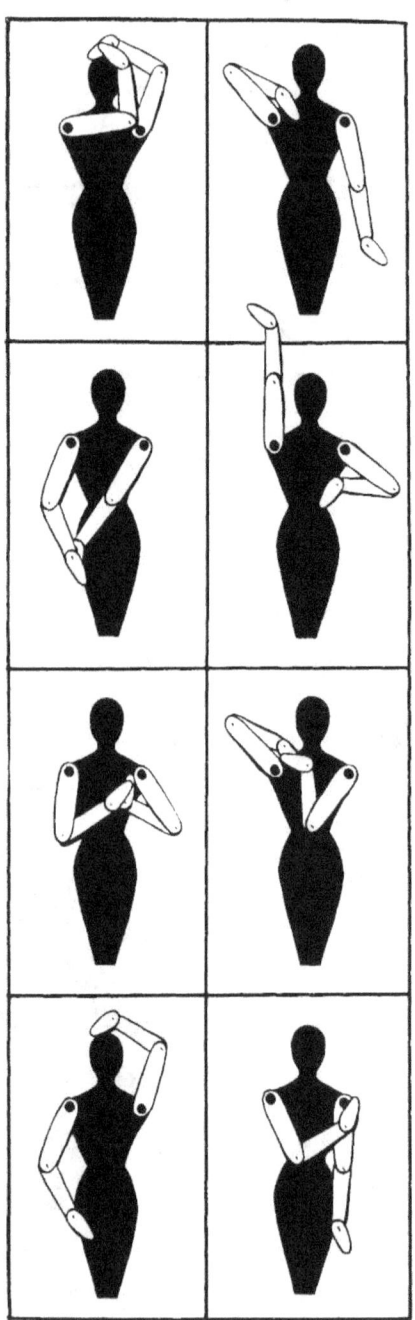

INFORMAL
ARM VARIATIONS

offer endless possibilities. They are interesting to work with and add definite artistry and impact to a pose.

As you experiment with informal arm patterns you must establish compatibility. One arm is usually of prime importance by its position (nearest the camera) or by its action, while the other is of secondary importance and is relatively unobtrusive.

When one arm moves in deference to the authority of the other, emphasis is gained in either design or impression or both.

Arms can add linear interest or become part of the design. They can combine to lengthen their own lines, with parts of the body to lengthen its contour lines, or with drapes or props to lengthen the lines of the latter.

Regardless of their purpose or pattern, the arms must stop somewhere. Think of the ten basic places at which hands stop (page 68) and arrange your cutout figure's arms with the *stops* in mind. Start by trying to ... put one hand behind the body while you move

the other to each position. ... use the same stops with different hand or

wrist positions.

... place both hands on the same hand-stop (both on the same pocket, same side of the neck, etc.). ... experiment with each hand on a different hand-stop

(one in a pocket while the other is touching a

lapel... etc.).

... have one arm send the eye in a specific direction while the other moves quietly to each of the stops. (Try not to confuse the eye by doing very separate and dramatic things with each hand.) ... see how many combined line arrangements you can make (or detect in our illustrations) in which the arm or a part of it extends the other arm, a part of the body or a prop.

FORMAL
ARM VARIATIONS

are primarily used for emphasis and decoration. They are frontal in form, often unnatural in position and usually perfect in design. Their arrangement can almost be deemed *architectonic*.

Formal patterns are created when each arm forms exactly the same pattern as the other at the same distance from the camera. Notice how much strength they imply when you arrange them symmetrically on your cut-out figure.

Let the hands stop simultaneously at:

... each of the ten basic hand-stops (page 68);

... ten different spots on the page in which the hand touches nothing (one hand on one side of the body and the other in a similar position on the other side);

... ten different positions on a vertical line extending directly through the center of the body.

By now you will have discovered both the *identical* and the *inverse* formal arrangements that fall within these strict limitations.

Identical (formal arm positions) not only form the same patterns within and around the body, but they do so in exactly the same way.

Inverse (formal arm positions) invert the patterns formed by the arms: one may go in one direction and the other, in exactly the opposite. We illustrate a few to encourage you to try some of your own. Many of them can be arranged by placing the upper arms in opposition to each other and then making the forearms parallel. At times, the hands do not complete this inverse pattern but send the eye off in a single direction by assuming identical positions.

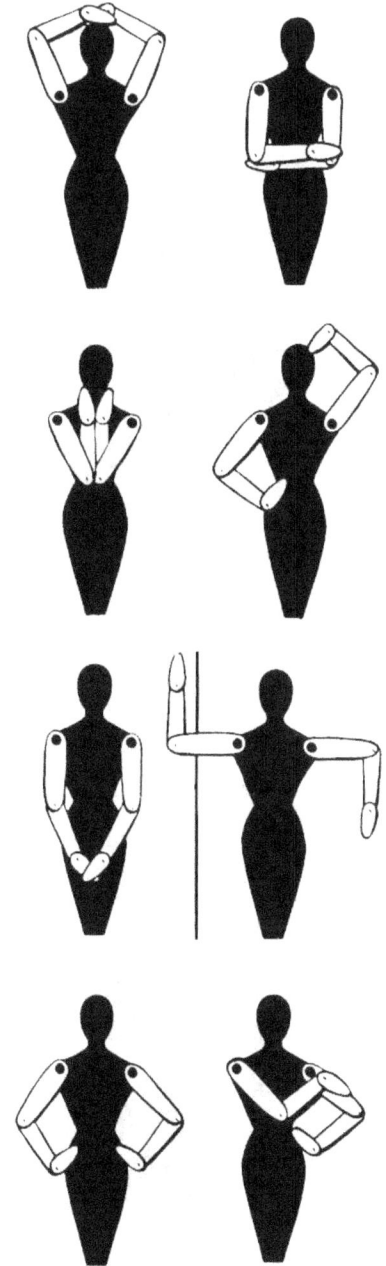

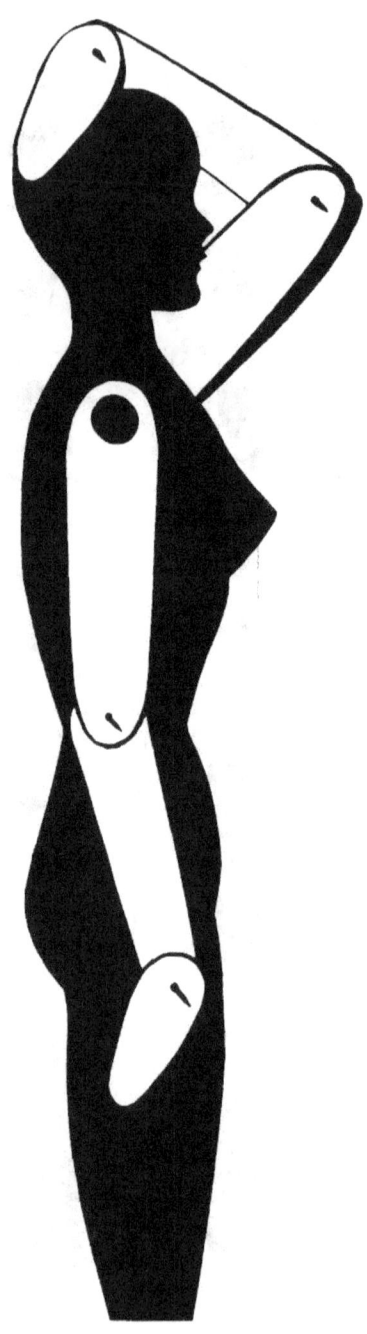

FURTHER
ARM VARIATIONS

become evident as the body turns in a side or J view to the camera.

If you care to experiment again with the cut-out idea, you can trace these additional body views and tack the original arms to either of them.

In the side view, the arms should be attached with one tack in the center of the shoulder. The 3/4 view seems more realistic if the arm furthest from the camera is placed behind the figure.

Once again the arms will perform for you camerawise and demonstrate the great variety of positions available to you in their pinwheel action.

Try arranging all arm positions with specific intent. Definite thought must be given to their relationship to each other. As in the full front views, one usually attracts more attention than the other and is placed in a way that will not detract from its effectiveness.

These pinwheel arms should send your creative ideas spinning into new variations and patterns. Give them a *whirl,* for arms are seldom used to the extent of their versatility and adaptability in creative arrangements.

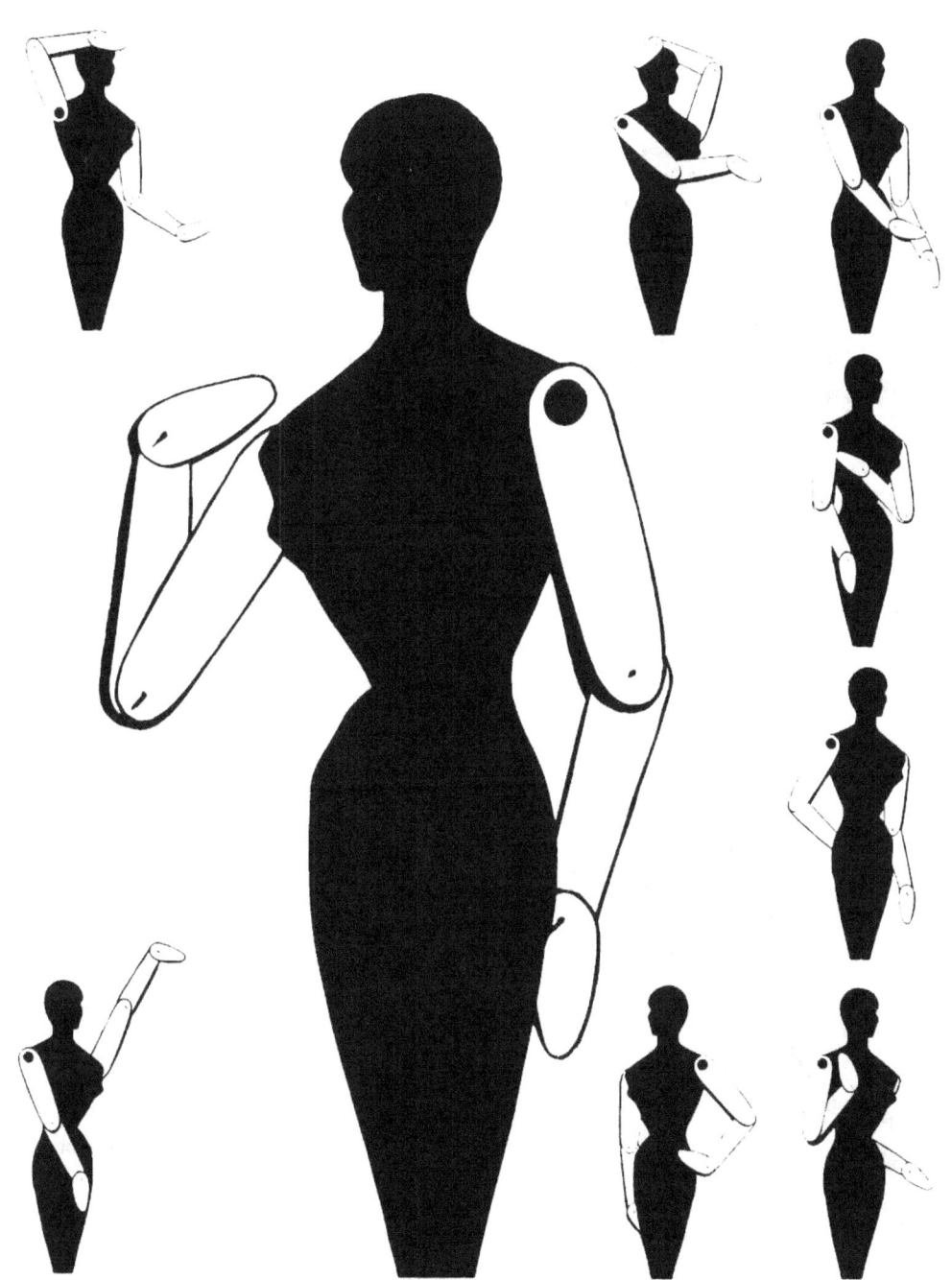

153

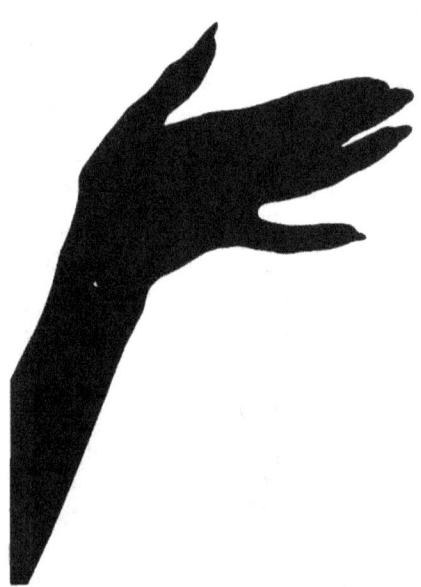

FINGERS SPACED AT EVEN INTERVALS

FINGERS GROUPED: ONE-THREE-ONE 154

LET'S TAKE THE HAND

out of its box. (If you remember, on page 65 we purposely enclosed it in a box to avoid confusing five-finger detail.)

But, let's not, while seeking variation, open the box too hastily - for a handful of thumbs may fly out! Release the hand from its compound bulk very carefully for odd finger arrangements can look like many things they are not. Remember the hand shadowgrams you made when you were a child? The donkey's head; the duck, the wolf! So it is in pictures, hands can take on the appearance of *unretouchable deformities* ... a handful of bananas, a snake's head or even a lobster's claw can appear from nowhere and cling to the end of the arm.

Release the fingers . . .

as though you were cutting the stitching on a glove in which all the fingers were sewn together. Release the thumb first and if you use the hand in this stage, be sure to watch where the thumb goes.

As you set the remaining fingers free, give them identity. You started with the thumb, release the *index* finger next; there's no mistaking that one. Next the *middle* finger and the *ring* finger and last and least the little finger, the *pinky*. When directing fingers, you'll find it much clearer to think of them in these terms rather than first finger, second finger, third ..., etc. in which one can very easily be mistaken for the other. Equipped with these descriptive terms, any model can take direction without looking at her fingers ... to see if she has the right number!

Finger spacing . . .

varies; it may be even or uneven ... one-two-two; one-three-one; three-two; etc.

FINGER FLEXION

is the simple movement of the fingers closing (or opening) shown here to the right in profile.

Finger arrangements are measured, not only by the degree of flexion (how much the fingers flex), but also by whether the flexing is simultaneous or heterogeneous.

When the fingers are clenched simultaneously in tight flexion, the fist becomes square and tense. As the hand opens and the fingers are but slightly flexed, it reaches its most relaxed and graceful state. The hand is longest when the fingers are fully extended.

Gradual finger flexion (from one edge of the hand to the other) terminates in an interesting diagonal. When the hands are fairly open and the fingers flex in different degrees at the same time (starting with the index finger flexed ever-so-slightly and the middle finger more-so, etc.) there is easy grace in the position. As this heterogeneous flexing continues and comes to the closed fist, we find a relaxed fist *closed on the diagonal* that denotes strength without depicting anger (like the squarely clenched fist).

Whichever edge of the hand is nearest the camera is the *leading edge.* When the thumb edge leads, the long line of the extended index finger is prominent (if the thumb does not separate too much and divert attention) and is considered an extension of the forearm. If, however, the index finger is crooked at the base (big-knuckle) joint, this elongating line is broken. A more photogenic curve results if this joint remains straight (or is slightly incurved) and the other joints of the index finger are flexed.

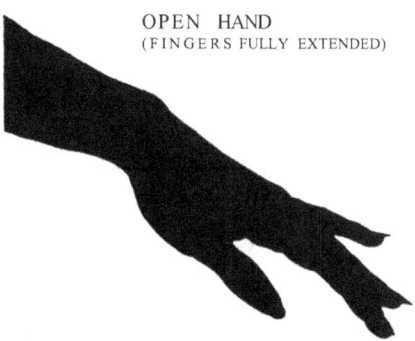

OPEN HAND
(FINGERS FULLY EXTENDED)

CLOSED HAND
(FINGERS CLENCHED)

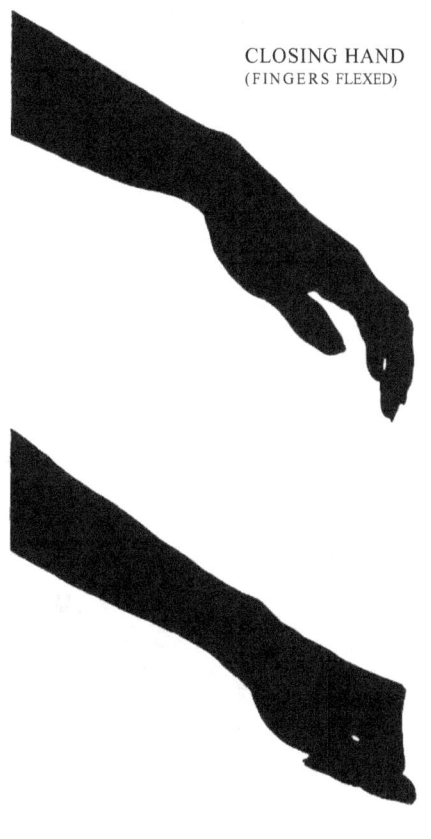

CLOSING HAND
(FINGERS FLEXED)

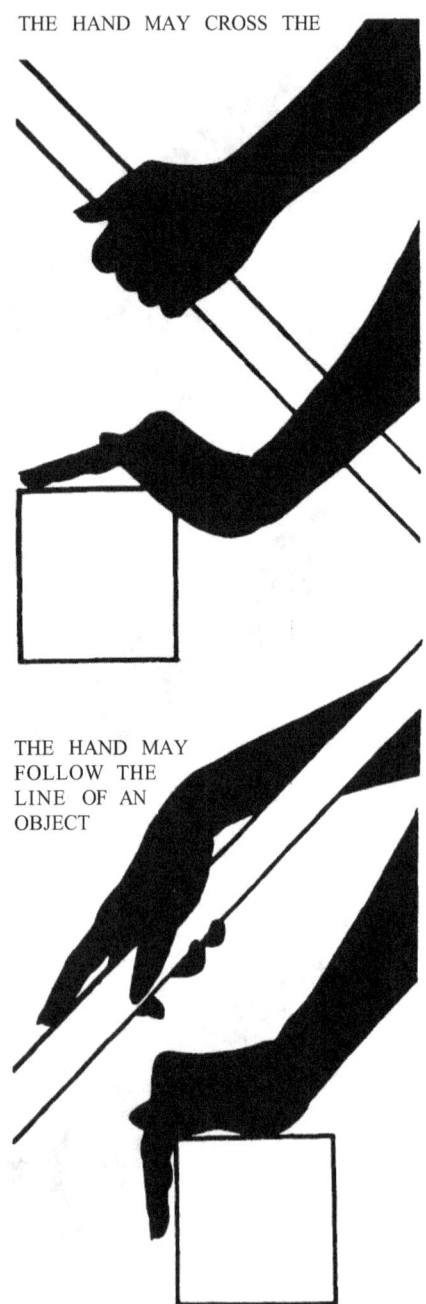

THE HAND MAY CROSS THE

THE HAND MAY
FOLLOW THE
LINE OF AN
OBJECT

HANDS AND OBJECTS

achieve a harmonious relationship in pictures through their line and import.

The line of an object . . .

is important. The line of the hand can flow with it or oppose it. If the object has only form, the hand either conforms to its shape or purposely goes counter to it. Each position creates a definite mood or pictorial pattern - or both.

Can you picture a child proudly displaying an apple on the flat palm of his hand? Compare this mental picture with the hand of the teacher, taking the apple.

When you visualize the child's flat palm in contrast to the rounded shape of the apple, your attention is attracted by the conflicting lines. You look at the apple to see what is causing these differences. The teacher's hand, cupping the apple and conforming unobtrusively to its shape, sends your eyes hurrying on to her face to see with what grace she is accepting the present.

Hands that follow the line or form of an object are usually unassuming ... easy in appearance; while hands that specifically set out to oppose the line will attract attention, invoke a mood, define a character, state a message or otherwise express more individuality.

Thus, a woman's hand might show grace and depict femininity or harmony by conforming to the long line of a boat railing, while the man beside her might show strength and project a feeling of masculinity by crossing the long line and grasping the railing at right angles with his hands.

Whenever a hand touches a drape, furniture, building, clothing, other people or props of any kind, its lines and those of the object it touches may be evaluated as a unit.

156

THE MEASURE OF OBJECTS

also governs us in the arrangement or use of the hands. The measure of the object may be its physical weight, its value, its texture, significance - any attribute which has a bearing upon its material being or inherent meaning.

Many factors dictate the manner in which a hand will contact or display an object... for the touch must be appropriate.

The weight of an object is significant when the viewer has a pretty good idea of the effort required to sustain its weight in comfort. When a picture shows this weight handled in its proper degree, we accept it. If it does not, we appraise it further and perhaps criticize it.

A model cannot strain to maintain grace while holding something heavy nor can she overpower a fragile object. Weight must be depicted realistically unless you want a comic effect or some dramatic position that will attract attention.

Each object must be considered in the light of its import. If the import of the object is its *value* it may be either of a pecuniary or sentimental nature. A dime store locket, received on a birthday, may be held with as much care as a diamond, but certainly they would both be held differently than would a paper clip. When a rose is held sentimentally or softly ... we feel it... and agree. If it is clutched, we are astonished and look to see why.

Handle all picture properties with care in acknowledgement of their full weight or import.

NOTE: Compare the top illustration on this and the preceding page for similarity of action and contrast in context.

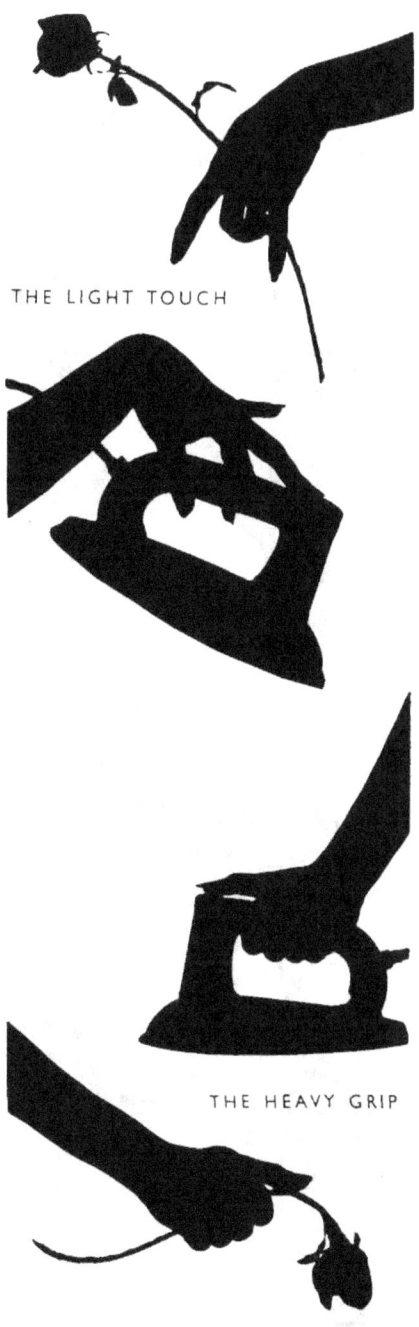

THE LIGHT TOUCH

THE HEAVY GRIP

157

'THAT-A-WAY'

'FIVE'

'I HOPE'

'NO'

'O.K.'

V FOR VICTORY

EXPRESSIVE HANDS

are used by both model and director to achieve greater meaning and believability in their pictures. The novice avoids the use of hands, while the skilled model and director appreciate them and relegate them to their duty with two questions:

... What must their action or position add to the picture?
... How can they do it best?

Hands talk. They can whisper secrets the mind is thinking or they can shout out messages they want the world to hear.

SHOUTING HANDS

seek to attract attention with a blatant gesture or cliche attitude that speaks in the place of a word or phrase. Hands can tell what a person wants *(three.. .four...)*, what the person is doing (hands folded in prayer), how they feel about a situation (two-finger ' V for Victory sign from World War II), a state of mind (palms flung up ... 'I don't know!') and many other gestures and symbols that speak as plainly as words.

These signs are universally understood, The hand has expressed itself unmistakably.

When the hand must be forceful in its message, be sure it rings clear by using the message most commonly associated with the idea the hand is expressing.

Vociferous hands belong in the foreground since their primary intent is to catch the eye. They must talk emphatically to the viewer!

TALKING HANDS

speak in more subdued tones ... but they are heard. Their message may be:

Ornamental and carry the line or design to a significant direction or termination. By repetition or unusual patterns they assert themselves without fanfare and aim to *please the eye.*

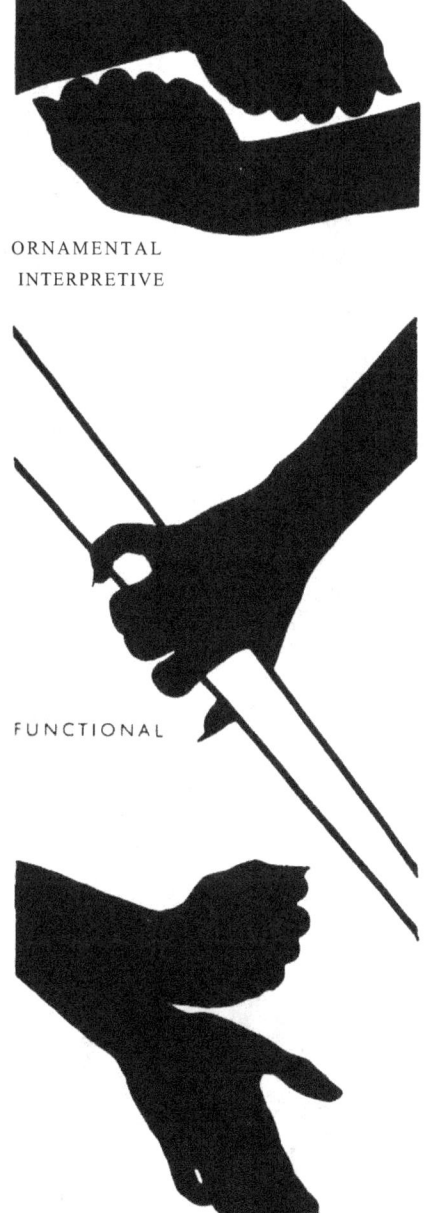

ORNAMENTAL

INTERPRETIVE

Functional and occupied in useful action. These hands go truthfully about their business in a natural way whether in grace or awkwardness. Functional hands, busy and unconcerned with the camera, are the delight of the photo-journalist whose alert eyes are always looking for and rejecting the *exaggerated hand a.nd* the *idealized hand.* Functional hand positions are based upon truthful possibility and can be posed in either deliberate or controlled-candid technique (though those who do either, will not readily admit it) as long as the finished picture finds them ultimately believable in their functional duties.

FUNCTIONAL

Interpretive and meaningful. Their action is significant in substantiating expression in the rest of the body. Their gestures are vibrant in revealing character and mood. Through changes of position, viewpoint and tension, they help the viewer understand the emotion of the person involved. They combine, at times, with the functional group but may have outbursts of expression themselves.

Talking hands go about their business naturally, never say, 'Look at me .... I'm different!' They reaffirm type of person, stage of life, social position, culture and feeling by their physical form, action and degree of tension.

159

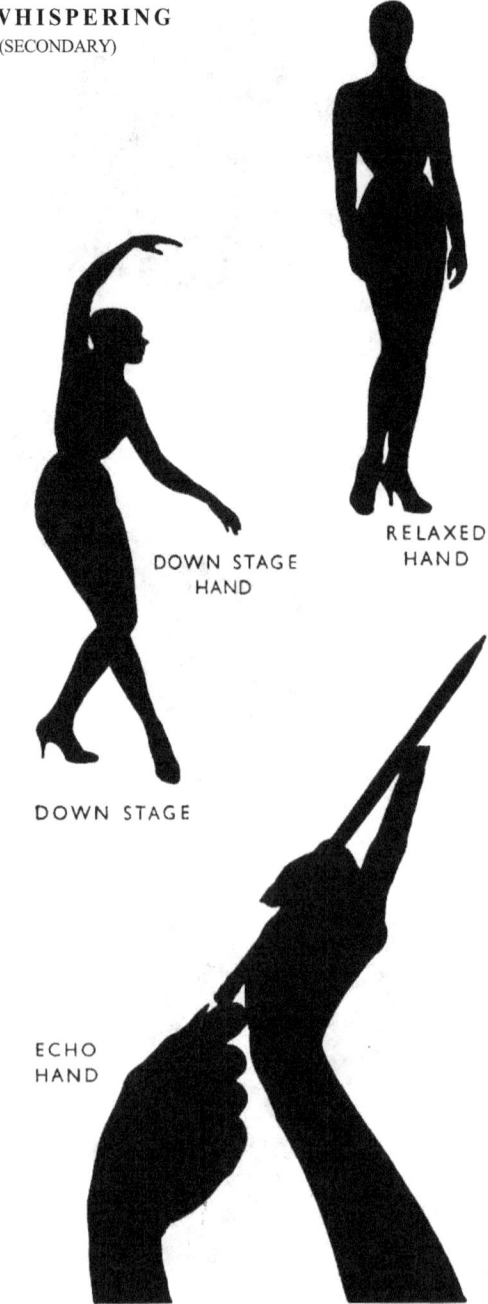

RELAXED
HAND

DOWN STAGE
HAND

DOWN STAGE

ECHO
HAND

QUIET HANDS

are discreet and unobtrusive. They listen and approve in passive ways. They never forget their place and speak of frivolous things.

Some are silent, muted and still, while others whisper in an appropriate, proprietary manner. They are always compatible with the other hand, for, as in a good marriage, the quiet hand never speaks when its partner is talking. It appears to listen with the proper interest and reaction, while the other is expressive. It echoes what the other says or remains silent too.

A father, pointing to an ink stain on the rug, might have one hand pointing downward to the stain in anger, while the other is tensely clenched in restraint ... thus, helping the viewer *read* the conflict and complex emotion going on inside the man. Had the secondary hand been relaxed limply at his side it would have stopped the story by attracting attention through fallacy.

Not all quiet hands whisper. Some are relaxed, completely silent and even retreat inconspicuously behind the back, the head, a doorway or a velvet skirt. Everyone knows they are there, but if they are very casual in hiding it may be advantageous for them to remain unseen.

The hands whose sounds are muted against the object they are occupied with or support, are quietly engaged in normal activity, in an ordinary way, with no lines of conflict and no dramatization of position or lighting. They remain wholly unemphatic.

As you reach for an appropriate hand position or its variation, remember what you want the hands to say ... and, how loudly you want them to say it. If you but ask the right question ... the hand will give you the right answer.

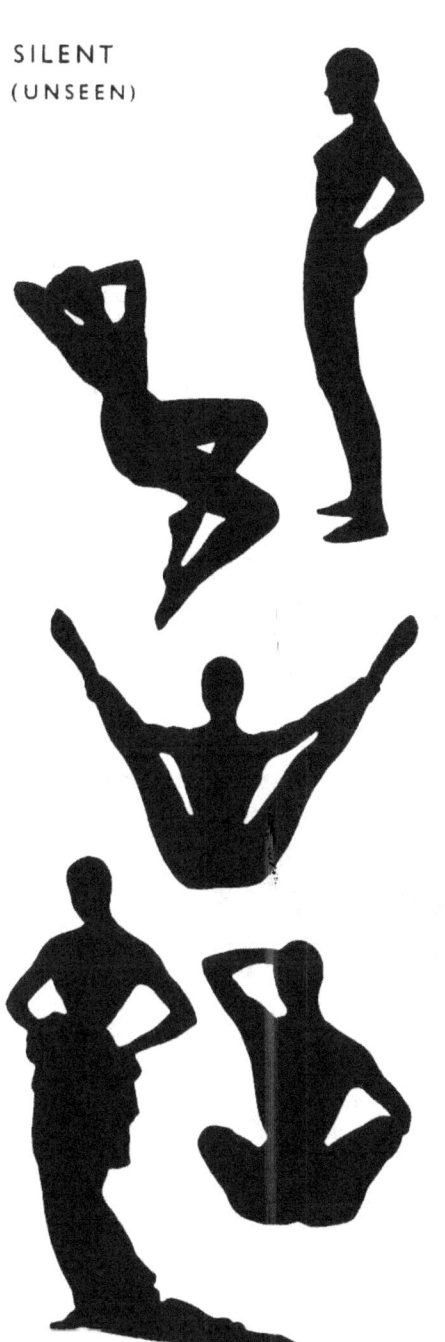
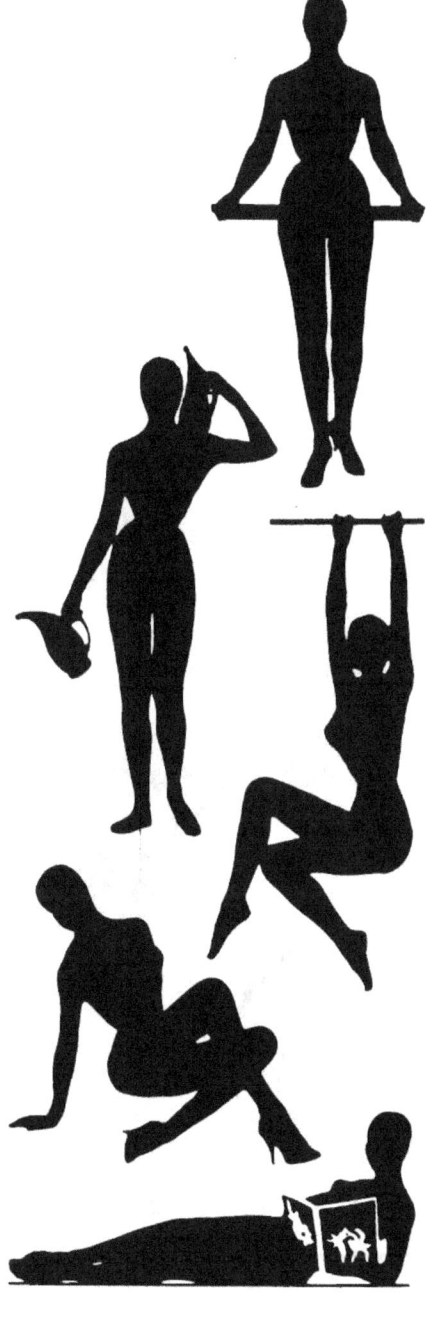

HEAD

placement, with a purpose, tells a story or creates au impression for the viewer even before the face gets into the picture. As the head turns, its very outline communicates mood and prepares the viewer for the message that expression will carry. A lift of the head may suggest hope or assurance; a drop ... pensiveness or sadness; a tilt ... concentration.

Extreme positions of lift, drop and tilt have an emotional quality usually associated with feminine or juvenile characters; conversely, conservative positions with but slight lift, drop or tilt give the impression of restraint, stability and strength.

Positions attained by combining the head movements, such as a lift-tilt or a turn-drop-tilt, are effective and add the style to a pose that distinguishes the work of the finished artist from that of the beginner.

When your purpose is to express specific character and feeling, immediate impression can be gained by starting with a position which, in its very outline, begins to tell your story.

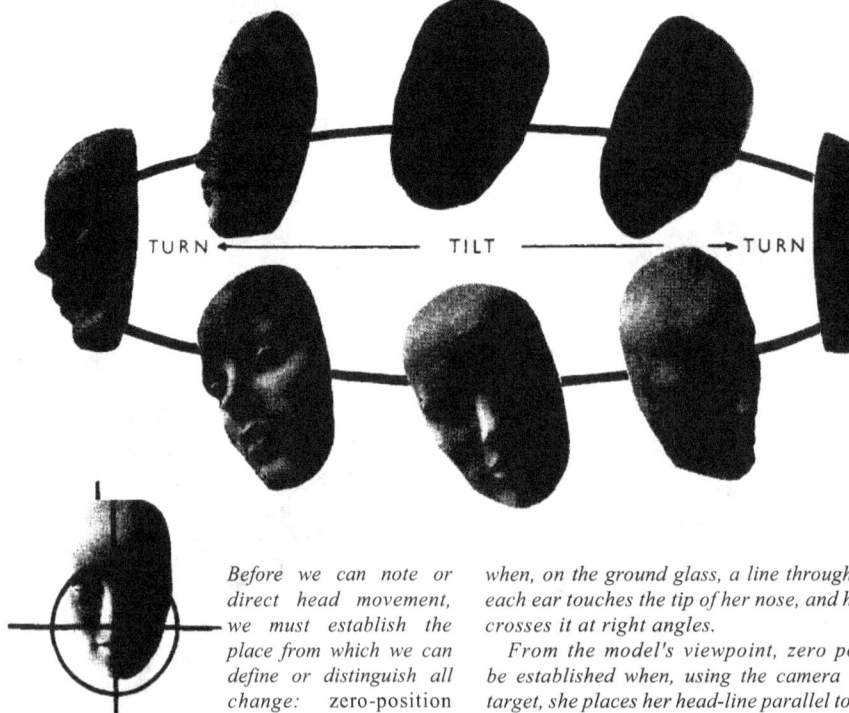

TURN ← ——————— TILT ——————— → TURN

Before we can note or direct head movement, we must establish the place from which we can define or distinguish all change: zero-position *or true center-front.*

From the photographer's point of view, zero is determined by the position of the model's head as viewed by the camera. Her head is true center-front

when, on the ground glass, a line through the lobe of each ear touches the tip of her nose, and her headline crosses it at right angles.

From the model's viewpoint, zero position can be established when, using the camera lens as her target, she places her head-line parallel to the sides of the camera and aims the tip of her nose at the direct center of the lens.

With zero position mutually established, all movement can be directed and executed with synchronized precision.

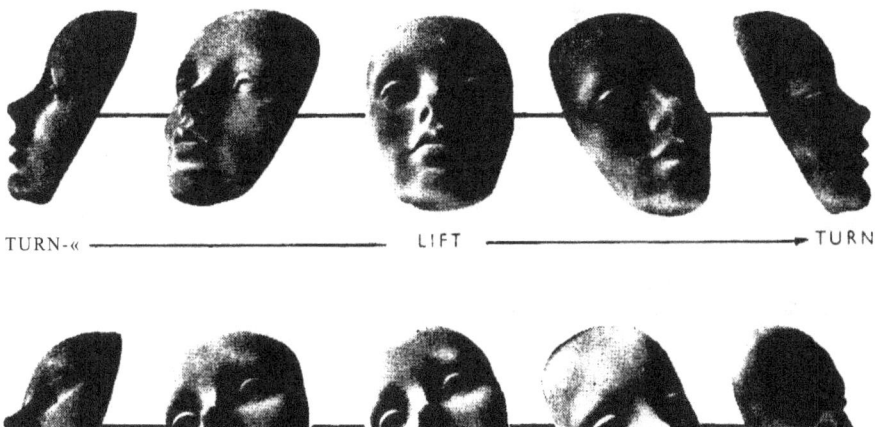

TURN-« ——————————— LIFT ——————————→ TURN

TURN -   LIFT-TILT   - TURN

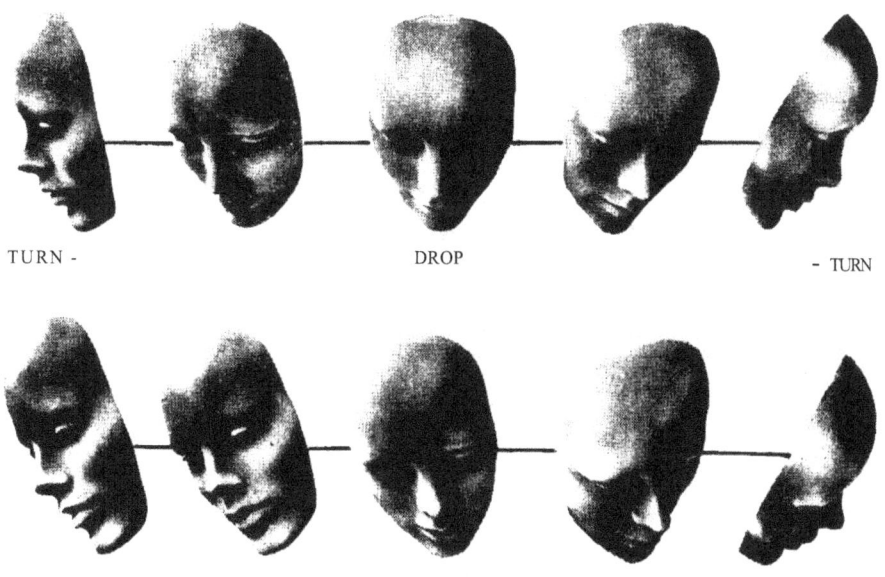

TURN -   DROP   - TURN

TURN -   DROP-TILT   - TURN

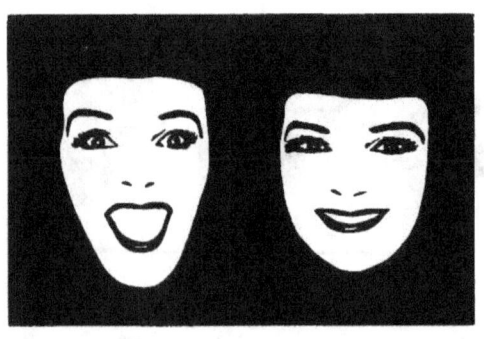

OPEN OR CLOSED POSITION OF MOUTH
MODIFIES SHAPE OF FACE

THE FACE

functions mechanically and emotionally. The mechanical arrangement of the features creates the impression of character and attitude, while expression gives the viewer insight into the model's mental and emotional processes. *Impression catches the eye, expression holds it.*

To a helpful degree, expression can be planned and facial elements placed for the compatible effect of impression *plus* expression!

THE MOUTH

effects a change in the shape of the face when it moves. Notice how a round, laughing face becomes oval-shaped when the mouth opens to form words such as *Hey!* or *Ah !*, and how a thin face appears rounder when the mouth is closed to say *Mmmmm* or *Whee!*

The right mouth position can also correct facial defects. For instance, when a smile exposes the upper gum, you will find that when the lips form the word *Gee,* the upper lip is restrained and the smile normalized.

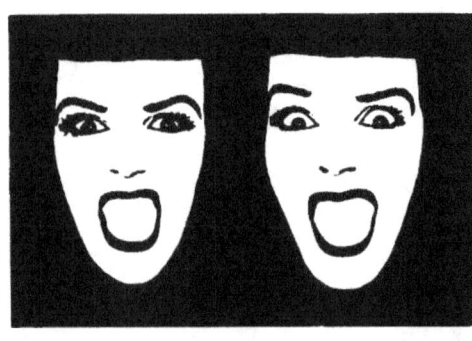

WIDELY SEPARATED EYELIDS COMBINE
SURPRISE WITH ANY BASIC EMOTION

THE EYELIDS

in extreme positions, project impressions which can be combined with basic expressions for mixed emotions. Slightly parted eyelids add contemplation to any given emotion. Widely parted lids add a feeling of surprise if the white space appears above the pupil or an element of voluptuousness if it appears below.

164

THE PUPILS OF THE EYE

direct a viewer's attention by their placement.

Here are four masks printed from the same negative. The first, without pupils in the eyes, is devoid of direction or message. Pupils were added to the other three masks, each pair focused differently. Study them. Notice how they orient attention and may even intimate expression.

Eyes are magnetic. Eyes gazing directly into the camera establish contact with the viewer of the finished picture, while pupils focused away from the camera direct attention to other areas.

The influence of the eyes' directional message should never be underestimated. It is a well-known dramatic fact that in group scenes, figures of secondary importance must gaze at the main point of interest. No matter how large the group or how small the individual figure appears, the pupils of the eyes add or detract from the picture.

The eyelids normally part to disclose the pupils equally. Sometimes, due to an eye's sensitivity to light, or poor muscular control of the lid, one eyelid droops more than the other. This inequality can be corrected if the other eye is closed for a moment or two and then opened slowly. As the strong eye reaccustoms itself to light, both pupils are revealed equal momentarily and can be photographed.

Except for comic effects, the pupils of the eyes should not disappear from view of the camera but should visibly aid expression and direct attention. If eyes leave the camera axis 90^0 or more, (as happens easily in 3/4 head and profile views) only the whites remain to startle the viewer.

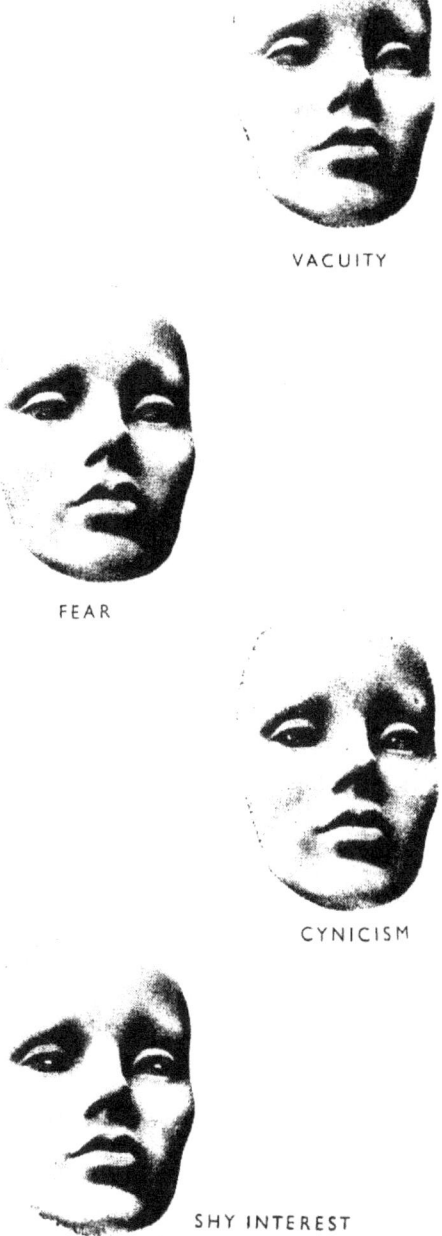

VACUITY

FEAR

CYNICISM

SHY INTEREST

165

EXPRESSION

can be approached tangibly through drama. Skill in combining subtleties with showmanship enriches both artisan and artist. Drama in still pictures differs from drama on stage or in moving pictures in one important aspect. Given time, an actor may portray an emotion with words and moving gestures, building the viewer up to a climactic moment. A photograph has no such previous support for its emotional impact. One picture must tell all. Character, mood and message must be capsuled into one inclusive expression.

Although we acknowledge the intangibility of emotions and their propensity for endless variety, for practical application, we have classified expression into four basic emotions: happiness, anger, sorrow and fear.

Each may be identified by the position of the eyebrows and intensified by the position of the mouth.

There is no single expression for any given emotion; each can be combined with other emotions for different shades of meaning. Our charts show not only the expressiveness of the face, but how facial muscles follow a pattern for the expression of each emotion. When the face is set in one of these emotional patterns, mental agility and showmanship on the part of the model can add spontaneity at any stage of its intensity.

Too simple to be true? Not at all. The expressions on pages 168 and 169 illustrate this point. The model was directed to the exact physical placement of her brows and mouth for each emotion, then at command she added reality and spontaneity to the expression. The results were consistent. Directing the illustrations for this chart of exact and comparative expressions ran smoothly for both model and photographer.

A convincing emotion can only be expressed with feeling from within. In many cases the thought used to stimulate a mood is unimportant as long as the expression conveys the desired message. For instance, if the assignment requires a model to express ecstasy over the gift of a new, super-deluxe washing machine and the model cares nothing for household appliances -she should be able to look at the machine and react to a ... Hollywood contract.

When intense expression is called for, *mugging* should be discouraged. The results are unconvincing and draw more attention to the manner in which the emotion is displayed than to the message or emotion itself. Expression should always be sincere without being grotesque.

In dramatic illustration, the nature of the character portrayed in any given situation plus the stimulus dictates the kind and degree of emotion displayed. This might be reduced to a simple formula:

CHARACTER + SITUATION = EMOTIONAL

nervous woman + new cat = apprehension
young child   + new cat = joy
grown man   + new cat = indifference

same woman + destructive cat = hysteria
same child   + destructive cat = fun
same man   + destructive cat — impatience

With the *right* expression, the viewer in turn, can correctly visualize the intended character and situation.

166

EYEBROWS IDENTIFY EMOTION - MOUTH INTENSIFIES EMOTION

HAPPINESS	ANGER	SORROW	FEAR
complacency	sarcasm	hopelessness	distrust
satisfaction	annoyance	dismay	timidity
mischief	contempt	pity	worry
sauciness	disgust	sympathy	cowardice
gratification	impudence	mourning	misgiving
triumph	petulence	contrition	premonition
teasing	cynicism	failure	insecurity
pride	indignation	longing	foreboding
contentment	irritation	penitence	doubt
hopefulness	disdain	humiliation	nervousness
cheerfulness	disagreeableness	loneliness	hesitation
amusement	impatience	pathos	perturbation
humor	spitefulness	regret	uneasiness
agreement	stubborness	despondency	anxiety
enthusiasm	accusation	fatigue	dread
merriment	animosity	distress	suspicion
zest	truculence	shame	awe
expectancy	meanness	dejection	suspense
piquancy	distaste	exhaustion	uncertainty
aspiration	hate	hurt	trepidation
delight	revenge	misery	apprehension
exhilaration	outrage	pain	shock
glee	exasperation	disappointment	alarm
joy	detestation	lamentation	excitement
anticipation	vehemence	pleading	consternation
enjoyment	loathing	yearning	turmoil
joviality	expostulation	suffering	fright
exultation	scolding	grief	agitation
hilarity	ferocity	tragedy	terror
abandonment	rage	torment	melodrama
ecstasy	violence	anguish	horror
jubilance	challenge	desolation	panic
laughter	tantrum	torture	frenzy
celebration	defiance	calamity	delirium
rapture	fury	agony	hysteria

167

HAPPINESS   **HAPPY-SURPRISE**   **ANGER**   **ANGRY-SURPRISE**

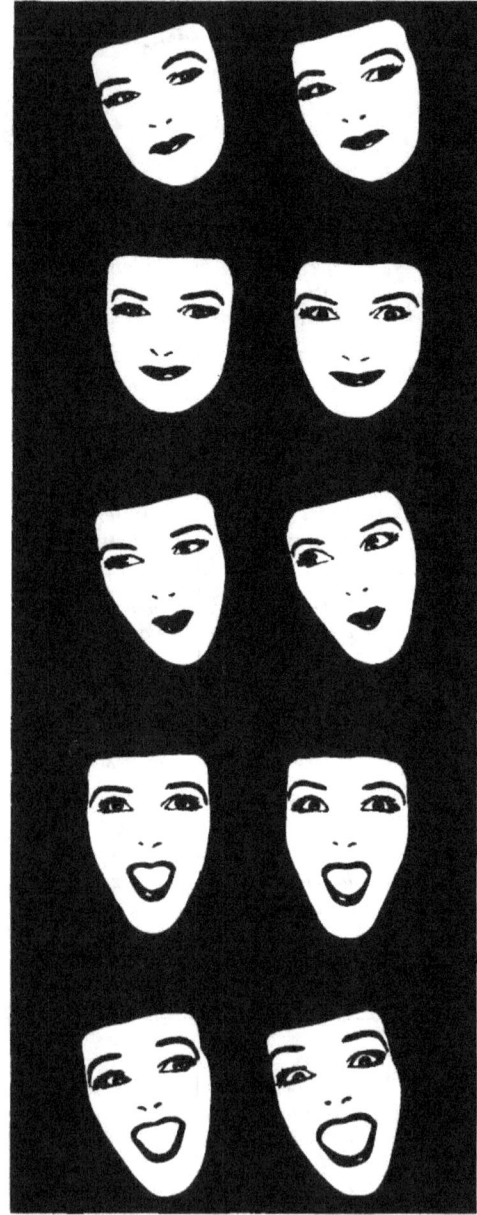
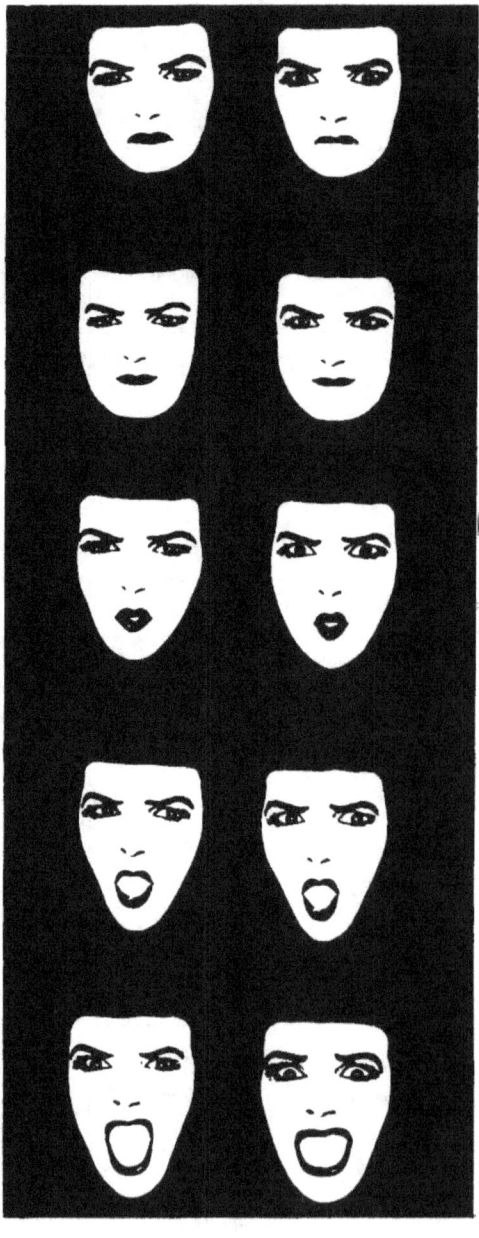

168

BASIC AND MIXED EMOTIONS

SORROW   SORROWFUL-SURPRISE   FEAR   FEARFUL-SURPRISE

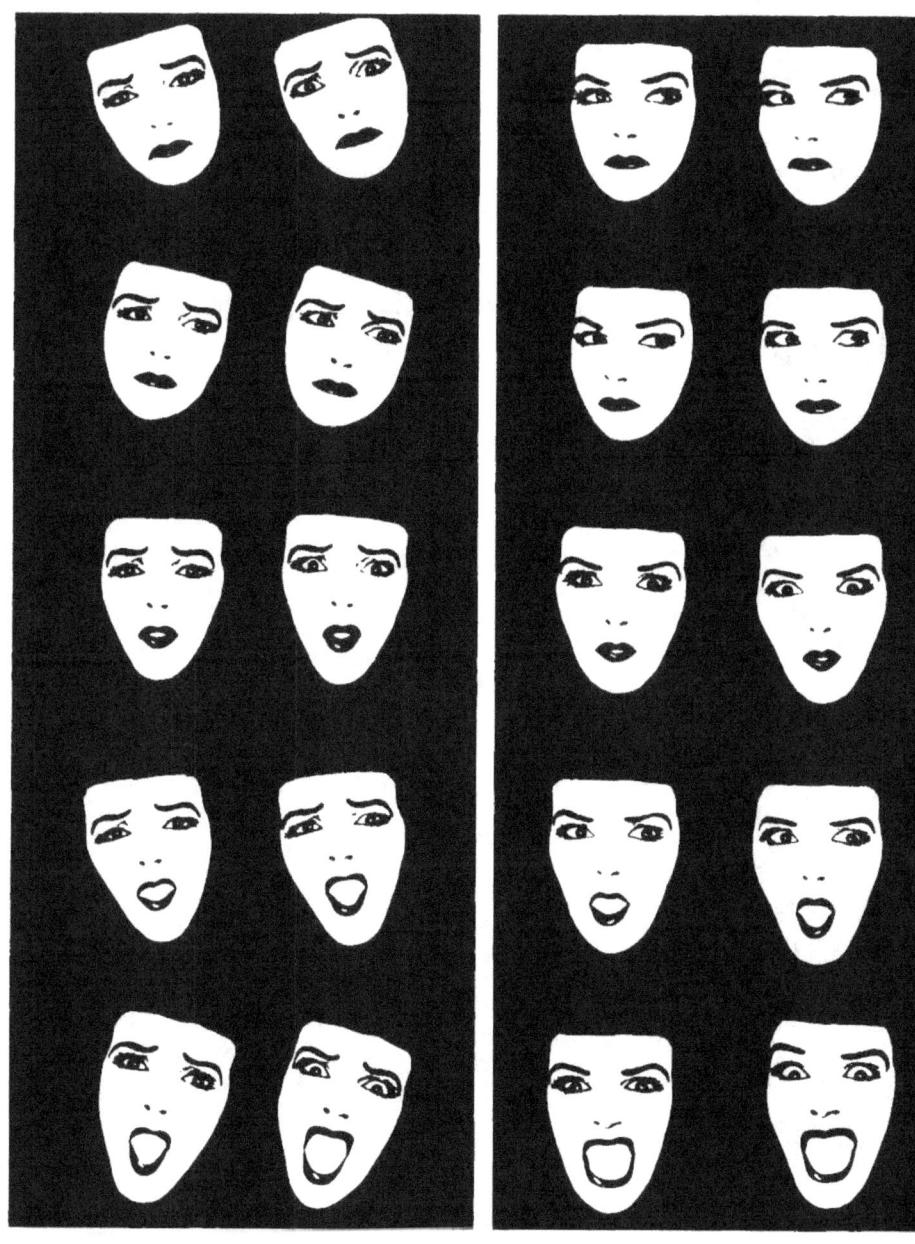

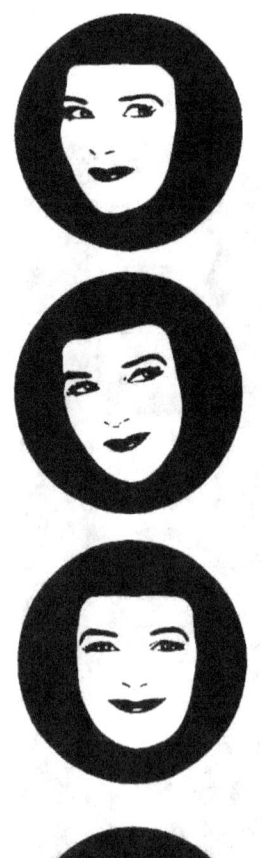

SMILES CAN BE
IDENTIFIED

1. S E E PAGE 171   Each of the five major types of smiles re-
veals personality in an attitude of its own.

Mischievous smiles are generally used by
the young or fun loving. They portray the
model flirting with tempting thoughts of
harmless play ... a trick ... a joke.

2. S E E PAG E 172   **Shy smiles** are generally used by the young,
the unsure. They intrigue by their
winsomeness. Their demure or coy attitude
expresses a happy but timid acceptance of
circumstances.

3. SEE PAGE 172 **Agreeing smiles** have a satisfied air becoming
to all ages. They state happy affirmation of
what one sees, feels or says. They put a
seal of approval on the situation.

4. S E E PAGE 173 **Questioning smiles** are the *tongue-in-cheek*
smile for all. They hint a ready wit and
sense of humor and wait for an answer
with a merry twinkle.

5. S E E PAGE 173   **Glad-to-be-alive smiles** are vivacious smiles
for all ages. They sparkle with a healthy
mental outlook appreciating the *joie de
vivre*.

*You would be
wise to realize
A smile is
started in the
eyes.*

"M-M-mm"

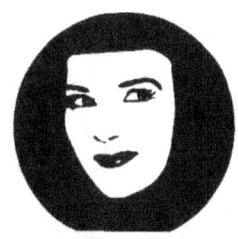

"Ummm!"

"Yes"

*If begun in proper
place It will
follow down
the face.*

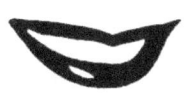

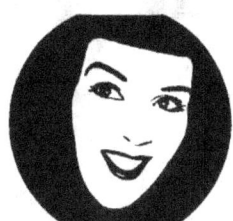

'Kiss? Yes!¹

"Eee"

*Mouth positions
quickly show
How a smile can beam
and grow!*

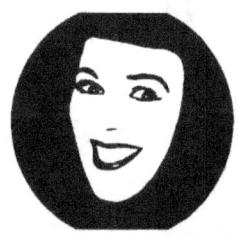

"Gee! Me!

"Hey"

*Form the word that
helps express
Your degree of
happiness!*

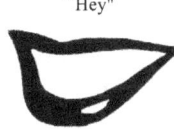

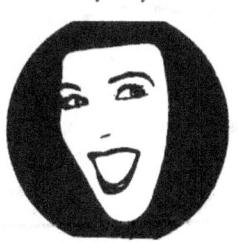

"Say! Hey*

"Ah!"

*Notice when mouth
opens wide
Laughter brims from
deep inside.*

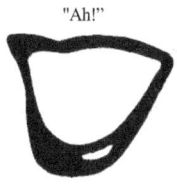

"Hah!"

SMILES CAN BE VIVIFIED!

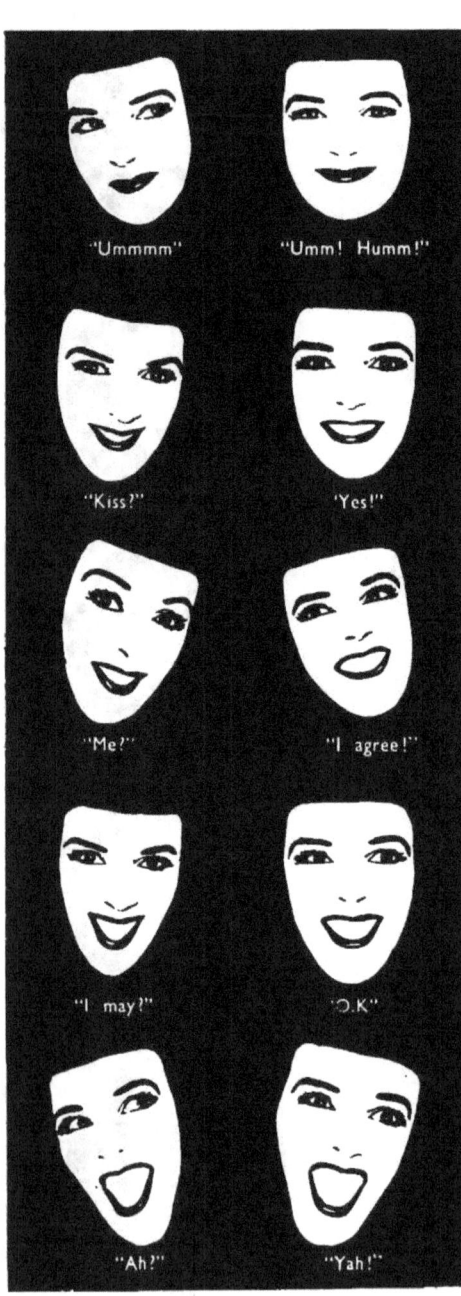

"Ummmm"   "Umm! Humm!"

"Kiss?"   "Yes!"

"Me?"   "I agree!"

"I may?"   "O.K."

"Ah?"   "Yah!"

Vivacity is a finishing touch, it is added after the face has already shaped the immediate impression of happiness. A clear conception of the basic personalities and intensities of smiles helps you to suggest, duplicate and alter any smile.

Eyes are the life of all smiles. They must say something ... and they must see something. Proper eye focus makes a smile flow in the right direction. When the director specifies a focal height or distance, the model must imagine something at that spot. Eyes focused on the floor might see a kitten; at eye-level... a person; upward ... a bird; or, in the distance ... a sailboat.

Sometimes dreamy eyes are not looking at anything in particular. They are actually searching for vacant spaces in which to paint pictures the mind sees. Dreamy eyes usually avoid direct contact with people and cameras.

Mouth positions can be prescribed by the use of words. Mouth-forming words of emotional value such as, *Kiss?* or *Hurrah I* have proved, in actual test, to have more

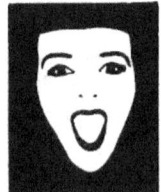 meaning than the old photographic standby *Cheese.* Even though smiles should appear easy, the model's mind must be on the job every moment. A temporary lapse may result in a picture showing that her mind walked off the scene leaving a blank smile to face the camera!

Contrary to common belief, the final success of a smile does not have to be left to chance.

Three simple steps build the right smile, to the right degree, at the right time:

1. Identify the type of smile wanted.
2. Intensify it to the degree desired.
3. Add for *plus value* ... vivacity.

Each smile in any of its five personalities and intensities has its own individual peak of freshness. It is the job of the model to produce its vivacity and the responsibility of the photographer to catch it.

Because enthusiasm is so contagious it befits each of those working together to put themselves, as quickly as possible, into the atmosphere and mood of the picture.

Positive comment on the part of the director and an enthusiastic frame of mind on the part of the model set the stage for climactic expressions.

The model creates while thinking, 'I know the shade of meaning ... I'm reaching for it ... I'm getting it!' The director encourages, 'Now you're getting it ... that ... that's ... *That's it!*'

The director's mind should be timed with the expression expanding within the model. Thus he can anticipate the approaching degree of the developing smile. Before it is reached (split seconds before he actually sees what he wants) he can start to press the shutter, allowing for the mental and mechanical time-lag necessary to stop the smile where he wants it.

A model rises to the peak of expression upon command when she steps out of her personal self and into the mood. She clears her mind of all else and is completely dedicated to that moment.

A director senses emotion to even a greater degree than his subject ... his very being exudes the atmosphere in which expression grows.

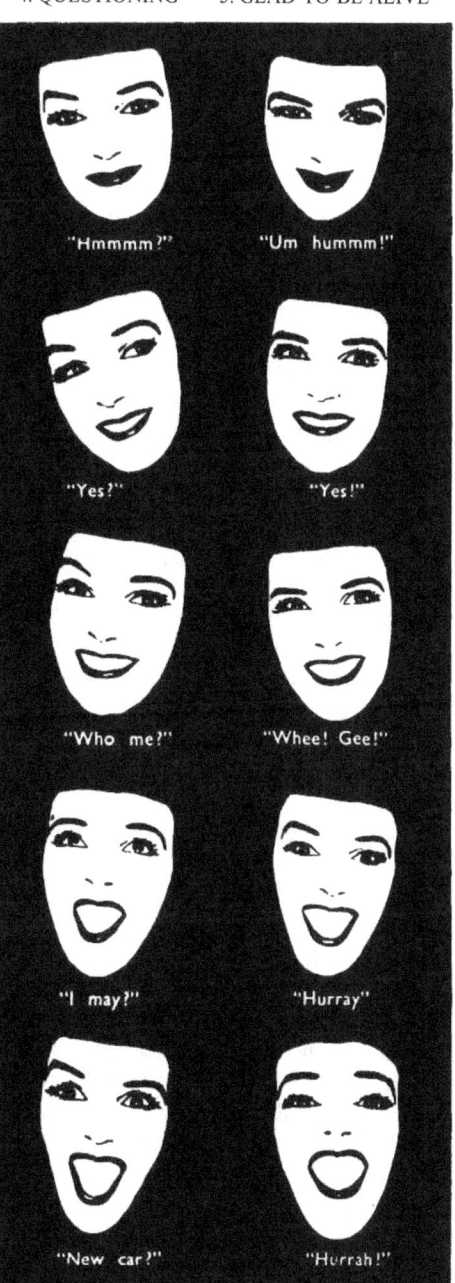

"Hmmmm?"   "Um hummm!"

"Yes?"   "Yes!"

"Who me?"   "Whee! Gee!"

"I may?"   "Hurray"

"New car?"   "Hurrah!"

CREATIVITY

is an awesome word. From a vague and amorphous beginning, results are produced. Those who are gifted and wish to remain alone and unchallenged on their imperious heights, would have you believe that creativity is for the chosen few and completely out of the attainable realm of the less fortunate.

They swathe their work in an aura of mystical inspiration. They may go so far as to tell you how they accomplish their work, but like a cook with a pet recipe, they leave out some important ingredients.

Or perhaps, they never realized *how* they became creative.

They haven't recognized the fact that their insatiable curiosity, instinctive delving beyond the obvious, their strong will, untiring drive, enthusiasm and even their sense of humor were the combustible qualities within that make their ideas explode in all directions. These qualities, these catalytic agents, some are born with but most must acquire. And anyone with determination can acquire them.

Creativity is not a vague product of a mood ... it can be made reliable and consistent. Yes, some results will be more inspired than others ... but the average will be high and successful!

There is a definite thought process, that can, if practised, start a person not naturally gifted, on the road to creative expression. This thought process, when consciously used can free the mind and send it reaching into higher spheres, start it producing. It embodies five logical steps:

1) Assembling information.
2) Relating it consciously to the subject at hand.

3) Incubation process.
4) Genesis of idea.
5) Evaluating and shaping to usefulness.

What are new ideas?

They are but unique variations of what somebody, somewhere has done before, seeing things in brand new relationships. The creative mind endows old facts with new significance, places them in fresh juxtapositions.

The non-creative mind accepts all facts as they have been given to him and cannot conceive anything that does not follow the time-worn pattern, while the creative mind sees new relationship in old facts.

You will sweep away the veils that obscure your horizons and limit you, recognize new relationships in well known facts and begin to produce usable ideas by practicing the definite steps that start creative thinking (if you have not already done so) when you ...

1) Gather Information ... reams and reams of it. (Here is where curiosity comes in handy.) There are two types of information you will require: general information and specific information.

General information concerns the world about you. Know what is going on. Be alive, be sensitive to and absorb interesting news and facts. You cannot be an implement of expression if you are oblivious to the world for which your creation is to be made.

Specific information (harvested by conscious effort) *pitches into* every phase of the subject or field in which you wish to become creative. Each aspect must be pursued as a subject in itself. Specific information does not mean general facts that satisfy a passing curiosity, it penetrates to the core and searches for the individual, the unique. The bit that sets each thing apart so it cannot be herded haphazardly into a faceless group.

If ideas are to spring from a new combination of general and specific information - you must have both.

2) Relate material to subject at hand.

When you collect general information and specific knowledge you have thrown the net that catches ideas but you must examine what you have caught and look for hidden facts. Rub the bits of information together, fit pieces to your personal usefulness; this is the refining process. Your mind must examine information in the light of what has gone before ... what others have presented. Relate the information you have collected to its bearing on life and all things that interest you. Do not view facts only within their own realm but see that basic truths are applicable to the truths in other fields.

3) Incubation process.
Shhhh ... subconscious at work. You have presented the facts to your subconscious, which along with other stored facts on the subject will be filing and shuffling them for orderly presentation at the propitious moment. Let the facts remain dormant until necessity or inspiration *of* the moment demands that the subconscious bring forth its stored treasure in a new light.

4) Genesis of the idea.
The actual birth of the idea (or series of ideas) is the product of spontaneous combustion within the mind. For, with enough general and specific information stored in the closet of our subconscious mind an outside idea or special problem (which would produce no reaction in an unsaturated mind) will fire your brain with searing ideas!

5) Shaping the idea
to practical usefulness requires the extra effort that separates the *doer* from the *dreamer*. Here you must demand from your subconscious, not only that which it is ready to give, but more and more. Draw forth each infinitesimal fact and applicable theory. Discipline your conscious mind to grasp the idea and shape it into practical usefulness: make it a reality!

You have evidenced vital interest in the subject of posing by reading this book. Take the facts we have offered. Qualify or disqualify them - but evaluate them to their fullest from your own standpoint. Explore their usability and adaptability to each field of posing: illustration, publicity, portraits, television, moving pictures, pictorial, fashion, photo-journalism and any other which incorporates the use of the camera. Each has its fine delineation. Each is a study in differences and each will generate further ideas for your work ... that are right!

If this book has proved a source of inspiration, we are happy. If it has been a source of irritation ... we are not unhappy. For in its very friction it has either strengthened your own convictions or deposited that grain of sand that may some day form a pearl of an idea for you.

This is not the end of the book, for as you progress further into your field, this book will serve as an ever-ready reference for posing variations, as well as an illustrated means of communicating with a beginner.

No, this is not the end; it is the beginning of your investigation into what makes the body tick. And what makes pictures click.

DATA ON SHADOWCRAMS

is here presented for those who are curious about how the illustrations for this book were made.

A roll of seamless paper, like the one illustrated below, was rolled down and forward to provide a large expanse of white surface. The lights were set on either side of the model to silhouette her figure against the background.

When feet were included in the shadow-gram (the model wore dark stockings and shoes in these shots) a back light was focused on her feet to separate them from the background.

Costume . . .

was varied according to the effect to be recorded. A full-length black leotard and black bathing cap was used for all the full length shadowgrams.

The full length frontispieces were made in a full length white leotard covered with black fish net (one inch mesh). The white legs were done in the same way, while the black legs had white net over the black leotard.

PHOTOGRAPHER'S
SHADOWGRAM

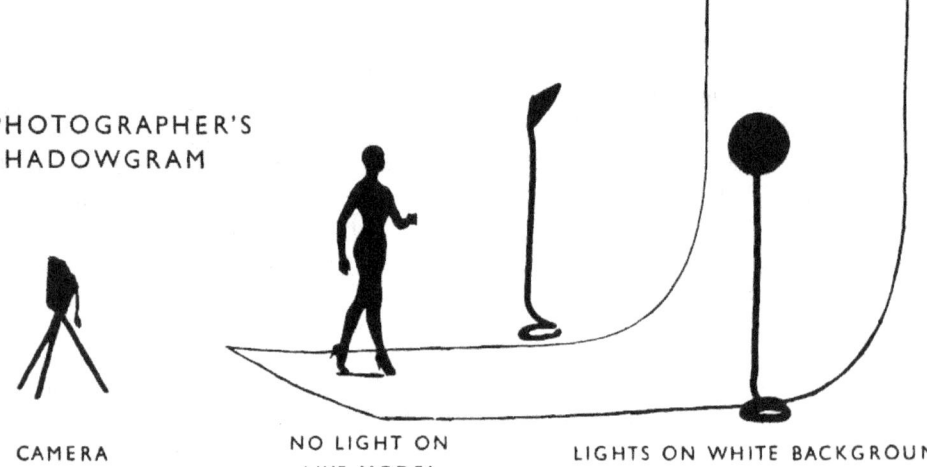

CAMERA   NO LIGHT ON
                LIVE MODEL   LIGHTS ON WHITE BACKGROUND

Film and paper

Contrast process film and top contrast paper were used for all pictures.

Props . . .

were the very ordinary things around any studio. They were eliminated on the negative, and replaced with a line.

The model . . .

was selected very carefully for the full-length pictures not only for her bust, waist and hip measurements, but for her proportions. She was eight and one half heads tall and was able to co-ordinate each part of her body under specific directions and tensions as outlined in this book.

176

Any model can make a shadowgram . . .

by standing on a sturdy platform of some sort in front of an uncovered light bulb. The resulting shadow can be intercepted by a sheet stretched and thumbtacked onto a frame or doorway. The closer the figure approaches the sheet the sharper the outline. However, if the model gets too close she cannot watch the shadow perform. If pictures made from the opposite side

Schematic diagrams (pages 60-61) . . .

were a combination of cut-out (from pictures of the mechanical arms) and art work done with Ben Day overlay and very narrow chart tape.

Faces (pages 168-173) . . .

in black and white were made to look like masks by painting the model's face with clown-white. Eyebrow pencil was used to pencil the brows, the lips and a line across the forehead to represent the top of the mask. Black mascara was used on the lashes and the contour of the face was outlined with a black drape.

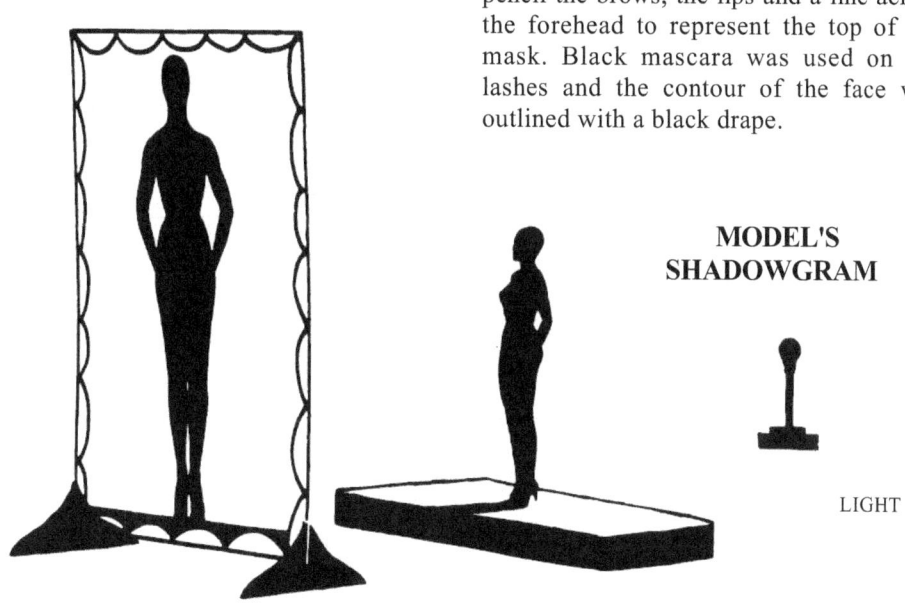

MODEL'S SHADOWGRAM

LIGHT

SHADOW OF MODEL ON S H E E T   LIVE MODEL

of the screen are to be sharp, the model should stand as close to it as possible.

Mechanical hand and shoulders . . .

were made of styrofoam, covered on one side with black paper and encased over-all in fish net of contrasting tone. (Same size mesh was used in all illustrations.)

Mechanical cut-out (page 148) . . .

was made exactly as described and photographed to produce the series of pictures on pages 150 and 151.

The two illustrations on this page were table-top set-ups (with figures printed and cut out to represent the real model).

The illustrations on pages 64 and 67 were also table-top set-ups.

BODY PARTS

EXERCISES	EXPRESSION (potential)	MOVEMENT & LIMITATIONS	PLANNING POSITIONS	SIGNIFICANT VALUE	TENSION	TERMS OF DIRECTION (also see 188)
71-77 148-153	74-76, 115, 150, 151	70-73, 75. 148-153	70, 72-74, 99-101, 1 15	I 1. 57, 70. 71 98. 104, 115. 1 19	63. 72, 77	57-74, 77
62-63, 149		62, 72, 76, 77	60-63, 76	62. 72	77	60-62
68, 77	155-161	154, 155	154-157	155-161	128, 155	154
62, 63, 74, 76		58-64, 72	61-72	57. 75	63	61-64, 73
68, 69, 74, 76, 77	66-71, 76. 155-161	64-73, 75, 154-159	68, 69, 73. 76, 148-161	57. 75, 155-161	77, 155-157	64, 65. 73. 74, 131. 154
74.76	71. 76	58-60, 72	60, 148-153	57. 75	63	60. 62, 65, 73
' 65, 76, 77	76	62, 65-69, 76	61-63, 76, 149	66-71	157	62-65, 77
32-35, US	16, 22, 26, 28, 30,	17, 22-27, 30, 31, 94. 95. 97. 98. 106-115,	96-131	1 1.97	125, 128-131, 183	19,22.29-35, 98, 106-109, 113, 129
(angles 33, 35) 110-111	30, 126, 127	30, 31. 38, 40, 106-113, 135	30, 31. 53. 101, 108, 109,	98. 104. 115, 116	126. 127	29, 112
110, 111	115, 116, 124-127	60, 62, 101, 106-III, 115,	106-111, 118, 119 126, 127	98. 104, 113, 124	125, 128	106-110, 125
86-89	81-85,87,162,173	80-83, 162, 163	18,86-91,94, 162, 166	11, 79, 162	(neck 128)	79-81, 86-90, 162, 163
90, 91	82-85, 88, 90, 91, 164-173	82-85, 165, 167	82-85, 90, 91, 165	164.165,167,172	(squint 90)	82, 84, 85, 88, 91, 171-173
88, 90, 91	n, 80-88, 90 91. 162-173	79-83, 90, 91, 162-165	80-91. 162-173	I I . 79. 84. 164	128	79, 82-91. 171-173
91	83, 88, 164, 166-169, I71-173	83, 91, 164, 166, 167	83, 88, 91, 167, 173	83. 164. 166,167	128	87, 88. 171-173
33, 35. 52-55. 145	30, 43, 47, 49-51, 132, 143-147	38-43, 51. 113, 132-140, 142, 143	46, 52-55, 138-141, 143, 145	11, 37, 39,43, 54. 100, 104, 136	147	39. 46, 52. 54, 55, 135, 136, 144. 145
55	48-50	38,48-51, 55	49, 50	48, 50	48	49. 50, 52. 53
55	16, 47	29-31, 38, 47, 55, 112, 113,	30, 3i, 47, 138, 142-145	47, 137	47, 55	47, 1 13. 134. 183
44-46, 54,	16, 49-51	38, 40, 41, 48-51, 133, 135	39, 46, 49-51	4i, 48, 49	49, 128	37, 46, 49-51. 133. 135
54, 55	30, 47	30,31,38,39,11 3, 134-140	29, 144-146	37. 113	147	37,39, 144, 145

179

MASTER INDEX

180

ORIGINATING POSES (see POINTS OF DEPARTURE: POSITIONS).

'P" (variables in count-down), 98 - (P)ositon of camera. 141 (also see CAMERA-view) - (P)rops, 156, 157 (also see PROPS) - (P)urpose, 97 (also see PiCTURE-purpose).

PARALLEL (limbs/page/props), 99, 107, 108, no, i n . 113, 126, 127 (also see LIMBS; LINE; TRACKS).

PATTERN, 9, 97 (also see DESIGN; PARALLEL), limb, 76, 1 15, 116, 143-145, 151 - paper cut-out, 148-153 - predetermined, 110, 1 1 1 (also see PREDETERMINED).

PERSPECTIVE, 29, 58, 73, 94. 95. 106. 108, 112, 137, 138, 141 (also see DISTORTION; FORESHORTENING).

PHOTOGENIC FEATURES, 89, 174-

PHOTOGRAPHER, 10 (also see DIRECTOR), shadowgram, 175-

PHOTOGRAPHIC STYLE, 10, 143.

PHOTO-JOURNALISM, 106, 159.

PICTURE, composition. 97, 143 (also see DESIGN) - feeling, 120, 121, 162 (also see VIEWER REACTION) - format (layout), 33 - mood, 97, 162 (also see MOOD) - planning, 12c, 166 (also see PREDETERMINED) - purpose, 97, 162, - view, 129.

POINTS OF (creative) DEPARTURE, 02, 93. 95, 97 (also see CREATIVE), alter body-line, 20, 2 1, 30, 31. 97, 99-105 (also see LONG-LINE; ZIGZAG) - apply imagination, 145 (also see IDEAS) - change support (or point of), 30, 31, 114-121 (also see SUPPORT) - combine angles, 30, 31, 113, 138 - compose lines, 97, 126, 127 (also see COORDINATING)
- convert contour (see SILHOUETTE; VIEW) - deviate degree (see DEGREE) - distort proportions (see DISTORTION; PRO PORTION) - diversify attitudes (see POSITIONS) - duplicate diagrams. 98-105, 110, 1 1 1, 113 (also see DIAGRAMS; DU PLICATING) - employ devices (see COUNT-DOWN; SYMBOLS) - exchange characteristics, 124 (see CHARACTER; PRE DETERMINED) - follow preferences (see IDEAS) - fluctuate tension (see TENSION) - inject inspiration, 119, 173 (also see CREATIVITY) - innovate action, 73, 118 (also see ACTION; DIRECTION) - modify movement (see DEGREE; MOVEMENT) - modulate expression, 129, 167-173 (also see EXPRESSION) - move tracks, 106-111 (also see TRACKS) - qualify mood (see MOOD) - shift position, 102-105 (also see DIAGONAL; HORIZONTAL; POSITION; VERTICAL) - substitute view. 22-27 (also see VIEW) - switch stops, 68, 69 (also see STOPS) - transfer balance, 52 (also see BALANCE) - vary camera station, 141 (also see CAMERA-view).

POINT OF SUPPORT (see SUPPORT).

PORTRAIT, 80-91, 162-165 (also see HEAD INDEX 178, 179).

POSE, 8.

POSING (also see ACTION; POSITION), balance, 33 (also see BALANCE) - believability, 128 (also see EXPRESSION-believa-bility; NATURAL) - consistent, 11, 86, 97, 106 - creative -fatigue, 33, 128 - formal, 30, 98, 99, 127, 144, 151 (also see POSITIONS geometric) — harmony, 93, 95, 128 (unity 97) -impact, 94 (also see IMPACT; IMPRESSIONS) - inspiration, 93
- informal, 31, 100, 101, 145, 150, 152, 153 - limitations, 72, 73, 104, 112 (also see LIMITATIONS) - natural (see NATU RAL) - problems (see PROBLEMS) - sensitive, 97 - skill, 11 (also see MODEL-skill) - stiff (frozen), 12, 13, 33 - style, 10, 162 (also see PHOTOGRAPHIC-style) - technique, 10 (basic 12-92), (advanced 93-173) - tension, 128, 129 (also see TENSION) - two-dimensional, 94, 95 (also see FORESHORTEN ING; PERSPECTIVE).

POSITIONS, acrobatic, 115, 118-120, 122, 123 - afi'ecting proportions, 108, 109 - basic (see BASIC TECHNIQUE INDEX) - bold, 30, 66, 67, 76,99, 129, 151, 158 - comic (see DEPICTING iMPRESSiONS-comedy) -controlled. 118-120 - correcting, 28, 97, 128 - crouching, 28, 116. 123, 131, 142 - dancing, 49, 120, 124. 146, 160 depth of, 94. 95 (also see DEPTH OF POSE) - diagonal, 21, 26, 27. 98, 101, 103, 155 - dia gramming, 19, 29 (also see DIAGRAMMING) - diving, 49, 70, 100. 101,114, 120 - duplicating, 17 (also see DUPLICATION) - falling. 101. 120. 121 - fashion, 32 (also see FASHION) - geometric, 30, 33, 99, 116, 144, 151 - hanging, 101, 103, 118, 161 - horizontal, 21, 24, 25, 31, 98, 100, 104, 105, 117, 123, 161 - improving, 35 - initiating, 52,86, 110-112 (also see CREATIVITY) - inverting, 24, 100 - kneeling. 28-31, 33, 35, 113, 1 14, 1 16, 122, 131, 142 - leaning, 26, 27, 31, 101, 103, 115, 116. 119, 120, 122, 127 - leaping, 100, 101, 114, 120, 123 - lengthening. 43, 49, 62, 67, 70-73, 76, 81, 119, 150, '55. '56 - neutral, 125, 162 - planning (see PLANNING POSITIONS INDEX) - reclining, 24, 25, 104, 105, 117, 137 (also see PosmoNS-horizontal) - reversing, 33, 35 - running, 120, 123, 145 - sitting. 28-35, 1¹²» 115. 136-141, 161 - standing. 16. 17, 20, 22, 23, 26, 27, 39-47. 99. 101-103, 106, 107. no, i n , 119, 122, 123, 126, 127, 131-135, 144-147, 160, 161 - supported, 26, 114-119 (also see SUPPORT) - talking, 124-131 (also see DEPICTING IMPRESSIONS) uncontrolled, 101, 121 - unnatural, 22, 30 99, 151 (also see POSITIONS-geometric) -unsupported, 114, 120, 121 - variations, 93 (also see VARIATIONS) - vertical, 22, 23, 102, 103 (also see POSITIONS-standing; VERTICAL) - walking, 17, 161.

PREDETERMINED, angles, 30, 31, 113, 138 (also see CCX>RDINATING) character, 124, 162, 166 - expression, 84, 85,87. 125-127, 167 (also see EXPRESSION)-external elements (see 'P"; PATTERN; PICTURE; POSING-style) - pose, 46, 72-74, 77, 90, 93, 145 (also see POINTS OF DEPARTURE; POSITION) — silhouette, 98-119. 123, 145 (also see LINE; SILHOUETTE) -unchangeable factors, 33 (also see CAMFRA-imposed limi-tations ; MODEL-imperfections) - variation (see COUNT-DOWN ; VARIATION).

PROBLEMS, in posing, 10, 11, 13, 33, 34 (also see COMPOSING PROBLEMS INDEX 178; LIMITATIONS) - to be solved, advanced, 110, in - beginner, 62, 71, 174.

PROFILE, 79, 80 (side-view 22-27).

PROJECTING, character, 124, 159, 162 - emotion, 167 -expression, 84, 85, 90, 51 128, 166, 167 (also see EXPRES-SION) - impressions, 124-127, 156-161, 165 (see DEPICTING IMPRESSIONS) - mood, 81 (also see MOOD) - technique, 128, 129.

PROPS, 98, 100, 101, 104. 113, 115, 119, 137, 156, 157.

PROPORTION, 58, 66, 67, 72, 75. 81, 94, 108, 109, 115, 137, 164.

RECLINING POSITIONS (see Positions-reclining).

ROTATION, of limbs, 38, 42, 43, 49, 59-63, 145, 148-153 -of pupils, 83, 165 (eyes) - on diagonal axis, 26, 27, 81, 103, 162, 163 - on horizontal axis, 24, 25, 81, 104, 105, 140 -on vertical axis, 22, 23, 51, 79, 80, 102, 106, 108, 109. 141 (also see MEWS).'S" SILHOUETTES (chart 98), diagonal, 21, 26, 27, 101, 103, - exercises, 33, 34, 35 - horizontal, 21, 25, 105 - inherent impressions, 22, 26, 101- reversed, 20, no, in - vertical 20, 22, 23, 102, no, in.

SHADOWGRAMS, 174, 175-

184

www.ingramcontent.com/pod-product-compliance
Lightning Source LLC
Chambersburg PA
CBHW081120170526
45165CB00008B/2499